Also by Carol Kahn

BEYOND THE HELIX: DNA and the Quest for Longevity

LIVING LONGER, GROWING YOUNGER

LIVING LONGER, GROWING YOUNGER

Remarkable Breakthroughs in Life Extension

By
PAUL SEGALL, Ph.D.
With
CAROL KAHN

Times
BOOKS

Grateful acknowledgment is made to New
Directions Publishing Corporation and David
Higham Associated Ltd. for permission to
reprint an excerpt from "Do not go gentle into
that good night" by Dylan Thomas from *Poems
of Dylan Thomas.* Copyright 1952 by Dylan
Thomas. Rights in the United States administered
by New Directions Publishing Corporation.
Rights in Canada and the open market
administered by David Higham Associates Ltd.
Reprinted by permission of New Directions
Publishing Corporation and David Higham
Associates Ltd.

Library of Congress Cataloging-in-Publication
Data
Segall, Paul.
    Living longer, growing younger.
    Bibliography: p.
    Includes index.
    1. Longevity.   I. Kahn, Carol.   II. Title.
QP85.S34   1989   612'.68   88-40164
ISBN 0-8129-1803-7

Book Design: Lorraine Hohman

Manufactured in the United States of America

9   8   7   6   5   4   3   2

First Edition

To Judy and Eileen

ACKNOWLEDGMENTS

I wish to thank my co-author Carol Kahn, for her help not merely in writing but in shaping and organizing this book, as well as her husband, Ira, for his patience and understanding during its lengthy preparation. Similarly, I would like to recognize the exemplary persistence of our agent, Susan Lee Cohen, and the wisdom, courage, and criticisms of our publisher, Jonathan Segal.

I would like to express my deep gratitude to Dr. P. S. Timiras of the Department of Physiology-Anatomy at the University of California at Berkeley for her guidance and encouragement as my professor, colleague, and friend, and as director of the laboratory in which much of our research, especially in gerontology, was carried out. I also wish to thank Dr. Doherty Hudson and Carole Miller for their many contributions to these studies.

The scientific understanding upon which much of this book is based could not have been reached without the help of many of my friends and colleagues, especially that of Dr. Timiras, Frosty (Dr. Harold Waitz), and Dr. Hal

Sternberg. I would also like to thank Professor Eugene Breznock, his wife, Dr. Ann Breznock, and Denny Strack, who made the work in large-animal ice-cold blood substitution both possible and successful.

Also central has been the role of many students in our laboratory on the Berkeley campus. Especially important in recent years was the assistance of Victoria Bellport, Cindi Cellucci, Teresa Jensen, Robyn Steinberg, Hoyt Yee, and Sandra Gan.

Additionally, I wish to thank the members of the Board of Governors of the American Cryonics Society, and the Board of Directors of Trans Time, Inc., for their determination to make the life extension sciences and cryonics a reality. I am thankful to Saul Kent and Professor Robert C. Ettinger for introducing me to the practice of cryonics, and to David L. Brown for the important contributions of his foundation to our investigations.

In particular, I would like to acknowledge the unending support given to me by my wife, Judy, who, besides her contributions too numerous to mention here, participated in many aspects of the research. I would also like to thank my sister, Janet, and my partner, Carl Abrams, who shared so much of their lives with me while I worked on the manuscript, and the research described therein. I also wish to acknowledge the continuing support of my mother, Helen, and the memories of my father, Joshua, who taught me the thrill of science, and my uncle, Dr. Morris B. Jacobs, who introduced me, by example, to its practice.

CONTENTS

PREFACE

The answer, of course, was very simple. He had a whole board of circuits for dealing with exactly this problem, in fact this was the very heart of his function. He would continue to believe in it whatever the facts turned out to be, what else was the meaning of belief?

—Douglas Adams, *Dirk Gently's Holistic Detective Agency*

I first met Paul Segall in November 1980 in San Diego when we were both attending the annual scientific meeting of the Gerontological Society of America. At that time I was researching my book *Beyond the Helix*, which would detail the lives and research of a group of scientists dedicated to unearthing the fundamental mechanisms of the aging process. Segall's approach was so different from that of his fellow researchers that I scarcely knew what to make of it. Almost every other researcher had staked out a territory that he or she was single-mindedly pursuing in the hope of coming up with *the* answer that would add years to a healthy life span. For them, the prospect of a vastly extended life lay somewhere off in the distant future. Segall, on the other hand, advocated a multiplicity of approaches that, he contended, could set us on the road to near immortality within our lifetime.

I still have the tape of our first interview, in which he

said with the force of conviction, "The life extension sciences taken as a total assault on death and aging, a multidisciplinary assault, is much more powerful than classical gerontology. If you just go with the classical gerontology approach, it is going to be long and slow [process]; if we go with all the life extension sciences together, there is no stopping it."

It wasn't just the loftiness of his goal but the specifics of getting there that intrigued me. He spoke of things—cloning human parts, operating on people placed in suspended animation, reviving those whose hearts had stopped many minutes after death, regenerating nerves and brain tissue—that sounded more fanciful than scientific. I was ready to write it off, and yet in the back of my mind I wondered if there might not be something to it. My skepticism and ambivalence were apparent in the one reference in my book to "Paul Segall, a research scientist, who calls himself an 'immortalist' and talks of cloning an embryo for each individual, placing it in suspended animation, growing it up to adult size with supernutritious I.V. feedings, and using the golemlike twin as a source for cannibalized parts."

I did not see Segall again until June 1985 in New York City. My book completed and about to be published, I was casting about for another project, when I happened to see a poster for a seminar that he was giving on life extension at the international AGE conference. To my great astonishment, he was now backing up every one of the ideas he had told me about five years earlier with impressive pieces of evidence. The newshound in me began to stir. I was determined to learn more about it.

It was not until another international meeting, this time of the Gerontological Society several days later, that we got together for a formal interview. I listened to what

he said with increasing excitement. Just as he had predicted when we first met, things were beginning to come
together. What had seemed almost like science fiction was
actually happening in the clinic and in the laboratory. We
spoke not only of the possibility of an indefinite life span,
but of the morality involved. To my great surprise, Segall
had given long and careful thought to the ethical considerations involved. And what he had to say made my head
spin. It meant rethinking what philosophers call my "life
stance" almost from ground zero. And yet if the things
that Segall insisted could be done were done, then one
was forced to consider if indeed they should be done. As
bioethicist Joseph Fletcher has written, "New knowledge
forces us uncomfortably to reappraise many things—
family relations, life and death, male and female, good and
evil, personal identity and integrity, parental ties, health
and disease—nearly everything." While I was still ponder-
ing this, Segall said to me abruptly, "When we're finished,
I have a proposition for you." As I put my notebook and
tape recorder away, he told me he had written the outline
for a book. Would I care to be co-author on it? Without
looking at a single word of it, I said yes.

In Douglas Adams's book quoted above, an alien population designed something called the Electric Monk as a
laborsaving device. Specifically, it saved you the trouble of
"what was becoming an increasingly onerous task, . . . believing all the things the world expected you to believe."
Its hardware having gone awry along the way, the Electric
Monk now believed everything at random and could be
counted on to persevere in its wrongheadedness in bla-
tant disregard of the facts. When faced with the facts that
Segall has assembled in this book, you too have two
choices: You can either act like the Electric Monk and
cling to the belief that aging is unstoppable and death inevitable, or you can open your mind to the possibility

that there is another way, that we stand on the threshold
of a new era in which aging and death will be increasingly
controlled, manipulated, and, finally, eradicated. All it requires now is the will to make it happen.

—Carol Kahn, 1988

LIVING LONGER, GROWING YOUNGER

1

DEATH, THOU
SHALT DIE

Do not go gentle into that good night,
Rage, rage against the dying of the light.

—Dylan Thomas, "Do Not Go Gentle," 1933

As far as we know, we have only one life to live, only one time in which our individual mix of genes comes together in a unique sequence never to be repeated, only one crack at realizing our hopes and dreams. Somewhere in mid-life, we start to change, to slide almost imperceptibly downward, to experience a gradual loss of power, tone, flexibility, energy, a gradual increase of aches and pains, of disability, of complaints small and large. And then it's over. The earth covers us and it's as though we had never been here, never smelled a flower, or kissed someone, or thrilled to a piece of music, or been enchanted by a smile. Aging, disease, death—inevitable, natural, a part of the human condition.

Or is it? I remember the first time I asked myself that question. It was a beautiful Long Island autumn afternoon and I was sitting in the darkened room of a freshman art history class. On the projection screen was a close-up of a herd of bison so perfectly executed it took your breath

3

away. If ever art seemed timeless, it was this painting done over twenty thousand years ago in a cave in southern Europe by one of our early ancestors. If I could be anything I wanted, I asked myself, what would I be? An artist whose work would be essentially immortal? Or, since I was studying engineering, a designer of rockets? A builder of bridges? No, I thought. Even though a work of art might enthrall viewers tens of thousands of years from now or my engineering designs be used for decades, perhaps spawning a new generation of design, I myself would be gone, just like the anonymous cave painter whose work now moved me so. Unthinkable!

I decided then to devote myself to the preservation of the artist rather than the art, the designer rather than the design, to study how aging might be prevented, whether death itself could be put on hold.

Far from being a new idea, life extension in some form has been practiced since the beginning of civilization. From the mummification of Egyptian Pharaohs to the alchemists' elixir of life to Ponce de Leon's Fountain of Youth, people have looked for ways to escape the fate that lies in store for all of us. But it was not until about one hundred years ago that science replaced magic and successfully extended human life. The accomplishments of the late nineteenth century and the first half of the twentieth century were impressive: the germ theory of disease, vaccines against a host of childhood illnesses, the discovery of vitamins (*vita* for "life"), and their role in nutrition and health, the development of "magic bullets" (specific medicines for specific diseases), and the most miraculous medicine of all, antibiotics. These, along with public health measures such as sanitation, added a quarter century to the life span. By 1900 the average person could expect to live forty-nine years, whereas a baby born today looks forward to seventy-five years.

In recent years we have started to hack away at the

much more difficult problem of chronic disease, the illnesses that accompany aging and may in part be caused by that same process. We have yet to conquer heart disease, stroke, cancer, diabetes, and other conditions, but with new drugs, techniques, and devices, we are making progress in all these areas, The result is that people over eighty now make up the fastest-growing segment of the population.

But this is only the beginning. Right now there is research going on in thousands of laboratories and clinics around the world that will have as great an impact on human health as the development of rockets had on transportation. *Destination Moon* was the name of one of the first movies I went to as a child. Two decades later, in 1969, I watched enthralled as the science fiction of my youth became a reality. Today we are embarked on a new kind of journey, one that will take us not to outer space but to the outer reaches of human survival.

The time has never been riper for such a thrust. We have the tools, the methods, and the knowledge for a longevity shot that will have far greater consequences for humankind than a moon shot. All we require is the will and the money.

I believe that we will conquer death and aging in the same way that we put a man on the moon or developed the atom bomb or wiped out childhood infectious diseases—through the combined efforts of many people working toward a single goal. It will come through a powerful, multidisciplinary approach using the findings of the life extension sciences. These are interventive gerontology (slowing aging and lengthening life), suspended animation (putting the body on hold in order to do state-of-the-art medicine and surgery), cloning (creating brain-absent genetically identical bodies for replacement parts), resuscitation (bringing people back from the dead), regeneration (regrowing damaged cells, tissues, and organs), artificial organs and transplantation (the use of synthetic, human, or animal replacement parts until cloning becomes a reality), and cryonics (freezing and thawing as an alternative to death), which incorporates the principles and procedures of all the others.

Each of these sciences by itself will produce lasting benefits for all of us. But added together they will become synergistic, the whole larger than the sum of its parts. Together they have the potential for extending life indefinitely.

There are five goals of life extension as I see it: slowing or reversing the aging process; restoring bodily functions lost through disease, aging, or accident; freezing people at death when there are no techniques available to help them; rewarming and reviving people after they have been frozen; providing new body parts when the old ones are no longer viable. The life extension sciences are the means by which these goals will be reached.

But how can I be so optimistic regarding such a sweeping program? As a scientist, my optimism must be based on the evidence, not on faith. And the evidence is overwhelming that the potential for vast extension of life span, perhaps approaching immortality, exists. In this short introduction, I can touch on only a few of the dramatic advances that have been made in my lab and many others that point the direction not only to the future but to steps that can be taken to improve human health and longevity right now. As you read through chapters 2 through 7 of this book, the scope, significance, and interlocking nature of these advances will become clear. Of course, barriers to the full realization of the goals in all these areas remain, but there is nothing to suggest that these barriers are insurmountable. Indeed, the opposite is true. Progress is occurring at such a rapid rate that the social, economic, and ethical questions raised by this work have to be considered now. Chapter 8, perhaps the most important chapter of all, is entirely devoted to a discussion of these issues. We will have to start thinking about the answers now, because the research I describe in this book is happening now. And much of it, perhaps all of it, will come to fruition in our own time, in yours and mine.

First, let me tell you about my own work. In 1959, when I made up my mind to study life extension, my first idea as a freshman preengineering student was to build a machine, an artificial body that would never wear out. But the best machine, according to my engineer father, was the human body, which has a quality not shared by any mechanical device: self-repair. It was, he liked to say, the closest thing to a perfect machine.

The next term, I switched my major to biology, in the hope of finding ways to slow or even arrest the deterioration of this near-perfect machine. Later I read of two developments that fired my imagination and gave me hope that radical life extension could be achieved in my own lifetime.

One was cryonics, Professor R. C. W. Ettinger's brilliant idea of using extreme cold to store the body after death until it could be repaired and revived. Ettinger's book *The Prospect of Immortality* launched the fledgling field of cryonics. The other development was an experiment in England in which a frog had been grown using the genetic material from a single tadpole cell. This was the first significant step toward cloning an animal, and I immediately recognized the potential that cloning had for trading in our old organs for new ones. This would provide the means to accomplish what I had first sought through engineering—an eternally self-replacing machine that would never wear out.

I have spent my entire adult life first as a graduate student in New York and then in Berkeley, California, where I received my doctorate and continue to do research, trying to answer two questions: Why do we grow old, and how can we stop it from happening? I believe that we now have some answers to both questions. Following the lead of earlier research which showed that drastically under-feeding rodents will delay aging and almost double the life span, I have put rats on a particular diet that has allowed me to duplicate these results. Dr. Paola S. Timiras, myself, and our co-workers have also gotten female rats to bear young at an age when almost all their littermates have died. At the same time, the diet we used allowed us to probe the underlying mechanism of aging. Since much of what we know about the brain and nervous system of humans comes from rats, and since the two species share a common mammalian heritage, we should be able to apply what we learn in the laboratory to ourselves. If we are right, then we have an explanation for how the brain controls the rate of aging and how long we live. This also suggests the means by which intervention in the aging process could be carried out. These ideas will be discussed at length in chapter 2.

But as a committed life extensionist, I am not so much interested in theory as in results. I experimented with diet restriction because it was the only known method for slowing the rate of aging. And I went into cryonics because it is the only known method of preserving the body after death with the hope of revival at some future date.

Here again, the results have been most encouraging. At this point we are able to revive hamsters and dogs after removing almost all their blood, replacing it with a substitute fluid that protects the cells against cold damage, and chilling them down to near-freezing temperatures. This experiment, as I will show in chapter 3, has immediate clinical applications in surgery and treatment of disease. In terms of freezing people, it means that the techniques of cryonic suspension right now are valid down to at least the ice point—the temperature at which water starts to freeze. In subsequent experiments we will attempt to revive animals from increasingly lower temperatures until we reach −320 degrees Fahrenheit, the temperature of liquid nitrogen, at which a body can be stored indefinitely.

The animals we use in our experiment are alive.* Will we be able to bring back people who have already died? And how far can interventive gerontology go if the means do not exist for rescuing organs that have been damaged by disease, accident, or aging? Fortunately, giant strides are being made concomitantly in all the other life extension sciences that will go hand in hand with cryonics and aging intervention in achieving the goals I have outlined above.

A truly extraordinary advance that will have implications in many areas of life extension is nerve cell transplantation. Researchers in a number of countries have now shown that embryonic brain cells can be implanted in an adult brain, where they will survive, take root, and function. This approach has already been used in rats and primates to cure drug-induced Parkinson's disease, and in rats to improve the kind of memory loss seen in Alzheimer's. In Mexico, human fetal cells have been used to treat people with Parkinson's, although the results are considered controversial. Research is now going on in the use of transplanted fetal cells for certain inherited diseases, epilepsy, and injury to the brain and spinal cord. In chapters 2, 4, and 5, I will show how brain cell transplants may play their biggest role in overcoming age, disability, and death itself.

But perhaps the most startling breakthroughs have oc-

---

* It is unfortunate that science and medicine must progress at the expense of the lives of research animals. But this expense is more than justified by the resulting human benefits. However, all the studies described herein have followed standard ethical practices and have been done in conjunction with veterinarians outstanding both in their abilities and in their compassion for animal subjects, with every possible precaution taken to preclude unnecessary pain and suffering.

curred in cloning. In 1984, two distinguished researchers declared in a much-quoted paper that cloning mammals was "biologically impossible." Only two years later this bit of scientific dogma was overturned in spectacular fashion by a Danish veterinarian working in Cambridge, England, who produced three cloned lambs. At least three high-tech agricultural companies are now racing to perfect the technique in order to mass-produce herds of cloned cattle. In spite of these very real advances, we are still literally at the beginning stage of cloning. Right now, we can duplicate animals only from very early embryos. Although cloning calves may be good for ranchers, to use this in medicine will require growing whole human beings from the instructions contained in a single adult cell. Body clones, identical in every respect except that they lack the one thing that makes us human—our higher brain —will be the greatest advancement in medicine ever achieved. In Chapter 4, I will discuss the obstacles that need to be overcome, the possibilities for success in the not-too-distant future, and why I believe that body clones, rather than being an ethical nightmare, will actually be a fulfillment of our highest moral aspirations.

What about reversing the dying process once it has begun? Here again medical progress has made such leaps and bounds that new records for survival after prolonged cardiac arrest are being set every day. The so-called five-minute limit for brain function after the heart has stopped beating has been shattered. Radical emergency procedures that I will discuss in Chapter 5 are bringing people back after twenty minutes; the possibility of pushing the limit to an hour is on the horizon. And that is only the beginning.

New drugs and procedures that will restart the brain the way we routinely restart the heart after death are now being tested. The name alone of a new class of experimental drugs—Lazeroids—tell the story. In chapter 5, I will describe the work of one man who practically single-handedly built the field of resuscitation medicine in the U.S. as well as detail the innovative measures he and others are now taking to restore lives *after* they have been lost. I will also show how a number of techniques now used in several different areas of medicine can be brought together to push back the boundary of survival after death hours, days, and even months.

Death can occur on many levels; from the whole organism down to local areas, like a part of the brain lost to stroke or loss of cells in a wound. Counteracting this local death is the science of regeneration. In the second part of chapter 5, I will talk about tapping the secrets of lower animals to regrow parts of our own body. In this area, a landmark series of experiments that are now going on show that injury to the central nervous system need not be forever, that spinal nerves can be made to regrow, and that permanent wheelchairs may become as obsolete as iron lungs.

Leases on life are now routinely being extended by transplanted kidneys, hearts, lungs, and livers. The biomedical trading post is open and active, with new organs being exchanged for old ones every few minutes. But the twin perils of rejection and the side effects of antirejection drugs continue to plague the recipient. Still, in this business it is better to receive than give, and the problem of supplying the demand has become ever more pressing. These considerations will be reviewed in chapter 6 along with a look at the high-tech solution of artificial organs. This field, which was recently given a shot in the arm by the National Institutes of Health decision to develop a wholly implantable synthetic heart, promises to make machine-man hookups the wave of the future.

All these advances are only a kind of preview to what lies ahead. In my most recent experiments I have begun to move from lowering the body temperature to the ice point to plunging below it—a very different prospect. When we can take an animal even just a few degrees below freezing and bring it back, the door will open to short-term cryonic suspension. To what frozen depths can we sink and still return? In chapter 7, I will tell the story of cryonics from the perspective of one who has been there almost from the beginning—the struggles, the triumphs and disasters, the recent progress, the exciting prospects for the future. It is in cryonics that all the life extension sciences will come together so that one day we can wake the frozen dead and cheat the grave altogether.

At this point, you may be saying, "But what about me? Will I live long enough to reach the promised land of vastly extended life and youth?" Nobody can answer that question for certain, but in this age of continuing medical miracles, it becomes ever more important to lead a prudent life to avoid dying prematurely. In chapter 9, I offer my own ten rules, and as I will demonstrate, with each incremental extension of our lives, the chances of living until an even longer, healthier life are increased. And if we can make it to the point where reversible cryonics becomes a reality, then we can make it back.

Advances in the life extension sciences make headlines and TV news practically every day. Interferon and interleukin 2, two disease-fighting substances that occur naturally in our bodies, have been synthesized by genetic engineering and are exciting scientists with their anticancer potential. The first promising drug against AIDS has been found; it actually blocks the AIDS virus from reaching and destroying the body's immune cells. Lifesaving bone marrow and red blood cells are maintained in frozen storage so that they may be thawed and used in places such as Chernobyl or in emergency wards. Hormone-like growth factors perform miracles of regeneration on the skin, blood, and brain cells. Couples who just a few years ago would have had to forgo having their own children have babies conceived in a test tube, frozen early in embryonic life, and then placed in the uterus of the biological mother or a surrogate mother until the time of birth. A patient is saved by an artificial heart until the right human heart is available. A toddler who surely would have been dead after pulling the plug in a Jacuzzi and being held fast in the escaping water for many minutes is restored to life by a series of new treatments. A young woman whose leg is severed by a crane at a construction site in New York City is made whole again, the limb having been sewed back in place by the wizard microsurgical team at Bellevue Hospital.

The life extension sciences grow, feeding on their own momentum, like a symphony building toward a finale. Perhaps we cannot cure a given cancer right away, but we may learn how to store the patient cryogenically until we can. Perhaps we will not soon be able to halt the underlying cause of aging, but we can discover how to replace aging hearts and kidneys and lungs with new ones grown from the cells of our own bodies. The beauty of the life extension approach is that it does not depend on progress in any one biomedical area. Since a body can be kept frozen indefinitely in liquid nitrogen, cryobiologists provide a fallback position for the gerontologists. The transplant and artificial organ surgeons keep the older individual functioning even after the vital organs have failed. The critical care and emergency medical teams routinely rescue the aged and infirm from certain death, giving them another shot at life and the possibility that they will be alive when the next dramatic advance in life span occurs.

But is life extension a good idea? When I asked the students in my class on the life extension sciences "How many people would like to be frozen when they die?" only one raised his hand. The others looked at him in horror. When I asked the others why they wouldn't, they said things like "It will never work," "One life is hard enough,"

"It will be boring," "It sounds evil," "My soul will be trapped," "God will get mad."

I have been told that life extension is unethical. People ask me, "Wouldn't the planet be overcrowded?" "Wouldn't birth be forbidden?" "Might there not be a small, privileged elite who would be allowed to live forever, while others died?"

I have been accused of being insolent, lacking humility, being greedy. I have even been told that life extension is unnatural. "Man was meant to grow old and die."

Listening to these criticisms, I can't help thinking of the Wright brothers. "Man was never meant to fly," they were told. "It will never leave the ground."

Perhaps the people hardest to understand are those who say they don't care. I have always assumed that one's body was a precious possession, whose health and integrity was to be protected at almost any cost. Aging violates that integrity and slowly and inexorably chips away at the very material of which we are composed. Look at the legacy of aging: cancer; heart disease; osteoporosis; arthritis; pain; disfigurement; loss of strength, energy, and movement; a dimming of the senses, "sans teeth, sans eyes, sans taste, sans everything." Who cares, indeed!

I realize that not everyone shares my values and perspective. In the end I cannot answer all criticisms or reply to every disagreement. There are many beliefs and the world can accommodate them all. Yet I have always felt that those who so easily accept aging do so either because they are afraid of being disappointed, believing that nothing can really be done about it, or else because they are basically unhappy and don't wish to live any longer.

Still, many of the objections I have encountered are valid and I will deal with each of them in this book. The possibility of greatly extended life is not something to be taken lightly. It brings up some of the most profound questions of human existence. For instance, What is ethi-

cal? Is it ethical to develop lifesaving drugs such as peni-
cillin and distribute them throughout the world, or is it
better that children die, as half of them under five do in
some underdeveloped countries, because they don't have
access to modern medicine? Is aging moral? Is there a
saving ethical grace in suffering the indignities and pain of
cancer, heart disease, and stroke? Is death ethical or
moral? Ask a child who has lost a beloved grandparent,
or a woman whose husband dies suddenly from a heart
attack, or a parent whose child dies of leukemia.

Perhaps there are those whose hearts are hardened
with a stern, Old Testament vision of propriety and order-
liness, of sacrifice for the sake of tradition and stability.
Often it is such disciplined and self-denying souls who
produce many of the benefits we all enjoy. I, myself, could
never turn away from such grief unaffected. I could never
accept such fate with equanimity. I personally feel that
every health professional should work as hard as possible
to rid the world of the sadness that comes with aging and
dying. I am confident that any deity that might be guiding
our actions has given us the minds and the tools to work
with so that we may proceed with this great endeavor.

In chapter 8, "Pandora's Icebox," I will deal with the
social, political, economic, religious, philosophical, ethical, and moral implications of the war against aging and
death. I hope that everyone will read it carefully and with
an open mind, because the way in which we answer the
question "Shall we do it?" will determine whether we carry
the burden of disease and aging into the future or whether
we try to end it now.

We have only one life to live. But that life may be lived
in ways that today seem as farfetched as a trip to the
moon did to the makers of the first airplanes. We may not
die in the next twenty-five or fifty years but go on to live
for what may now be considered many lifetimes, or our
lives may be placed on hold at some point, to be contin-

ued at a future date. There is much to accomplish, but each new medical advance makes our lives a little better. And surely the day will come when we no longer live in fear of aging and death, and the undertaker and stonecutter will shutter their shops and leave their outmoded occupations.

2

FOREVER YOUNG:

THE SECRET

OF THE MICE

His life became a quest
To find the secret of eternal life
Which he might carry back to give his friend.

—Epic of Gilgamesh, third
millenneum B.C. (Sumeria)

T he bellow that greeted me upon entering Ginty's Tavern was unmistakable. It was Wild Bill, an amateur naturalist who kept ocelots, alligators, and other exotic beasts in his small cottage at the edge of East Rockaway, Long Island. "Your search for the scientific fountain of youth is over," he roared, waving a newspaper in front of my face. I followed him to his habitual stool in the dimly lit recesses of the bar, where he revealed the fruits of his latest research.

YOU WILL LIVE FOREVER, proclaimed the headline unblushingly in the centerfold of the *National Enquirer*. Even more theatrically, a box in the upper right-hand corner stated that the experiments were under tight government security because they contained a secret more potent than that behind the atomic bomb. While this supermarket tabloid hardly qualifies as scientific literature, on that night in

17

1963 I was thunderstruck. Several years earlier my uncle Dr. Morris Jacobs, a professor at Columbia University's School of Public Health who knew of my interest in aging, showed me an article in the Sunday *New York Times* Week in Review section. It was about the same experiment. It would be more than a decade, during which I would study at four universities, before I would be able to validate the findings in those articles, and yet another decade before I realized that this research, while not containing the formula for eternal life, might hold the key to understanding and controlling the aging process.

I was twenty-one at that time, and a man obsessed. At seventeen I had made up my mind not to "go gentle into that good night." With the arrogance of youth, I assumed that a society that was talking about putting men on the moon, seeing into the heart of the atom, and swapping vital organs, both natural and manmade, as if they were new or used auto parts, had the technology and the brainpower to conquer aging and death.

Science is a balancing act between faith and reason, skepticism and belief, evidence and speculation. You must be ready to abandon your favorite hypothesis when the numbers on a graph or the cells on a slide or the animals you are working with tell you otherwise. But you must also be ready to set your course, hold on for dear life, and ride out the storm when you are convinced that it is the only way to get where you are going. It is this blind faith that the world is reasonable and that answers do exist that provides the passion, the drive, and the persistence to see things through to their conclusion. I do not think that there is a scientist worth his salt who has not felt this.

In my case there were two sets of experiments that were to allow me to hold on all these years. One, carried out by a courageous, pioneering woman in England, I will describe in the next chapter. The other is what many researchers consider to be the most fundamental experiment in gerontology.

In the 1930s, Clive McCay, a nutritionist at Cornell Medical Center, showed that putting rats on a severe diet right after weaning allowed them to live 50 percent longer than rats allowed to eat all they wanted. Maximum life span, like maximum size, is built into a species. For rats raised in the laboratory, this is about 3 years or 1,000 days, and one no more sees a 6-year-old rat than one sees a horse-size rodent. The same is true of humans, whose maximum life span is about 105 years. The oldest documented age at death is 120, reports of Methuselah, Soviet Georgians, and yogurt eaters notwithstanding. So when McCay actually increased the maximum life span of rats—fellow mammals whose biochemistry is not all that different from our own—he made scientific history.

Some of the diet-restricted animals have lived more than 1,800 days, or 800 days longer than the controls. In human terms, it is as though we had found a treatment that allowed a person to occasionally reach 150 years of age. But while McCay's experiments were clearly interesting, they could not be adapted for human use. Who would want to put a child of 5 on a near-starvation diet that would leave him stunted and sterile, even if he might gain another 50 years of life? It seemed to gerontologists too high a price to pay, so they ignored these experiments for 40 years.

But when I read about this research while still an undergraduate, I had a different reaction. To me the importance lay not in a possible life-extending diet, but in what the results said about aging and death. Perhaps these two endpoints were not as certain as taxes, as immutable as the tides. They could be postponed, arrested, perhaps even reversed one day.

But try as I might, I could not get others to think the same way. Almost everyone, my family and friends in-

cluded, assumed that you could no more stop aging and
death than reroute the earth's orbit. What was the reason
for their attitude? Why were they resigned to eventual disfigurement and death as though it was a sentence imposed
on us from birth? I vowed I would not let the same thing
happen to me.

I would avoid the conditioning that says aging and
death are inevitable by questioning every underlying tenet
in science, memorizing nothing, ridding my mind of all
preconceived notions. My aim was total liberation from
any intellectual, cultural, or conceptual blinders that
would make me prematurely discard any piece of information that might bring me closer to the secret of life
extension. To this end, I read everything I could get my
hands on in biology, development, and aging. I even studied philosophy and logic, thinking that perhaps the answer lay in this realm. And I hounded everyone with my
unceasing concern with longevity and immortality.

My obsession nearly finished me before I had begun.
Since I refused to memorize lecture notes or facts from
the assigned texts, my marks were abysmal. At the same
time I succeeded in alienating everyone around me. I grad-
uated from the New York State University at Stony Brook
with the lowest grade in the history of the school in biology, my major: a solid D.

I was floored. What was I going to do? I had to go to
graduate school if I was to continue my search for life
extension. I took the Graduate Record Exam and scored
only in the upper quarter in the biology section. Not
good enough. And then I figured out a little secret (known
to almost every successful student). Mass testing, like the
GRE, must rely on a common base of accepted knowledge, the kind one would find in a standard textbook. And
that is what I did the week before I retook the exam—read
a freshman biology text from cover to cover. Most of the
material was familiar to me from either classroom work

or independent reading, but now I was able to organize it in a coherent, manageable whole. This time I scored in the upper reaches of the upper one percentile in biology, the highest score ever achieved in my school.

On the strength of my GRE scores I was accepted into a second-rate master's degree program at a local Long Island college. I compromised my attitude about memorizing facts—and received grades high enough to gain acceptance into a doctoral program in biology at New York University. My doctoral dissertation would explore the antiaging effect of the experiments I first read about in the clipping that my uncle showed me while I was still in my teens and that Wild Bill had flashed in my face that night in Ginty's Tavern.

The experiments, carried out in the late 1950s and early 1960s under the direction of Dr. Richard Gordon, director of research at the Monsanto Corporation, were actually a variation of McCay's diet-restriction experiments. But instead of cutting back on total calories, Gordon severely restricted intake of a single dietary ingredient—tryptophan. An amino acid, tryptophan is an essential building block in the construction of many of the body's vital proteins. Working with chickens and mice, Gordon found that a diet low in tryptophan elongated their lives by stretching out the period of development from infancy to adulthood. He believed that this extraordinary effect was somehow regulated by the pituitary gland, the "master gland" that regulates many of the body's hormones.

I expected that Dr. Gordon, like most scientists, would freely share the results of his research with me. But while he was willing to discuss his findings in chickens, he refused to say anything about the mouse experiments. Recalling the strange box in the *National Enquirer* story that declared that the experiments contained some vital secret that the government refused to divulge, I asked him whether the work was somehow classified. Again he refused to answer, saying that I would not have access to that information. Angered by his repeated refusals, I told him I would duplicate his experiments and slammed down the phone.

I began by switching my doctoral studies from NYU, where there was little interest in gerontology at the time, to the University of Pittsburgh, where a prominent researcher in aging, Dr. Albert Lansing, headed the Department of Anatomy and Cell Biology. I would work under the direction of Dr. Irving Lieberman, an expert in the fledging science of molecular genetics, which is now the basis for genetic engineering.

Although I was originally promised that I would work on diet restriction and aging, I was given the job of performing measurements on DNA, the stuff the genes are made of. This meant I had to do my tryptophan experiment in my free time. I set up the cages for the rats in a deserted corner of the laboratory. On Sundays, I would bring in ingredients from a local supermarket, trying one preparation after another, noting the changes that took place in the animals. After weeks of work I arrived at a low-tryptophan diet that would not kill the rats but would delay growth and maturation. But no sooner was the experiment running smoothly than I was told my animals were an embarrassment to the laboratory and that I should stow their cages underneath the table if I intended to pursue my work.

Discouraged, I called Dr. Fleur Strand, my advisor at New York University, and asked permission to leave Pittsburgh and return to NYU. Although there was no money to support my research there either, I had finished my studies and needed only to complete the experiments for my dissertation. I planned to get a job in the New York area, find a house, and set up my laboratory there.

Dr. Strand agreed. My Aunt Margaret, the wife of the Columbia University scientist, who had since died, loaned me the down payment for a cottage on Long Island, and my longtime friends Harry Waitz and Bruce Cohen helped me build a small laboratory in the garage. Once again I started my low-tryptophan experiments, only this time on mice, and soon found I was able to dramatically delay their growth without killing them. The catch was that even on their deprived diet the mice were eating better than I was. They lived on food, prepared by a commercial nutritional biochemical company, that cost six dollars per pound, while I made do with hamburgers. When I heard that the University of California at Berkeley had a program on aging, I decided to apply for a graduate fellowship.

For the first time, I would be in a situation where my experiments would be part of a program and not treated as something extraneous, I would have a real laboratory to work in instead of a garage, and as a fellow, I would get my tuition paid and have a stipend. Rather than lead two separate lives, I would be able to integrate my research and my studies. And best of all, I would be working with the head of the program, Dr. Paola Timiras, who was a pioneer in aging research. She herself was a former student of Hans Selye, the founder of stress theory who had also made several contributions to aging theory. My acceptance arrived and I moved to California.

Berkeley turned out to be the answer to my dreams. Dr. Timiras had a keen interest in aging research. Like Selye, she is a bold, well-informed, insightful investigator with a strong background in both theoretical and medical physiology. While most scientists would run for cover when I told them what I was interested in, she just smiled. Unlike many of her peers, she is not afraid of the unknown. Over the years she has been of invaluable help to me, defending me from the attacks of colleagues less enamored of my goals while gently directing my efforts toward the achievable. She has an uncanny sense of what can or cannot be done. And she is almost always right.

I was also fortunate in having at Berkeley a strain of especially hardy rats. The diet placed an enormous strain on the animals, and I suspected that a good percentage of the colony would not make it through the first year. Dr. Timiras and I ordered our low-tryptophan diets and began our study.

We started most of the animals on the diet at three weeks of age, the earliest we could safely wean them from their mothers. But with three rats we waited until they were three months of age before placing them on the diet because we wanted to see what role the age at which we began the regimen played in life extension. Within the first few weeks we began seeing growth differences between the normally fed and the low-tryptophan (T-minus) group.

By this time, Harry had moved to Berkeley and was once again working with me. The first hint we had that the diet was slowing aging came when the T-minus rats had reached midlife. We found that these animals handled stress better than their well-fed counterparts. We tested this by returning the rats to normal diets and giving them a brief bath in icy water. We had previously shown that the older the animal was, the more slowly its body temperature recovered from this cold-induced stress. Rats are survivors and will adapt to icy rivers and sewers when forced to swim in them, but they lose this adaptive ability with age. Our tryptophan-deprived animals bounced back much more rapidly than the age-matched controls.

But the real excitement was yet to come. That happened the day I walked into the lab and saw an unmistakable swelling in the abdomen of the twenty-month-old rat. This female had been fed the low-tryptophan diet from the time of weaning until fourteen months of age. Because I thought the diet would make the animals sterile, we began feeding her normally when she was fourteen months old and mated her at nineteen months. Now she was obviously pregnant at twenty months—five months after most rats of her strain had already become infertile.

Within a few days we had the intense pleasure of seeing her nurse healthy pups. We mated her three more times, and each time she bore litters. The last time was when she was twenty-eight months old. Nearly half of her normally fed littermates had already died of old age. We mated her again at thirty-two months, but she died a few days later, perhaps of old age or perhaps of a lover's quarrel with the male rat in her cage.

This experiment was one of the high points of my life. So much of science is dealing with abstractions. There are broad theoretical issues that are difficult to pin down, findings that lend themselves to various interpretations, results that are not clear-cut, measurements that can be used to prove anything you want. But when you see an animal at twenty-eight months—the equivalent of a seventy-year-old woman—bearing young, there is no doubt that you have arrested reproductive aging. Academic committees and review boards can debate until the cows come home, but the results of our experiment cannot be denied.

Meanwhile, one of the rats that had been started on the low-tryptophan diet at three months of age died at seventeen months. Because our supply of animals was low, we put the other two rats started at three months back on a normal diet. These two rats both had pups at twenty months but could not bear pups at twenty-four months. Their reproductive aging had been delayed but perhaps not by as much as those rats placed on low tryptophan earlier in life, before puberty.

Next we wanted to zero in on exactly what difference the low-tryptophan diet was making on aging and life extension. We planned a new series of experiments, in which we would use two different levels of low tryptophan, but both higher than that in the original diet. And we would start the diet immediately after weaning because other studies had shown that the diet had the strongest effect when it was started very early in life. Some of the animals were maintained on the low-tryptophan diet for two years, others for thirty months. Then they were fed normally.

When we had our answer, we were in for a big surprise. The diet that was lowest in tryptophan was the one that made Methuselahs out of the rats. Although nearly half the population raised on the most severe diet died within the first year, the rats who survived did far better than the controls. They lived longer, aged more slowly, and had more pups at later ages. In other words, the diet that had the most lethal effect on the population was the one that allowed a few lucky individuals to survive and outperform all their contemporaries.

In some instances the aging process was so delayed that we were able to double the age at which a female rat gave birth. Normally rats are infertile after fifteen months of age, but when we took a few rats off the low-tryptophan regimen (the diet itself was assumed to make them sterile) they went on to give birth at twenty-seven months and even older. Our oldest rat mother had pups at thirty-three months. It was as if an eighty-year-old woman had children and then lived on to raise them. This elderly rat mother lived to four years of age, when 90 percent of her brothers and sisters had died by the age of three years. It was impossible to deny the evidence before our eyes: The aging process could be slowed. It was not immutable. It needed only to be better understood.

Similar experiments in which the total number of calories, rather than one amino acid, is reduced have been carried out in dozens of laboratories around the world. In each case, the results have been similar—and in some cases spectacular. Diet restrictions started soon after weaning has led to near doubling of the maximum life span in mice and rats.

Roy Walford, a leading gerontologist at UCLA who has carried out many diet restriction experiments in mice, points out that it has worked in every species so far tested, including worms, flies, fish, rodents, and, preliminarily, cattle. The National Institute on Aging is now trying it in monkeys, although the results won't be available for years. There is even some scattered evidence that eating less increases the life span of human beings, says Walford. The people of Okinwa have the highest percentage of centenarians among the Japanese, while eating a diet that is only about 60 percent of the "recommended intake" for Japan.

Interestingly, Roy Walford and others have shown that starting the diet later in life can also increase the life span over that of normally fed animals, but to a far lesser extent than when the diet is started early in life. If caloric restriction is less strict or a diet higher in tryptophan is used, the maximum life span attained is also not as great as with the most severely restricted diets. It is as though better feeding in early life and more food later on is harmful rather than helpful in terms of slowing aging—just the opposite of what you would expect.

What is going on? Should we drastically reduce the amount of food we take in or greatly cut down on the intake of tryptophan? Restricting our own calories to the extent necessary to slow aging, according to the rodent studies, has not been explored carefully enough in higher mammals and humans to assume it can be done safely without special guidance and instruction. However, Walford, a highly respected researcher, has designed and advocated a low-calorie, high-nutrition diet for adults in two of his books.

Lowering our intake of tryptophan is downright dangerous. As I stated earlier, tryptophan is an essential amino acid, needed for the production of most proteins. Reducing or eliminating it from the diet would have drastic health consequences. The highly sophisticated laboratory experiments I have described here were done on rats and mice, not people. I am not championing withholding food from children or in any way abusing or maltreating them in an attempt to add years to their life span. In fact, people who are well off economically and socially usually have had better nutrition than those who are not, and they are the people who have longer, not shorter, lives.

I have always believed that the true importance of these studies lies not in an antiaging remedy but in what they can tell us about what is really going on in the body as we grow old. This in turn will allow us to design interventions that are safer, more effective, and certainly more appealing than a lifelong stringent diet.

For the past few years in our laboratory, my colleague Dr. Hal Sternberg, a biochemist, and my student Victoria Bellport have been using the low-tryptophan diet to dissect the aging process. I believe that we now have a coherent scenario to explain the process that is the final act of the drama begun at the moment of conception.

How a single fertilized egg develops into a human being with sixty trillion cells remains one of life's greatest mysteries. At the other end of the life cycle, the disintegration and death of what was once a supremely fit person is also a puzzle. Development and aging are the two extremes of the life span—and yet, perhaps they are not so very different after all.

What they have in common, I believe, is a life script written in the genes. It is this genetic program, inscribed in the DNA of the nucleus of almost every cell in the body, that determines the destiny of every organism. Not only does it control the making of a tadpole, a caterpillar, or a human baby, but it also directs the metamorphosis of the frog from the tadpole, the butterfly from the caterpillar, the man or woman from the boy or girl. There are those scientists who maintain that the program stops with the fully mature organism and that aging is an unraveling of that tightly regulated process. But there are others, like myself, who hold that the genetic script, like a well-made play, has the end written into the beginning.

Look what happens with the developing embryo. Like the product of Penelope's loom, it is constantly being made and unmade at the same time. Some cells are dividing and growing, while other cells are dying in great numbers. This massive loss of specific populations of cells is preprogrammed. It is part of the design. For instance, the hand of the human fetus starts out embedded in a web like a duck's foot. In the same way that a sculptor chisels a statue from stone, the death of cells sculpt the fingers from the surrounding web. Large-scale cell loss also occurs with maturation as a young animal attains its adult form. The tadpole loses its tail to become a frog, the caterpillar spins its cocoon and forms the pupa. Small populations of cells called imaginal discs survive, while most of the others die off and are completely replaced.

Cell death in a particular area of the brain may act the same way in the sexual maturation of human beings, signaling the onset of puberty. I base this idea partly on work done twenty years ago in our laboratory at Berkeley by Dr. Nancy Sherwood and Cheryl Ellis. They cut the nerve tracts in certain areas of the brain, the anterior hypothalamus and the arcuate nucleus, and brought on signs of puberty at a much earlier age in laboratory animals. I have suggested that by destroying these nerve tracks, they mimicked the cell death that occurs naturally with maturation. The result was that they triggered premature sexual development.

Another striking example of cell death, which we know occurs, is the incredibly shrinking thymus. Starting out as a rather large gland during childhood, the thymus, which lies above the heart, begins to shrink in response to hormones released during puberty. By the time we are forty years of age it is only a shadow of its former self. Again, this is preprogrammed development, and the only way to stop it is to interfere with the program: If one removes the ovaries from juvenile rats, their thymuses weigh *more* than usual when the rats reach full size.

The loss of thymic cells with age takes its toll in the body. The thymus gland, a major organ of the immune system, is responsible for defending the body against a variety of harmful microorganisms such as viruses, bacteria, and fungi. This gland is also a main target of the deadly AIDS virus. In fact, as with AIDS, the diminishing power of the thymus and the thymus-influenced cells allows normally unthreatening microorganisms to invade and produce devastating effects. This doesn't mean that from puberty on we are thrown into an AIDS-like condition—we're talking about a process of cell death that takes place over decades—but the gradual loss of cells from the thymus weakens our resistance to disease as we age. Only the modern magic of antibiotics keeps many middle-aged people today from succumbing to such illnesses as pneumonia and tuberculosis, illnesses that routinely killed their grandparents.

But where does food restriction or tryptophan deprivation fit into all of this? This is the question I asked myself when I looked at the scrawny, undeveloped, almost sickly rats in my laboratory that, like some ornery codgers, were living to be the equivalent of centenarians. And why was it that the more severe the diet, the longer the life span attained?

One idea we have come up with is that underfeeding sends a signal to the body that says in effect: "Resources are in short supply. There is not enough energy for growth. Stop making new cells. Hang on to the ones you have." The body stops killing off cells. And as we have seen, cell death sets in motion the processes of maturation and aging. If cell death is prevented, maturity is delayed, and aging is arrested.

What is the evidence for the idea that diet restriction works by slowing or halting cell death? For one thing, this has actually been shown in the reproductive cells of animals. Normally the ovaries of both rodents and humans lose egg cells with age. But the underfed animals lose these cells far more slowly than their well-fed, age-matched sisters.

Second, researchers have found that the rate of cell division in diet-restricted animals is generally decreased, although not in all parts of the body. Since underfed animals outlive the controls, we have to assume that they lose cells at a far slower rate. If this were not the case, and cells died off at a normal rate, the slower cell division rate of the dieting animals would mean that they would not be able to replace their lost cells fast enough. Their tissues would become depleted and they would die earlier rather than later.

Finally, there is our own study of tryptophan deprivation, which shows that the longest-lived animals are the ones on the the most severe diet. It makes sense that the more deprived the diet, the more the animal has to preserve the cells that it has. So by stalling cell death we are stalling the program for both maturation and aging.

To summarize, then, in our view, aging, whether it is in rats, mice, or humans, is due to a *cascade of specific cell population losses in the various tissues of the body*, and especially in its three major control systems: the brain, the glands, and the immune system. By *cascade* I mean the waterfall effect, in which one stream flows into another, each time increasing its flow and destructive force. In this case, the first trickle begins with the normal cell death of maturation. This in turn initiates the onset of puberty, which releases hormones that cause further cell death in areas such as the thymus. As we age, more cells are lost, more are inactivated. The cascade continues, spilling over the systems of the body until the tissues are depleted of cells vital to its function and support. Performance deficits appear. Energy declines. The runner slows, the batter connects less often. Aging comes slowly but insidiously until a major support or defense system fails. The result is a heart attack, cancer, kidney failure. The trickle has become a torrent.

But we are not helpless in the face of this onslaught. The nutritional-restriction experiments point the way to how we can fight back. It may have taken more than half a century for McCay's experiments on underfeeding to be accorded a central place in aging research, but that has finally happened. The federal government has now launched a massive multimillion-dollar, ten-year study of diet restriction in mice and rats. The study, which is being directed jointly by the National Institute on Aging and the FDA's National Center for Toxicological Research, is designed to pinpoint the crucial differences in aging between the long-lived diet-restricted rodents and normally fed controls who die on schedule. To do this, they will award contracts to various laboratories around the country that will look at the problem in terms of their own area of expertise. Immunologists will look at differences in the ability to mount an immune defense, specialists in neurological aging will look at differences in neuroendocrine functioning, molecular biologists will look at what is happening at the level of the genes, and so on. Through this study and similar ones going on independently in various laboratories, including my own, we should be able to get a handle on the aging process as well as test the various competing theories of aging that have been around for decades. And since nutritional restriction is also known to be a most effective means for eliminating or greatly reducing the incidence of cancer in animals, we should get double our money's worth from this research.

My own approach is to look at why the tryptophan-deprived female rats in my laboratory are able to bear pups at an age when most of their contemporaries have already died. We have shown that severely restricting the diet of juvenile rodents can drastically delay female reproductive aging. We also know that a particular area of the brain in the hypothalamus plays a leading role in this process. By comparing the differences between the hypothalamus of diet-restricted rodents and the normal controls, we may learn how the restricted group is able to produce offspring well into old age. Finally, since there are many parallels between aging in mice and men, we should be able to apply much of what we learn in the laboratory to the world outside and thus greatly accelerate our understanding and control of human female reproductive aging.

The benefits of such research do not stop there. Since reproductive aging is likely to have the same causes as other kinds of aging, particularly those functions directed by our brain, we may be able to use this research to overcome such age-related losses as the slowing of our reflexes and the dimming of our senses. If the animal experiments are any guide, women may even escape the tyranny of the biological clock and be able to have children at much later ages than is now possible. By understanding the sequence of hormonal events, where they occur, how they are timed, and why they unfold, we will be better able to defend ourselves. As we learn the exact pattern of cell losses and inactivation, especially in the control systems of our body, we will find ways to slow, stop, or reverse the tide of age changes.

How will we do this? By picking up where nature leaves off. Using an array of biomedical technology such as genetic engineering, organ transplantation, and embryonic nerve cell implants, we will replace the cells that have been lost, turn on the cells that have been inactivated, provide the products that are no longer supplied. A revolutionary approach to pharmaceuticals, which is already under way, will base drugs on our own proteins and hormones. Such drugs will work even better than the originals, delivering benefits without the backlash of side effects. In this way we will accomplish what I call *partial rejuvenation.*

A prime example of partial rejuvenation, which is now being used by many women, is estrogen replacement therapy (ERT). In the normal course of events the ovarian cells that produce the hormone estrogen are lost after menopause. Estrogen plays an essential role in protecting the bones from being eroded by osteoclasts, tiny cells embedded in the matrix of the bones themselves. Without estrogen, many women suffer osteoporosis and hip fractures when they are in their fifties and older.

Estrogen replacement does more than stop hip fractures. It stems the loss of bone mass, gets rid of the "hot flashes" that can make a misery of menopause, and restores the lost vaginal secretions that protect against infection and abrasion. Recent studies show that it halves the risk of dying from heart disease after menopause. The risk of endometrial cancer remains a statistically small but potentially dangerous side effect. Other bodily substances, such as vitamin D and parathyroid hormones, have also shown promise in building up bone mass and stopping fractures in men as well as women.

A new day is dawning for men as well in realizing the age-old dream of hair restoration. The first hair tonic ever to be based on something other than snake oil is minoxidil. In a nationwide test, 40 percent of the volunteers had "moderate" hair regrowth, while 8 percent actually got a "dense" bush of hair. In the wings are still more products that may soon make male-pattern baldness (the kind that looks like a lawn mower went down the middle of your scalp) obsolete.

Genetic engineering promises to provide in abundance substances that are lost to the body with aging. In some cases the cells that are the source of these vital factors are lost, and in others the cells are still present but are unable to synthesize or release the needed molecules. These include proteins like interferon, which prevents viruses from colonizing cells; interleukin 2, an immune system protein that is effective against cancer; and thymosin, a substance secreted by the thymus gland. Doctors are now testing genetically engineered interferon and interleukin to fight cancer, while thymosin extract has successfully boosted the resistance of healthy elderly people to pneumonia. Mass-produced hormones and hormonelike substances called growth factors are enhancing, increasing, or speeding up natural processes that slow with age. Growth hormone, which now ensures normal growth for abnormally short children, has actually reconstituted the thymus gland and restored youthful immune function in rats. Theoretically, a recombinant growth hormone could do the same for humans while avoiding undesirable overgrowth. Epidermal growth factor, a remarkable substance that controls the growth of certain cells of the skin and mucous membranes, is already being used clinically to accelerate wound healing and grow sheets of skin for burn victims. About twenty other growth factors have been discovered that are now being tested in the laboratory for a mind-boggling variety of growth effects, including regenerating nerve cells, healing ulcers, replenishing bone, and creating capillaries. There are even indications that growth factors may halt cancer, reverse male infertility, and prevent skin wrinkling.

Perhaps the most encouraging news on the antiaging front is the use of brain implants to fight the terrifying neurological diseases of later life. The first clinical use of this technique has been in Parkinson's disease, where cells from the patient's own adrenal gland have been transplanted to the brain. There they appear to restart the production of dopamine, a brain chemical whose deficiency is believed to cause Parkinson's. Although there are reports that the treatment may have relieved the tremors, slurred speech, and difficulty of movement associated with Parkinson's, many experts believe that cells taken from aborted human fetuses will be even more effective. A great debate is now raging over the use of fetal tissue (see chapter 4), but such use provides the one means of potentially curing not only Parkinson's but also Alzheimer's and stroke, two diseases of brain cell loss that make a mockery of old age.

All of these strategies are designed to replace, piece by piece, the losses that occur with age. They are, as I have said, *partial* rejuvenations. But there is one approach that has the potential for global replacement, a complete rejuvenation, a literal new body in place of the old one. This is cloning, the subject of chapter 4.

Cloning is the ultimate weapon in the battle against aging. It will allow us to become our own organ donors, replacing every old, diseased, or damaged bodily organ or tissue with a genetic duplicate. Unlike any transplant that exists today, there will be no rejection, because it will be made of the same stuff we are. There will be no need for powerful immunosuppressants, which weaken the body's defenses, no waiting list for cadaver parts, no search for a "good" tissue match, no last-minute desperate newspaper and TV appeals by a parent, or child, or spouse, for the donation of a heart or lung or bone marrow. We will be able to exchange any aged, diseased, or damaged organ or tissue for a young and healthy replacement. We will have the biomedical counterpart to the Fountain of Youth.

The motion picture *Cocoon* was a milestone for life extensionists. It marked the first favorable presentation by Hollywood of the concepts of rejuvenation and immortality. Although the picture was a fantasy, the characters were sympathetic, caring, identifiable people, not cartoons. Bernie, the one holdout, who believed that "we should play the cards we are dealt," rather than flee from old age, was portrayed in an almost nostalgic light, as though he was literally the last of a dying breed. The rest of the old people were not punished for their vain and selfish wish to be young again, as has usually been portrayed. Although they were leaving behind what remained of their families and friends, they were seen as going forward with great joy and anticipation to an unknown but limitless future. But there is one crucial difference between this movie and real life. *Cocoon* involved the intervention of aliens from a distant star. Youth extension and rejuvenation on earth will require intervention from human beings like you and me if we are to realize the dream of being forever young.

3

SUSPENDED ANIMATION:

BREAKING

THE ICE

"What is that thing that whirls around so merrily?"
asked the princess. And she took the spindle and tried
to spin too. But she had scarcely touched it before the
curse was fulfilled, and she pricked her finger with the
spindle. The instant she felt the prick she fell upon the
bed, which was standing near, and lay still in a deep
sleep which spread over the whole castle.

—The Brothers Grimm, "Briar Rose"
("Sleeping Beauty")

P eople magazine called him a hero. The Phil Donahue
show gave him a coveted spot on their stage. The
National Enquirer featured him begging a biscuit from my
daughter, Eileen. But Miles, an adorable, friendly beagle, is
unaware of his fame. He just lives his doggy life in my
backyard at Berkeley and occasionally sneaks into the
house, where he can get into mischief (like the time he
took a big chunk out of a multitiered wedding cake on
our kitchen table that a professional chef had just finished
icing for a friend of mine). Then he lies down, his long
ears flopping over his paws, looks at you with those big
brown beagle eyes, and you just have to forgive him.

Miles is a survivor. In 1987 he emerged intact from an experiment in which Harry Waitz (nicknamed Frosty for his work on cryonics and cryobiology) and I removed almost all of his blood for more than one hour, perfused his veins with a blood substitute, and chilled his body to near-freezing temperatures. For fifteen minutes he was clinically dead, his heart stilled, his brain deprived of oxygen. Like his namesake in the Woody Allen movie *Sleeper*, who awoke from a 200-year cryonics nap, Miles is fully recovered and happily discovering a new world, in this case the one outside laboratory walls.

Chilled bloodless perfusion—three words that represent a process it has taken us many years to achieve. First we did it on hamsters, then on dogs. Now the veterinary medical team that performed the actual surgical procedures on Miles and cared for him during his recovery is gearing up to perform the same experiment on monkeys. If we are successful in chilling and reviving man's closest relative, the benefits of chilled bloodless surgery to human beings will be immense.

Operations that are now too difficult or dangerous to perform will become routine. New avenues for treating cancer and liver disease will be opened up. The nation's blood supply, at risk because of underdonation and fears of contaminated transfusions, will be revitalized. People with terminal organ disease will not have to grow sicker each day, wondering whether a tissue-matched organ or death will arrive first. Even medicine in space will be affected.

The successful revival of Miles from a near-frozen state is only one of the advances that has been made recently on the cold front. At about the same time we were doing this work, another laboratory three thousand miles away was having a breakthrough that may revolutionize the field of organ preservation. Greg Fahy, a world-renowned cryobiologist at the American Red Cross transplantation laboratory in Bethesda, Maryland, accomplished a crucial step in his pioneering attempt to open up the world of vitrification.

It is a world where liquids become solid, where temperatures are well below the freezing point of water but no ice forms, where organs are stored at the kind of pressures you find at the bottom of the Mariana Trench six miles down in the Pacific Ocean. Vitrification is literally glassmaking. Glass itself is a liquid, but one that flows at such a slow rate it appears to be completely solid. Fahy, who became interested in vitrification when he tried to freeze kidney slices, describes the phenomenon as "a snapshot of a solution, a stiff liquid, molasses in January, only more so."

With vitrification, a kidney or a liver or a brain becomes a sculpture of frozen glass. At that point it can be placed in a liquid-storage tank at a temperature of − 6 degrees centigrade and stored forever. Fahy's team has also invented an electromagnetic heater capable of rewarming the organ in a matter of seconds. Although still in the experimental stage, Fahy's work shows that the day may soon be near when a physician will be able to call up an organ bank; order a heart, lung, kidney, pancreas, or other body part that is practically a custom fit in terms of size and tissue match; and have that organ ready for delivery in about the time it takes to remove a frozen dinner from the fridge, pop it into the microwave, and then serve it up.

Ice is our ally but also our enemy. While it can preserve matter for centuries, it can also cause damage, as anyone knows who has ever taken a badly wrapped piece of meat from the freezer. The expansion of ice crystals can crack cells and tear tissue. But with vitrification and other forms of cryopreservation under development at our lab and elsewhere, we may be able to break the ice in the struggle to store and revive human organs and bodies.

That struggle is very real to the scientists like Harry Waitz and me who are on the research team at Trans Time, Inc., in Oakland, California. There the towering stainless steel capsules containing the frozen "patients" remind us of our obligation to learn everything we can about freezing and reviving people. It has not been easy and it has taken us many years of intense effort during which we lived, breathed, talked, and thought of little else but how we could freeze a small animal and then bring it back to life again.

It was not like any Christmas I had ever experienced— the sun was shining, the air was balmy, the flowers were in bloom. It was 1971 and I had just arrived from New York City to continue my doctoral studies at Berkeley. On the campus it was a time of ferment, excitement, and possibility. Added to that was the pioneering spirit, the lack of tradition, the openness to experience that I thought of as California. And to top it all off I was at one of the greatest universities in the world, privy to some of the finest minds of our time. It seemed the perfect setting for what I wanted to do—find a way to cheat death.

I was soon joined by an equally enthusiastic Frosty, who also wanted to complete his education. I had already been accepted into the Department of Physiology-Anatomy. The next step was to get Frosty into the university as well.

We asked our friends who among the senior faculty would be receptive to the adventurous ideas Frosty wanted to pursue for his doctoral studies. When the same name kept coming up, we knew we had our man: Dr. Melvin Calvin, winner of a Nobel Prize for discovering the chemical pathways that plants use to convert sunlight into energy for growth and survival. When the three of us met and Frosty described his engineering experience and plans for his doctoral research, Calvin agreed to recommend his acceptance as a graduate student in the Berkeley bio-physics group.

Calvin's word was better than gold, and Frosty began his studies immediately. Meanwhile, I had been assigned a laboratory course that involved working on an original team project with a small group of students. I persuaded the group to help me discover how to chill a mouse to the ice point and revive it. Since Frosty was an expert in materials science and shared my hot-blooded passion for cold temperatures, he jumped at my offer.

We were young, we were game, and we were sure we could do it. In fact we even knew how to go about it. We would follow the lead of a lucky Yugoslav and a coura-geous Englishwoman.

During the Second World War, when the Germans were attacking Yugoslavia, the library of a researcher named R. K. Andjus was destroyed in a bombing raid. Had it not been, he would have no doubt read the considered opin-ion of physiologists around the world, who all said that animals that maintain a constant body temperature could not survive being chilled to near-freezing temperatures, and thus may never have achieved the result he did: the first suspended animation of a warm-blooded animal.

In his experiments, he placed a rodent into a jar, closed the top, and put the jar into ice water. As the animal used up the oxygen in the container, its body temperature began to drop and its hypothalamus—the temperature regulator inside the brain—began to fall down on the job. After about an hour, when both the body temperature and the available oxygen were so low that the animal was los-ing consciousness, Andjus removed the animal from the jar and buried it in a bed of crushed ice. The rodent's temperature plummeted to the ice point, its body became immobile, its skin turned gray, its heart stopped beating. It had entered the deathlike state of suspended animation.

When Andjus rewarmed it with the heat from his desk

lamp, its heart started ticking like a watch rewound. Like a rescuer breathing life into a drowned person, he respirated, or breathed for, the animal by squeezing air into a mask placed over its nose. As the rodent warmed and its paws became a deepening pink, it took its first deep, irregular breaths, and began to shiver—sporadically at first and then violently. A few hours later it was running around in its cage as though nothing had happened.

A few years after the war, Andjus moved to England, where he joined forces with Dr. Audrey Smith, of the National Institute for Medical Research in London. Several years earlier, Smith had made the all-important discovery that adding glycerol before freezing cells acted as a *cryoprotectant*, a kind of antifreeze that protected them against cold damage. For many years in her laboratory in Mill Hill, she, Andjus, and James Lovelock, an engineer and inventor, chilled and rewarmed hundreds of animals. Rats, mice, hamsters, rabbits, and even galagos, a distant primate relative of the monkey, were brought down to freezing temperatures of about 0 degrees centigrade—the point at which water starts to turn into ice. Emboldened by their success, they plunged further, taking a number of animals to below the ice point, where a substantial percentage of their body water actually froze solid.

In one study involving several hundred hamsters, Smith and Lovelock were able to revive some animals whose body water was more than 50 percent ice—an astounding feat. They had shown conclusively that a mammal could survive cooling to the point where it was largely a solid block of ice. There is a precedent for survival in a frozen state in nature, but this was not to be known until decades later. Unfortunately, Smith and her colleagues were skating on thin ice here. In a classic series of papers published in the *Proceedings* of the Royal Society in July 1956, Lovelock and Smith concluded: "Some means of permeating the whole animal with glycerol or propylene glycol or some other neutral solute so that 10 percent or more of its body water is replaced thereby will doubtless be devised. Before this is done there is little prospect of preserving whole animals in a state of suspended animation for long periods in the frozen state at very low temperatures." Having exhausted every means they could think of to introduce cryoprotectants into the body, including putting them in the animal's food and even injecting them into their blood, the team finally abandoned the project altogether.

Twenty-five years later, well after Audrey Smith had died and Jim Lovelock had turned to other pursuits, we began our own experiments in reviving mice from low temperatures.

We started with the closed-jar technique described by Smith and Andjus. Since we were on a small budget, we used objects close at hand—a vacuum-sealed canning jar for the mouse and a small fishbowl filled with ice water to immerse both mouse and jar. The mouse would move around for an hour or so and then would slow down and become nearly unconscious. We would remove the animal from the jar, attach a thermometer and EKG leads to detect heart activity, and immerse it in crushed ice.

About an hour later, when its body temperature was near the ice point and its heart had stopped beating, we would warm it up, using a desk lamp and a simple respirator consisting of a tube connected to a hand-held squeeze bulb like a nasal aspirator. The tube ended in an attachment that fit the animal's nose. By squeezing the bulb rhythmically, we would respire the animals for a period of hours after it had been chilled.

Over and over we tried the experiment. As each mouse warmed up, its heart beat slowly at first, then faster and faster. We thought it might be reviving; but then the heart-beat became erratic, slowed down, and finally stopped altogether. Each experiment took hours of work. And each one failed.

One day we made a mistake. We accidentally kept the mouse in the jar too long and it stopped breathing. We did the only thing we could under the circumstances—removed the mouse and used the respirator to get it breathing on its own. To ensure that the mouse was getting enough air, we continued to respirate it even after we had packed it in ice and had begun to chill it. When its body temperature reached the ice point, we let it stay that way for a few minutes before we warmed it up. And this was how we got back our first mouse—purely by accident.

We were elated but mystified. Why should this mouse, which had nearly died before we even started chilling it, be the one to revive? Frosty found the answer in a paper published in 1970 by two scientists, P. D. Rogers and H. Hillman from England's University of Surrey, who described similar experiments inducing reversible suspended animation in rats and mice. They, too, had found that they needed to respirate their animals on the way down to the ice point as well as on the way back up. This respiration was necessary because as rats and mice cool, their brain activity shuts off and they stop breathing even though their hearts continue to beat. The beating heart uses energy, and energy consumption in the absence of oxygen produces an acid buildup in the bloodstream.

A similar thing happens to humans when we run too fast and outstrip our body's ability to deliver oxygenated blood to the muscles. Acids start to accumulate and we gasp and pant in an effort to blow off the waste products formed.

With the chilled mouse, the situation becomes lethal. When the mouse stops breathing, its heart and other tissues continue to function. The animal's blood becomes acid and waste products accumulate. This acid buildup, or *acidosis*, was what prevented our animals from recovering.

Smith's work had led us astray, as it would again. Since most of her work had been done on hamsters—natural hibernators that can breathe on their own at much lower temperatures than rats or mice—she did not need to pre-respirate them and therefore did not include this step in her experimental procedures. Taking our clue from Rogers and Hillman, we respirated every mouse before as well as after chilling. And every mouse came back.

Meanwhile, Frosty's doctoral work was progressing. He was investigating the possibility of freezing animals into an almost magical state of ice called Ice III. Discovered by another Nobel Prize winner, P. W. Bridgeman, Ice III is a kind of ice that forms at unusually low temperatures under crushing pressure.

When water freezes, it expands with the kind of force that can burst pipes and crack car engines. But, as Bridgeman discovered, when water is cooled under 2,000 atmospheres of pressure, rather than turning into ice at 32 degrees Fahrenheit, it just gets colder and colder. It is caught in a vise in which the tremendous pressure prevents the molecules of water from expanding enough to snap into the ice position. Finally, at −4 degrees Fahrenheit, 36 degrees below freezing, water turns into Ice III. In topsy-turvy fashion, Ice III actually shrinks.

Frosty and I thought that Ice III might be the answer to freezing living organisms—no ice expansion, no bursting cells. It occurred to us that Ice III could be used to preserve food as well. Meats and vegetables that are now damaged by ordinary freezing processes might be frozen and thawed without loss of texture or taste. They could even be stockpiled in liquid nitrogen for years or decades as a hedge against crop failure and famine.

The beauty of Ice III was that pressure, rather than a cryoprotectant such as glycerol, acted to prevent freezing damage. We hoped that this approach would do away with the need for cryoprotectants, which can taste bad in food and are toxic in large concentrations. But first we had to test our theory in the laboratory. We had to learn how to put small animals and mice under high pressure so that they could be frozen and thawed without damage.

In science you have to go one step at a time. Before we actually froze an animal, we had to learn how to revive it from the ice point. Buoyed by our success with mice, we decided to switch to hamsters, the tough little hibernators that can frisk across the Syrian deserts in the summer and curl up in their burrows in winter until the warm weather returns. With them we hoped to unlock the secrets of chilling and thawing that would allow us to move into larger animals, such as dogs and monkeys. We found that the Syrian golden hamsters, *Mesocricetus auratus*, lived as long as four hours after their hearts were stopped at the ice point, while mice and rats could only survive for one hour. The same animal could be chilled over and over without any obvious lasting effects. We cooled and rewarmed a hamster ten times in one month and then watched him for a year thereafter, during which he displayed no unusual effects from the experiments.

It was now the mid 1970s, and cryonics was beginning to attract national attention. Television stations would call Art Quaife, president of Trans Time, and ask what was new in the body-freezing business and whether there was any research being done on animals. Art would refer them to Frosty and me. Reporters and cameramen would come to our lab, where we'd demonstrate our techniques for reviving chilled hamsters. Sometimes they would even interview my wife, Judy, as she patiently respirated the hamsters during rewarming and explained what was going on in words everyone could understand. Footage of these experiments appeared on "In Search Of" and other science-oriented TV programs.

So great was public interest that ABC television offered to furnish Trans Time with $1,000 to film both a hamster and a dog revived from ice point temperatures for its nationally televised "Second Edition." We wanted to go even further with dogs, taking out the animal's own blood and replacing it with a blood substitute. This blood replacement would serve two purposes: It would remove the possibility of the blood's clumping during the cooling process, and it would provide a means of delivering a cryoprotectant agent throughout the body, which would be essential when we wanted actually to freeze an animal.

I am aware that many people find the idea of using dogs or cats as research subjects particularly abhorrent. I have shared my life with many pets, and am aware of the profound love that can exist between a cat or dog and its master. But studies on laboratory animals, including those higher up on the intelligence scale, such as a dog, cat, or monkey, are vital to medical research and practice not only for people but for their pets as well. In the same way that few people would volunteer to take a drug that had not been first tested for its toxicity on animals, few pet owners would want their cat or dog to be the first animal that the vet has ever operated on. Although tissue culture is an important tool in testing new compounds, it can never replace a whole living organism in its complexity. And for certain procedures, such as research on surgery or freezing and thawing a living system, such use is patently absurd. No scientist in his or her right mind willingly puts up with the expense and potential danger of caring for and handling laboratory animals unless there is a payoff in terms of actual benefit for humans. And, as the following paragraph graphically illustrates, techniques worked out on dogs and other animals can be successfully translated to human beings.

We were fairly confident that we could perform a blood substitution. During the late 1960s and early 1970s, Dr. Gerald Klebanoff, a colonel at the Lackland Air Force Base in San Antonio, Texas, chilled and revived a small group of dogs to temperatures ranging from 50 degrees Fahrenheit to 64 degrees Fahrenheit. In these experiments he would remove their blood, replace it with a blood substitute, and keep the animals chilled for up to eight hours. He then replaced the blood substitute with the dog's own blood cells and those of other dogs, rewarmed the animals, and revived them. One of these animals lived for a year before it was sacrificed and autopsied.

Not only did Klebanoff explore bloodless chilled perfusion in dogs, he had actually used it in human beings. In one memorable case described both in the *Journal of Surgical Research* and in the national press, he used his blood substitute on a comatose soldier afflicted with a terminal case of hepatitis. Bringing his patient's temperature down to 80 degrees Fahrenheit, Klebanoff flushed out the virus-infected blood with the blood substitute for ten minutes and then replaced it with transfusions of whole blood. The soldier regained consciousness, sat up, and made a dramatic recovery. Klebanoff had demonstrated that a technique first developed in dogs could be applied to people.

Wishing to follow up on his work, we tried to contact him. But by the time we tracked him down to his place of retirement, he had died of a heart attack. We had no choice but to proceed with only what he had written in his papers.

We invited the ABC crew in and went to work. The hamster was the easy part. Then came the dog. The Trans Time team, consisting of a perfusionist, biophysicist (Frosty), physiologist (myself), mathematician (Art Quaife), computer scientist, and a number of technicians and helpers, managed to replace the dog's blood with a balanced salt solution similar to the one we were using at the time in the initial steps of cryonic suspension after death. Even though we had had almost no experience with dogs, we were able to maintain the animal for more than one hour at 20 degrees Celsius (68 degrees Fahrenheit) and then replace the artificial solution with the animal's own blood. Although the dog never regained consciousness, it breathed on its own for seventeen hours, proving that at least the part of the brain necessary for respiration was intact.

Thanks to ABC, we were briefly $1,000 richer but overall a lot poorer. The actual cost of caring for the dogs and paying each member of the team was much higher, and this did not even begin to touch the cost of providing the substantial quantities of expensive and sterile chemicals for the blood substitute. The bottom line was that an experiment on a dog cost $3,000—while the same one on a hamster cost $10. We could do three hundred hamsters for the price of one dog. If we were to develop a workable blood substitute, it would have to be on the hamster, the Model-T of research.

Realizing the application of this work to freezing people, the American Cryonics Society scraped together a few thousand dollars to provide set-up money and a prize of $2,000 for the investigator who could revive a small animal following removal of its blood and its replacement with a blood substitute.

Frosty and I went for that prize. But from the start we ran into trouble. We needed to cannulate an artery so that we could replace the blood with blood substitutes. But slipping the thin plastic tubes called microcannulae into the tiny arteries of the teacup-size animal was like trying to thread a needle with a toothpick. Even the comparatively large femoral artery in the animal's groin proved too small to penetrate. Luckily, two things happened in 1982 that got us on the right track.

One day I received a phone call in my laboratory from someone with a thick Russian accent. "This is Dr. Moysey Puvshitkov," the caller informed me. "I have come from Russia to help Trans Time freeze people. I would like to meet with you as soon as possible."

Somehow Misha, as he called himself, while working at an institute in a remote area in the Soviet Union, had heard of a place called Trans Time that was freezing people. One of Russia's finest cardiovascular physiologists, he held three doctoral degrees, was the author of a number of books and dozens of scientific papers, and had been the director of a Soviet air force hospital. Chucking all that, and leaving his oldest son in the U.S.S.R. to complete his medical education, Misha set out with his wife and youngest child to find Trans Time.

When he arrived in London, he asked for "Trans Time, where they freeze people." Told it was in New York, he boarded another plane and headed for New York, where he again asked for Trans Time. This time he was directed to San Francisco, where someone was able to give him our number. He arrived at our laboratory on the Berkeley campus, excited and ready to work. "Could we please go right away to Trans Time?" he asked.

Trans Time was then located in tiny, cramped quarters in the nearby town of Emeryville. I tried to warn our distinguished visitor that he should not expect too much. We were a small organization with an almost nonexistent research budget. Since Frosty was working on the hamster perfusion project, while I was concentrating on the arrest of aging using low-tryptophan diets, I asked Frosty to take him over.

When he showed Misha the facilities at Trans Time, the Russian refused to believe his eyes. "Where are all the technicians?" he cried. "Where is the institute?" All of Trans Time was crammed into 1,100 square feet of a warehouse, including an office, a few large metal cylinders (called cryocapsules) that contained the frozen bodies, and some research and medical equipment. He obviously had expected something far grander.

But Misha's arrival turned out to be a godsend. Frosty told him about our hamster project and the problems we were having with cannulation. At the time Misha was living on a modest stipend provided by an organization that supported Jewish immigrants from the Soviet Union. We offered him a small salary to work at our laboratory, which was all we could raise but more than anyone at Trans Time was getting, including Art Quaife, the president. He turned us down but agreed to help anyway. Having worked in Russia on hamsters, where he learned how to measure their blood flow by injecting small quantities of chilled blood and following its flow through the animal, he was an expert on cannulation. He taught us some tricks and we were again on our way. Unfortunately for us so was he, having obtained a lucrative position in a Los Angeles research hospital.

The second thing that happened was a stunning discovery in cryobiology that showed that Audrey Smith's instincts about the need for cryoprotectants were right on target. In the North Country of Minnesota and up into Canada live several species of frogs that have evolved an unusual means of adapting to the formidable winters. As the days become shorter and frost covers the ground, the frogs nestle into the leaf cover of the forest floor and allow between one third and one half of their body water to harden into ice. The cells of their body do not freeze, but remain dehydrated, surrounded by an ice matrix of frozen body fluids. They can remain in this partially frozen state for months, until nature's heat lamp, the sun, thaws them out in the spring and they go about their lives.

In the winter of 1982, Dr. William Schmid, of the University of Minnesota, published an account in *Science* of experiments in which he froze some of the overwintering frogs until one third of their body water was ice, and then revived them. When he and his colleagues analyzed the body fluids of these frogs, they found that substantial amounts of glycerol were present. (Other frogs made glucose, the common sugar found in our blood.) As the ice crystals began to form in the frogs' blood, the frogs' liver cells produced large quantities of these cryoprotectant chemicals and released them into the bloodstream. Audrey Smith had been right: Cryoprotectants were the key to survival in the icy state.

When we read about this experiment, I and the other scientists at Trans Time were ecstatic. Our thesis, that complex vertebrates with organ systems like our own could at least be partially frozen and stored in suspended animation—without heartbeat, breathing, or any other integrated body activity—had been supported. It was a true suspension of life, accomplished by freezing down below the ice point, chemically protected, and capable of reversibility even months later.

Although hamsters, unlike frogs, do not manufacture their own cryoprotectant, we believed that if we could find a way to distribute such an agent throughout the body, hamsters, too, could survive icy repose. Unlike frogs, which are amphibians, hamsters are mammals like ourselves and therefore provide a much better model for human responses in like situations.

By this time, the grant that I had to do the nutritional-restriction (low-tryptophan) experiments had run out, and I had become increasingly interested in the blood-substitution experiment. During his brief stay, Misha had shown us that it was much easier to cannulate the carotid artery in the hamster's neck than the femoral artery in the leg, and Frosty and I had designed a special microcannula for the job. Now that Schmid had provided evidence that we were on the right track, I decided to devote full time to the hamster work. It took many experiments, but we finally got a hamster to survive for one hour after chilling it to the ice point and replacing its blood with a blood substitute.

Our excitement was intense. We had shown that we could perfuse an animal with a blood substitute and get it to survive, if only for an hour, in a state of suspended animation at ice point temperatures. We felt as though we were at the doorway to the solid state.

I reported our success to the Board of Governors of the American Cryonics Society (then known as the Bay Area Cryonics Society), but the prize was not yet ours. We had agreed that the hamster had to survive *two* hours after regaining consciousness. This would take another year's work and another accident.

Over and over we repeated the experiment to no avail. In spite of all our efforts not one animal revived. It is hard to describe just how tantalizing and frustrating this experiment was. We had done it, we knew it could be done again, and yet we kept failing. Finally, in desperation, we took our hamsters to a microsurgeon at the Pacific Medical Center in San Francisco to see if perhaps our surgical technique was somehow at fault.

We boxed up our animals and equipment, but had to leave our bulky EKG machine behind. Since the lab we went to did not have an EKG machine of its own, we had no way of determining the state of the animal's heart. Although the surgeon was highly skilled, he was not familiar with the operation. While he struggled to cannulate the hamster, the cooled animal stopped breathing. Fortunately, we had brought along our hand-held respirator and were able to get the animal breathing again.

Finally the surgeon got the microcannula into the animal's artery and we plunged its temperature to the ice point, flushed out its blood, and replaced it with the blood substitute we had developed. After a short period at the ice point, we transfused the hamster with blood taken from other hamsters and warmed it up. Although we were unable to record the animal's heartbeat, we noticed that it had started breathing on its own. At this point, we began to get excited. Through our long experience in front of the TV cameras in chilling and reviving hamsters that had not been blood-substituted, we had learned that the animals that began breathing on their own and did not require artificial respiration went on to recover. As it happened, this hamster never fully recovered; still, we had again accidentally learned something important.

Although it was true, as we had learned previously, that hamsters could breathe on their own at much lower temperatures than mice or rats, and therefore did not have to be respirated as they were chilled, this did not appear to be true of those hamsters that were perfused with a blood substitute. These animals had to be prerespirated just like the mice and rats. They had to go into the bloodless state with their tissues loaded with oxygen and reduced in carbon dioxide. They also had to maintain a proper acid balance. In other words, we had to provide them with what they would normally get from their own circulating blood.

The hamster's blood, just like that of people, has enzymes and buffers that protect the cells of its body from acids produced when oxygen is not available. These acids build up when body temperature is lowered and respiration slows. If we neutralized the acids by respirating the animal during the cooling stage, we could remove its blood, replace it with a blood substitute, and store the animal at the ice point for some time before the acids accumulated again.

Once we began respirating the hamsters during the cooling phase, we began to get more of our animals back for longer periods of time. Finally, we revived a chilled blood-substituted hamster that lived for two hours—just long enough for us to win the prize money from the Cryonics Society.

Things began to look up. Saul Kent, president of the Life Extension Foundation, agreed to support our research. He gave us a $5,000 donation and we set out to improve our ability to "bring them back alive."

In the spring of 1984 I received a letter by Federal Express from David Brown, an entrepreneurial genius who had built a multimillion-dollar energy efficiency company in Texas using programs he had devised on an early model Apple microcomputer. David had previously made a name for himself in Houston as an engineer at NASA, where he had worked on the landing gear of the Lunar Excursion Module.

In the letter he invited me to join him for lunch when he came to San Francisco in a few weeks time. He had read about my work and ideas in a recent issue of *Science Digest.* In the article I had implied that the life extension field needed an entrepreneur who would support research and development.

Tall, good-looking, David was a striking combination of dynamic executive and courteous gentleman. He struck me as someone who cared greatly for the welfare of others. Over lunch, I learned that he had long been interested in prolongevity, extended youth, and cryonics, and was particularly attracted to the idea of a multidisciplinary approach to life extension. He asked me to show him around our laboratory on the Berkeley campus and to introduce him to several faculty members with whose work he was familiar.

After several more meetings, which included an unforgettable banquet in his luxurious home in a posh Houston suburb, David offered to back our research. Although now wealthy, he had grown up in rural Pennsylvania, attending a small country schoolhouse. He had worked hard for his success and was not averse to enjoying it in those few hours when he could get away from business. As we drank wine from cut crystal and ate with gold silverware, we talked of a future when death would be conquered by cryonics, age would be reversed by youthful organs harvested from clones, and life would be extended indefinitely. Having recently played a role in the birth of the space age, he was now ready to engage in a new and to him even more exciting challenge: the conquest of death and aging.

Armed with generous monthly checks from David's Foundation for the Enhancement and Extension of Life, our laboratory on the Berkeley campus flew into high gear. But, after nearly another year of research, we could revive only one of every ten of the chilled blood-substituted hamsters. My student assistant became nervous. She was pre-med and wanted an A from me for her part in our research, which she was using for university credit. Although I assured her that her work was excellent and that she would get my highest recommendation, she was still upset that one experiment would succeed and the next five to ten would fail when we did the same thing every time.

Frosty, too, grew anxious. He sensed there was something wrong. Meanwhile, a group from Rome's Channel One television station contacted us and wanted to make a videotape of one of our chilled blood-substituted hamsters reviving. We did several preliminary experiments, and when each of the hamsters came back, we agreed to let them film an experiment in progress. They flew in from Italy and set up their lights and cameras in our laboratory. Frosty performed the delicate and demanding microsurgery without a hitch. The animal never recovered. Frosty did a second experiment as the film crew worked on expensive overtime. By ten o'clock that evening it was clear that the second hamster had gone the way of the first. The film crew returned to Italy empty-handed. We were devastated and embarrassed.

While we were trying to figure out what had gone wrong, we received a call from the Italian filmmakers. They had decided to use the footage from our laboratory and to add on some clips of a more successful experiment, which we had videotaped on our own and sent to them. Now they wanted to know, would I appear live on their show in Rome? I accepted eagerly, and my wife and I arrived during the week before Easter of 1985. Tucked into our bags were several papers on hypothermia in hamsters, which I had not yet gotten around to reading.

This was my first trip to Rome, a city not unfamiliar with the concept of preservation. Here one is continually surrounded by art and architecture of past millennia. The remains of popes from past centuries lay in state below the floor of the Vatican. The Colosseum, the Forum, and all Rome's other ancient wonders gave one a sense of the past that flowed seamlessly into the present. It was in a hotel in the Eternal City, while I was reading the papers of Joseph Musacchia, a professor at the University of Louisville in Kentucky, that I realized what I needed to do to make my hamsters live again.

Musacchia, who was interested in what hamster hypothermia could contribute to the space program, had cooled hamsters to a few degrees above the ice point and then studied what happened to their blood in the near-frozen state. He and his co-workers had found that if they lowered the temperature to seven centigrade degrees above freezing and maintained it at that point, the animals would last anywhere between several hours and one day. However, if they continually infused small amounts of glucose into the animals' bloodstream, the hamsters would live for three days. When they looked at the animals that were dying, the blood glucose levels had dropped to nearly zero. My God. It hit me. All my chilled hamsters needed was glucose.

I returned to Berkeley in a state of excitement, convinced that I had the answer. We chilled seven hamsters in a row, replaced their blood with a blood substitute containing glucose, and revived all seven. Frosty set up a series of experiments, which we would report on at the upcoming Cryobiology Society conference. Five hamsters were to be chilled and revived using a blood substitute containing glucose and five would go through the same procedures but with no glucose in their blood substitute. All the glucose-treated hamsters revived to the point of breathing spontaneously, and all but one regained full consciousness. Of the non-glucose-treated, only one animal revived fully, while the others failed even to breathe on their own.

For the first time we had a technique that could be reliably repeated. But sticky problems remained. Some people were skeptical about the application of a technique worked out in animals that were natural hibernators and therefore adapted to low temperatures. After all, they said pointedly, humans do not hibernate. They claimed that such experiments had little relevance to any potential use in medicine.

Second, most of our hamsters died within a day of their suspension, although Frosty did manage to revive one hamster that lasted at least six weeks. We never found out how long this animal actually lived, because we caged it with a male to see if it would reproduce and together the pair was strong enough to knock the lid off their cage and escape, never to be seen again. But obviously a medical technique that killed most of its subjects within twenty-four hours would have little value in the clinic.

I was certain, however, that all these complications arose from the surgical limitations of working with a tiny animal. Our technique, I believed, would actually work better on a large, more humanlike animal. The hamsters had been most useful in allowing us to discover the answers to fundamental physiological questions, such as what the most important components of the blood substitute were, and what general procedures had to be followed during cooling and warming. Now that we could reliably bring back hamsters from states of bloodless cold, could we apply the technique we had worked out on these small animals to a dog?

Although several laboratories had already succeeded in reviving dogs from extended periods of bloodless perfusion, some of the animals did not fully recover. Many of Colonel Klebanoff's dogs, in the experiment mentioned earlier, had developed breathing problems and died, while dogs in other experiments have had seizures and convulsions indicating sustained brain damage.

While these types of experiments are extremely distressing to some dog owners, medical researchers are compelled to use them for preventing human death and suffering. Our knowledge of circulatory physiology is based largely on the use of dogs. Without this knowledge, it would be impossible to treat such life-threatening conditions as heart attack, stroke, and shock.

Our chance came sooner than we anticipated. We found a veterinary surgeon, Dr. Eric Schertel, at the University of California at Davis, to do the surgery. As luck would have it, a research project at Davis involving a number of dogs had been canceled and we were allowed access to the animals that would have otherwise ended up as teaching specimens in student laboratory demonstrations.

We carried out several preliminary experiments in which we showed that we could successfully get a dog to breathe on its own after chilled bloodless substitution. In one experiment the dog's temperature dropped too rapidly and its heart went into fibrillation, a useless writhing

motion that can be rapidly fatal. But Eric was able to stabilize the animal, reviving it from a hypothermia so deep
we thought it was dead. In another experiment, which
failed, the animal literally drowned in its own fluid. In
these early experiments, which were done solely as explor-
atory investigations, we did not use sterile procedures. All
the animals were humanely sacrificed to avoid needless
pain. But with each experiment we learned something. At
Davis, we were also fortunate to obtain the services of Dr.
Eugene Breznock, Schertel's mentor, an experienced physiologist and a master veterinary surgeon. Now we believed
we were ready for a full-scale demonstration that the procedures we had worked out in the hamsters could be
transferred to a large animal such as a dog.

When Frosty and I arrived at the Davis campus that
morning, we knew we were in for a full day's work. We
struggled into Gene's lab with the ice-filled cooler containing bottles of crystal-clear, sterile blood substitute that we
had made up the previous day. Shortly thereafter the dog
was brought in, a little beagle that was shaking all over as
if he knew he was about to embark on a strange journey.
As Gene gently administered the barbiturate solution, the
dog's quivering stopped and he fell asleep.

We then placed him on his back on a iron grating
suspended above a tub of ice water slush. After securing
the dog's paws, Gene inserted one end of an endotracheal
tube into the animal's airway and connected the other end
of the tube to a respirator. He then turned on the respirator, which began rhythmically inflating and deflating the
beagle's lungs, filling them with a mixture of oxygen and
anesthetic. Since ether is a highly explosive gas that can
fuel a blast from one spark of static electricity from a
nurse's nylons, we used Flether, ether tamed with a fluo-
rocarbon anesthetic called halothane.

While the animal slept, Gene hooked up thin plastic
tubes called catheters to the femoral vein and artery in the

right side of his groin, so that we could monitor the blood pressure in these vessels, take samples of blood, and administer lifesaving drugs intravenously, if necessary.

Next we carefully lowered the iron grating on which the dog was lying until he was in the tub of ice water. His body temperature rocketed downward. Gene inserted larger tubes, called cannulae, into the carotid artery and jugular vein in the right side of the dog's neck. These giant vessels, which come up both sides of the neck, supply blood to the brain. In a human, obstructing one of these vessels even briefly could spell disaster. In the dog, however, two vessels in the back of the neck called the vertebral arteries supplement this blood supply to a greater degree than they do in man. This could be an evolutionary adaptation for fighting in these animals, who literally "go for the throat."

Now came a crucial moment in the surgery—the insertion of the Swan-Ganz catheter. Although its name derives from the two surgeons who invented it, the catheter does somewhat resemble a swan's neck in the way the tube, which has an inflatable tip at the end, is curved. This was not an easy procedure. Gene had to first thread the "swan" through the jugular vein and into the right side of the heart itself, finally wedging it into a branch of the pulmonary artery, the blood vessel supplying oxygen-poor blood to the lungs.

Gene's associate, Denny Strack, followed his progress on the polygraph, a multichannel strip of electronic recordings, like an EKG machine, that monitored what was happening inside the dog's heart. There were some tense moments while Gene fiddled with the catheter and Denny tried to figure out if it had reached its target. Finally, after a period that seemed to last forever, but was probably no more than five to ten minutes, the polygraph reading indicated that the catheter was in place.

It was Gene's idea to use the Swan-Ganz catheter to

monitor the pressure of the blood as it flowed into the lungs. This allowed us to regulate the delivery of the blood, or rather the blood substitute, as it circulated through the heart and into the lungs. We had to keep the pressure below a certain point to prevent fluid from spilling across the walls of the capillaries in the lungs, filling the millions of tiny air spaces with liquid, and thus drowning the animal in its own fluids. In this way we hoped to avoid losing our beagle as we had lost the second dog in the series.

When our animal's temperature had fallen below 70 degrees Fahrenheit, his heart stopped beating. With the dog hooked up to a heart-lung machine, the same kind that is used to oxygenate and circulate blood during human cardiac bypass surgery, we began pumping the blood substitute throughout his body. At the same time we drained his own blood into a sterile container. When we had collected almost all his blood, we placed the container in the refrigerator. At this point we were cooling the dog inside and out—with chilled blood substitute circulating in his arteries and veins and an ice bath encasing his body.

By the time the beagle's temperature was a frigid 50 degrees Fahrenheit, his blood was 90 percent artificial solution. We continued to circulate and oxygenate the blood substitute, allowing his temperature to sink slowly to 38 degrees Fahrenheit, just six Fahrenheit degrees above the freezing point of water. Then we turned off the pump and the oxygen supply. For fifteen minutes the dog stayed like that, his heart stopped, his blood in the refrigerator, the blood substitute no longer circulating. He had no vital signs and was to all appearances dead.

We then began the warm-up, a cool-down in reverse. Again we worked both inside and out, replacing the ice water slush with water heated to 104 degrees Fahrenheit and warming up the artificial solution in his circulation with the heat exchanger in the bypass machine. His temperature began to climb, soon reaching 50 degrees Fahrenheit. He had spent an hour and ten minutes below that temperature.

At about 55 degrees we began feeding the beagle's own blood back through his veins and arteries, replacing the blood substitute. As we warmed him, we added more and more blood, filling the vessels with a few units of blood that had been collected from other dogs. Near 80 degrees Fahrenheit, Gene applied the electric paddles of the defibrillator to the dog's chest. The current changed the heart motion from the useless writhing pattern of fibrillation into a regular coordinated beat. Our dog was coming back from a truly deathlike state.

Finally, the beagle's chest heaved as he started breathing on his own. We shut down the respirator, removed the catheters and cannulae, and closed the surgical incisions. I took a good look at the dog. Often I have a sixth sense about whether an animal is going to come back. Everything had proceeded smoothly but I was still worried. The dog was so deeply asleep in his surgical field he seemed comatose.

When I last saw the beagle around seven o'clock that evening, packed off into a carrying case for his ride to the clinic, I had a sinking feeling in my stomach. Although his blood measurements indicated that he was a healthy animal, he had yet to stir. I was certain I had seen the last of him.

I couldn't have been more wrong. He regained consciousness sometime during the night, and after an uneventful recovery lasting approximately a week his condition was excellent.

What would we name him? I liked Birdseye, a name suggested by a friend visiting from Oregon. Frosty, however, insisted on Miles, after Woody Allen's character in *Sleeper*. The name stuck, and Miles came to live with us, a refugee laboratory dog with a Hollywood label.

More than two years have now passed. Miles is a scrappy young male who loves to venture forth in my suburban neighborhood, poking his nose into everyone's business. He has been carefully observed by many people who can find no aftereffect of his trip to the other side and back. Miles's complete recovery is a lesson for us all. We have now chilled and revived a second beagle, Misty, with equally good results, the entire procedure recorded permanently by a Japanese film crew and shown on Tokyo's Nippon TV. Although this work is very preliminary, the fact that these and similar operations by other groups have succeeded has tremendous implications for human health.

First, chilled bloodless surgery could make operations such as coronary bypass, which involves a high degree of blood loss, immeasurably safer. With a patient's temperature near the ice point, and his blood safely tucked away in the refrigerator, the surgeon could work in a clean, bloodless field without the everpresent danger that one tiny nick could trigger massive blood loss and irreversible shock. Indeed, the thirty-five to forty pints of transfused blood often required in bypass operations would become a thing of the past.

The near-freezing temperatures would also protect the brain and other organs during surgery. In one striking case, surgeons successfully repaired an aneurysm pressing on the brain of a 61-year-old woman in an operation that involved chilling her body to 58 degrees Fahrenheit, removing her blood, and stopping her heart for 40 minutes. "It may be the surgery of the future in cases where bleeding poses the greatest risk to the operation," says Julian Bailes, who uses low-temperature medicine in his neurosurgery practice at Pittsburgh's Allegheny General Hospital. "Bleeding is the biggest cause of death in surgery," he says. "If you could put someone in a state of suspended animation, you could operate in a totally bloodless field."

Second, bloodless cold could make possible operations in virtually inaccessible regions of the body: tumors close to a large artery or vein—where the patient is at risk of bleeding to death—or in a vital organ, such as the brain, that cannot survive oxygen deprivation.

Third, it would allow procedures that are unthinkable at present. For instance, disseminated cancer of the liver, which is now all but hopeless, could be treated by cooling the entire body. The liver could then be selectively rewarmed and bombarded with high concentrations of anticancer agents, while the near-freezing temperatures protect the bone marrow, intestines, skin, and other highly vulnerable organs from the toxic chemicals.

Finally, the use of blood substitutes could revitalize our endangered blood supply. Our nation is faced with a massive shortage of donated blood. People must choose daily between the need for this blood, which is becoming ever more scarce, and the risks of transfusion-borne infection. The development of a surgical technique that allowed blood to be removed and stored during an operation, and then put back (along with a few pints of one's own predonated frozen blood), would go a long way toward solving the problem. These are just some of the possible benefits we may owe in part to a little beagle somewhat overfond of wedding cake.

But Miles is only the first step into the future. What are the possibilities of reviving people from temperatures below the ice point? Here, too, we are convinced that advances made in studying hamsters will pay off in larger animals, first in experiments in monkeys that I and my colleagues are now carrying out, and eventually in human beings.

We have frozen a small number of hamsters in dry ice

until their deep body temperature dipped as low as 11 degrees centigrade below the freezing point, and then quickly warmed them up. Although they did not recover, their heartbeat returned, reaching a rate of up to sixty beats a minute, as measured by their EKGs. We had flushed these animals with glycerol solutions as concentrated as those found in overwintering frogs. We are now pursuing this avenue of research for several reasons.

Frogs are not all that different from the more highly evolved hamsters. Their lungs, kidneys, livers, brains, and basic cell structures are very similar, although there are some differences. We believe that if we could learn to perfuse the body of the hamster with a cold-protecting substance similar to that synthesized by the freeze-tolerant frogs, we could revive the warm-blooded rodents from frozen states just as the cold-blooded frogs revive themselves each spring.

What would successful revival from below the ice point mean for human beings? An accident victim, who donated his organs to others, could be stored for a month while the most effective use of his lifesaving gifts could be determined. A little girl, needing a heart or liver, could rest, safely frozen, until an organ best suited to her small body became available. An astronaut who fell dangerously ill or suffered a serious accident in space could be held in suspended animation until he or she was returned to an earthside hospital.

Could reversible prolonged storage in cryogenic temperatures be achieved? The scientists at Trans Time and the American Cryonics Society are optimistic that the answer is yes. They point to the accelerating progress in techniques for freezing and thawing tissues and organs and the ease with which these breakthroughs can be rapidly and inexpensively screened in small test animals. When a pioneering technique such as vitrification proves effective in reviving frozen kidneys, similar protocols could be applied first to blood-substituted hamsters, then to dogs and monkeys. Ultimately, people dying of incurable diseases—young men with AIDS, women with breast cancer, those whose minds are wasting away with Alzheimer's—could be painlessly stored in the cold until a cure for their condition was found.

And, finally, what about revival from a much longer winter? Will those in cryonic suspension ever emerge from their stainless steel cocoons? Is resurrection from death a dream or a possibility? When I think of the progress we have already made and the hurtling speed with which biological, medical, and technological advances are being made every day, I believe it is only a matter of time before the aging process is vanquished and death itself becomes a temporary state. But that is for another chapter, in which I will look at cryonics—the world of ice and the second spring.

There is a sign at the entrance to the Capuchin Monastery at the base of the Via Veneto in Rome in which the bones of its inhabitants of the last three hundred years are displayed in a variety of truly grotesque designs and poses. The sign reads: "As you are now, so once we were. As we are now, so will you be." For those of us who would rather not, cryonics is the answer.

4

CLONING:
BORN AGAIN

*If we refuse to do a thing which bears the possibility
of abuse for fear we shall find it easier and easier to
tolerate the evil, then we will by the same token find
it easier and easier to tolerate the loss of the good.*

—Joseph Fletcher, *The Ethics of Genetic Control,*
1988

She looked at her face in the mirror the way a jeweler
examines a diamond: facet by facet. The petal-fresh
skin, the cresting cheekbones, the sapphire eyes, the
straight-arrow nose ending in a pert tilt, the bow-shape
upper lip, the pouting lower one, the sculpted jaw. It was
the most sought-after, most photographed, highest-
priced model's face in the world.

But while diamonds were forever, her beauty was starting to chip. A faint mottling of her flawless skin, tiny ver-
tical cracks in her lips, slight puffiness around the eyes, the
unmistakable tracks of crow's feet, the suggestion of a sag
in the firm foundation of her jawline. Age had her in its
viselike grip.

Not for long. Thank God, she was living at a time when
she did not have to put up with growing old. "Dr. Blake,"
she said into the phone, "it's Xanthia [the one name she
was known by throughout the world]. I want a clone."

"It's good that you've come to me now," said Dr. Blake as they sat in his office later that morning, "so we can start the process right away." He dimmed the lights and turned on the full-color computerized display. Xanthia's perfect face filled the wall-size screen. Then it dissolved into a surgical-gloved hand holding a forceps with a tiny snippet of skin. With the 3-D animated images as background, the doctor outlined what was involved: He would need a few of her skin cells to "seed" an egg cell. The embryo would grow in a lab dish until it was ready to implant into a chimpanzee especially bred for this purpose. After six weeks he would remove the embryo and extract a small portion of its brain cells so that it would never develop into a conscious, feeling human being. He would freeze the embryonic brain cells and reimplant the brain-absent body clone into the chimp's womb, where it would remain until it was ready for Caesarean delivery. Then they would have to wait a year or two while the body clone was "grown up" by supernutrient feeding and hormone injections so that it could fulfill the purpose for which it was created.

Xanthia watched fascinated as her aging face and body were reconstructed on the screen. "Using each part of the body clone," Dr. Blake explained, "we will replace every organ and every tissue that has begun to age. Since the body clone is your genetic double, there will be no possibility of rejecting the transplanted body parts. Your skin, your hair, your bones, will not be *like* new, they will *be* new again. As fresh and glowing with youth as when you were twenty. We'll even use some of those frozen brain cells we set aside during the early embryonic stage to replace some of your aging neurons. You will be able to move and dance down the runway with the same grace, agility, and control that you had as a teenager. And here's the best part. At the same time as we make the first body clone, we'll create two other ones. These will be frozen and stored for future use if your liver or heart or any other organ should fail, or when you want another total renovation."

Mutilated embryos, brainless babies dissected for their parts, ape surrogate mothers, spare body clones kept on ice—is this a blueprint for the future or a horror movie? Even if all this were possible, would we want it? Are we to cast aside all considerations of ethics and morals, the concept of motherhood, the uniqueness of the individual, the very sanctity of life because some aging woman can't bear losing her looks? Before you make up your mind, consider a second scenario.

Tears stream down the face of the young mother as she almost collapses against her husband, who struggles to maintain his own composure. In the hospital bed lies their little daughter, Michelle, horribly burned and poisoned from the explosion and fire at the airport. She was flying home after a visit to her grandparents when the airplane she was on crashed and burst into flames. Although she was thrown clear, 70 percent of her body received third-degree burns and her lungs were seared with noxious gases. In a few hours she would beg for water as the shell of skin that was left could no longer contain the vital fluids necessary for life. Her cries would be muffled because her muscles were too weak and her oxygen supply too inadequate to support a scream.

Dr. Norman, head of the multidisciplinary team assigned to Michelle, enters and says that the body clone is ready. Later in his office, he assures the anxious couple that their worries are over. "There was a time not too long ago when I would have told you that your daughter was in for very rough times. Even if she survived the burning of three quarters of her skin, she would spend weeks battling infection and would then have to go through an extended series of painful skin grafts. The damage to her lungs would be irreparable. She would need a lung transplant and over the next weeks and months as her body tried to reject the 'foreign' organ she would require immunosuppressant drugs with unpleasant and dangerous side effects. As for her looks, even with plastic surgery she would have been mutilated for life.

"But now, with cloning, that outcome is as obsolete as smallpox or polio was in your generation. In fact, thanks to your forethought when Michelle was born, we can begin right away."

David and Jenny glance at each other at the same moment, each thinking the same thought. When their pediatrician had first broached the subject of body clones after Michelle was born, their first reaction was horror. They had read about such things, of course, but it seemed to them so unnatural, spooky even. And there was the expense. As a working-class couple, the addition of a baby alone would strain their budget. But their doctor had persisted, saying that the creation of two body clones for Michelle was "literally life insurance." If the occasion ever arose when they needed one, the cost would seem small indeed.

Now, as they hold hands and listen to Dr. Norman's calm explanations, they breathe a silent prayer of gratitude that they took the pediatrician's advice. While one of Michelle's body clones had been frozen early in life, the other had been grown in parallel with her so that the organs were just the right size. Their daughter would treat the transplanted tissue as if it were her own tissue—which it was. The nightmare, as Dr. Norman assured them, would soon be over.

A few weeks later it was all as he had predicted. Michelle breathed easily with her replacement lungs, her shouts of delight as lusty as ever. Her new skin was a glowing pink, the burned areas having been discarded and the bare patches covered with grafts from a body clone. She was completely healed. The only evidences of her ordeal were the nearly invisible lines where the transplanted skin patches had grown together, and even these would soon disappear.

Cloning could make both of these scenarios come true. It could restore a model's beauty and a child's life. It could heal damaged organs and reverse the losses of age. It could give us new bodies for old. It could provide the basis for a literal reincarnation, the reconstruction of the mind and body after the cryonic sleep. What cloning offers is simply this: an endlessly renewable supply of body parts—redundancy as immortality.

This is not just blue-skying. Large animals like cattle and sheep have already been cloned from cells taken from embryos at the beginning stages of development. Many scientists believe that it is just a matter of time before mature cells from a young or adult animal, including a human being, could be used. In fact, Steen Willadsen, who cloned the first farm animals, concluded in his report of this feat in the prestigious British journal *Nature* that his results indicated that "large-scale cloning of domestic animals" is feasible.

But the ability to genetically duplicate a human being will not come without a price. It will impose choices on us that are as fearsome and awe-inspiring as those the ability to harness atomic power imposed on an earlier generation. It will force us to question our most fundamental concepts, our most cherished moral stances. How we decide to proceed in the next few years, whether to carry this research forward or abandon it, whether to apply it to human beings, whether to pursue the goal of cloned parts for organ transplantation, will determine whether we continue the present-day acceptance of disease, disfigurement, and death or go forward into a future where the true potential of human existence can finally be realized.

The word *clone* comes from the Greek for "twig." When you take a cutting from a friend's plant and root it in your own garden, you have created a clone. The same leaves, the same flowers, are now yours to enjoy. It is a clone because it has been asexually produced. You haven't mixed the genetic information from a stamen and a pistil. In the animal kingdom, nature occasionally produces its own clone, splitting the egg after sexual reproduction and fertilization has taken place so that each half contains the same information. The result is a twin, an exact copy down to the acquiline twist of a nose or the corkscrew curl of the hair.

Second selves have always been a source of fascination both in life—which of us does not stop to stare at identical twins?—and in literature. Often the concept of a double has had sinister overtones. The doppelgänger of German legend usually represented one's dark side, a demonic Mr. Hyde reflecting the good Dr. Jekyll. With twentieth-century technology, science joined hands with legend to create the literary version of the clone. In Aldous Huxley's *Brave New World*, the Hatchery and Conditioning centers used assembly line techniques to process subpopulations of humans. Like cars, they came in models ranging from the Model-T Epsilon, the workhorses of society, to the deluxe model, the Alpha Plus Intellectual. *The Boys from Brazil* featured ninety-four Hitler clones from which the notorious Joseph Mengele hoped would spring the new fuehrer. At least one book, however, depicted cloning in a more favorable light, as a means of reincarnating the genes of greatness. Here the clonee, as he was called in *Joshua, Son of None*, was a copy of none other than President John F. Kennedy, cast from the cellular matter of his fatal wound. Cloning even made

headlines when writer David Rorvik claimed in his book
In His Image that an unidentified millionaire had bank-
rolled unnamed scientists to create an undocumented
clone. This was pure fiction masquerading as nonfiction.
In this case, the clone served neither an economic nor
imperial nor messianic purpose, as in the earlier examples,
but a purely personal one—the ultimate ego trip.

The idea of cookie cutter colonies of subhuman populations, or a second-generation Hitler, or even a literal
chip off the old block, as in the Rorvik book, is truly
science fiction. It has no basis in reality. A clone starts out
the same way the offspring of a sexual union does—as an
infant. He or she will develop according to the particular
circumstances in which he or she is raised. The result will
be an entirely separate individual, more different in personality from the person from whom its cells were derived than twins are who were raised at the same time by
the same set of parents.

The kind of cloning I am proposing is entirely different. It is not creating a person in any sense of the word.
It is a body clone, a collection of tissues and organs, a
repository of spare parts. It will never see the light of day,
walk among us, have a conversation, feel an emotion,
think a single thought. There will be no Society for the
Protection of Body Clones, no uprising among its numbers, no clonal collectives with nonnegotiable demands.
What cloning will do is liberate human life from the chains
of disease, disability, and death itself. This is not science
fiction, but science.

My own interest in cloning began with frogs. When we
were boys, my cousin Roger and I spent many dreamy
summer mornings in the creeks of upstate New York,
where my Uncle Morris owned a country house, searching
for frogs. When we finally managed to catch one, we'd
bring it home and play with it, watching its every move,

wondering at the process that turned the streamlined tadpole swimming in the stream into the tailless, four-legged, hopping creature before us. It was not until much later that I realized that somewhere in that program for metamorphosis lay the secret of cloning.

Years later, when Roger and I went to college, both majoring in biology and both hoping to find the fountain of youth, I still retained my interest in frogs. For my first independent college laboratory experiment, I decided to study the growth and development of tadpoles.

As students we bought our frogs rather than caught them. When they arrived from the supplier, we put them into the refrigerator, where they could stay for weeks without food. When we needed them for an experiment, we simply warmed them up. This was my introduction to cryonics, a graphic lesson in how cold slowed biological time.

I learned how to remove the pituitary glands from frogs and inject them into female frogs. The hormones released by the pituitary glands caused the females' bellies to swell with ripe eggs. I then squeezed the eggs out into a dish of pond water and added a paste made from testes of male frogs. As the sperm penetrated the egg, it would rotate, forming the zygote, or fertilized egg. A short while later, as I watched through my low-power stereomicroscope, the egg would divide. The first cleavage plane sliced the egg down the middle, dividing it into two separate cells sharing a common wall. The embryo had begun to form.

Two, four, eight cells; soon there would be too many cells for me to count. The embryo would begin to change its shape, becoming elongated, like a football rather than a little basketball. A groove appeared across its top, the sides of which grew together and sealed. By four days it had formed a head and a tail. Soon there were eyes and a beating heart. Six days after fertilization, the tadpoles would hatch from their clear, sticky shells and swim about freely.

I was not the first to be fascinated by frog embryology. More than half a century ago, biologists learned to divide a fertilized frog egg down the middle. Using a fine hair from the head of a baby, they would circle the egg, drawing the loop tighter and tighter until the egg was split into two separate parts joined only by a little cuff in the middle. Then they would watch. One half of the embryo developed, the other half stayed an egg. Why? Because only the half with the nucleus contained the instruction book for making a new frog.

The story of sexual reproduction is the same for man as for frog, indeed for all multicellular animals. During fertilization the sperm gets so excited that it literally loses its head. Its tail stays stuck to the egg's outer membrane and only the head gains entrance. The egg actually swallows up the head of the sperm, which now forms a round body called the male pronucleus. Wrapped in this little package are the father's genes, which are lined up on tiny threads called chromosomes, like data on a reel of computer tape.

The egg has a pronucleus gene package of its own, which carries the mother's genes. Both the sperm and the egg cells, called gametes, contain only half the chromosomes of the immature cells from which they were formed. The cells of the body, the somatic cells, have two matching sets of chromosomes. In the usual form of division called mitosis, the chromosomes first double and then divide, so that the two sets are passed on, one to each of the daughter cells. But in the special form of division called meiosis, in which the gametes are formed, the two sets of chromosomes are broken up and only half are parceled out to each of the daughter cells. This means that if you carry genes for both blue eyes and brown eyes,

50 percent of your gametes would carry the blue-eye gene and 50 percent would carry the brown-eye gene. The same distribution would occur in your genes for skin color, hair color, height, and body build. For the purposes of cloning, these reproductive cells are less desirable. They would give rise to an individual that resembled you but was no more identical to you than your son or daughter. (However, deriving a body clone from a reproductive cell is a possibility that I will discuss later.)

After fertilization, the male and female pronuclei fuse to form the zygote nucleus, and their chromosomes mingle. The double set of chromosomes is restored, a fifty-fifty combination of mother and father, a unique mix of traits different from any other individual that has ever existed. All the information is now in place for the drama of development to begin.

The zygote, or fertilized egg, divides. Two identical sets of chromosomes form from one. Each of the two daughter embryonic cells, called blastomeres, gets an exact copy of the chromosomes, which are packed into two identical nuclei, one nucleus in each cell. Sometimes during the development of the embryo, these two blastomeres, instead of staying joined, separate. They become two individual organisms—identical twins. They share the same genes. In humans, you can transplant organs from one identical twin to another without the terrible problem of rejection. Their immune systems recognize the transplanted part as "self" rather than "foreign." Twins are members of the same clone.

As embryonic development proceeds, the cells divide over and over again, their chromosomes replicating exactly during each division. The result is that each cell in the body contains the same genetic instructions as all the others, a complete library of all the organism's genes. All the cells of the body are actually members of the same clone, because they all descended from the same fertilized egg. It is this exactness of genetic replication, built into the basic design of the double helix of DNA, that makes cloning possible.

DNA is the stuff that genes are made of. It is the chemical computer tape on which our body's genetic information is stored. One gene carries the instructions for making one protein. Each cell of the body, except the red blood cells, has a nucleus. Each nucleus contains a set of chromosomes housing the same DNA molecules. We resemble our parents because we inherit half of our DNA from each of them. Thus, our eye, hair, and skin color, our facial features, our height and build, possibly even our temperament and intelligence, may reflect that of one parent or another, or be a fifty-fifty mixture of the two. Each of us is genetically different because the DNA of our chromosomes is a unique combination of our parents' DNA. Each of us, that is, except for identical twins, both of whom share the same DNA information within all of their cells.

Something else happens during the process of embryonic development. Through a process that some experts have termed the Central Mystery of Biology, a fertilized egg turns into a multicellular organism whose individual cells have different functions. Every cell of the body, as we have noted, contains the same information as every other cell, yet, depending on the tissue to which it belongs, it does different things. We have liver cells and brain cells and stomach cells and blood cells, and they all look different and behave differently. What is it that makes a liver cell a liver cell and not a brain cell? The answer is differentiation.

The fertilized egg and the very early embryonic cells are totipotent—that is, they have the potential to develop into a complete organism. They are like a college freshman who hasn't yet taken a single course. All his options are open. As the student moves through the curriculum taking various prerequisites and finally choosing a major, his options become increasingly narrowed. At some point he becomes committed to a specialization and turning back becomes very difficult.

Commitment to the differentiated state, in a nutshell, is the major obstacle to cloning. In order to make a new you, one would need to use a somatic cell, which contains the complete complement of two sets of chromosomes, rather than a reproductive cell, which has only one set. But while reproductive cells are totipotent, somatic cells are totally committed. Is it possible to take a somatic cell and return it to the point where all options are open and begin again? Or is commitment forever—a one-way ticket?

In the early 1950s, in a classic series of experiments, Drs. Robert Briggs and Thomas King, working at the Institute for Cancer Research in Philadelphia, set out to explore that question. Their experimental model was the leopard frog *(Rana pipiens)*, a common species. To create their clones, they developed the technique of nuclear transfer, which is still the prototype of cloning today. Peering through a microscope that has dials or joysticks to allow precision control, the cloner sucks up an isolated cell into a hollow glass needle. The opening of the needle, which must be hand-forged to the exact thinness, is just wide enough to break the cell wall but leave the nucleus with some of its surrounding cytoplasm intact. Then the nucleus is injected into the egg cell, whose own chromosomes have been removed. So demanding is the technique that even today few are skilled at it.

During the first stages of amphibian development, known as the morula and early blastula, there is little activity within the chromosomes of the cells. The evidence is that most, if not all, the genes are quiescent, doing little more than allowing the cells to divide. As the morula stage gives way to the blastula, the embryo becomes a little ball populated with hundreds and later thousands of cells.

Marie DiBerardino, a petite woman with a quick smile and a keen look in her eye who worked with Briggs and King during those years, recalls the first memorable moment of success. She came to work one February morning and found Tom King dancing down the corridor. Pulling her into his lab, he pointed triumphantly to his microscope. He had been trying to get a clone to reach the blastula stage, a sure sign that he was on the way to normal development. But each time, some of the seven to eight thousand cells making up the hollow ball failed to divide properly. Now she looked down to see a perfectly formed sphere with bumps and raises on the surface like a basketball, indicating that the cells had fully cleaved. Hearing the excitement in the lab, another colleague wandered in. King handed the newcomer a pair of forceps with which to turn the blastula and see that its cells had divided all the way around. "This person, I won't use the name or gender, looked, was duly impressed, and left," says DiBerardino. "Then Tom sat down to look at his favorite little first and found that the person had *squashed it* and walked away without saying a word. We all slapped him on the back and said, 'If it's real, you'll do it again.' " It *was* real, and in 1952, Briggs and King published their historic paper on the first successful cloning of a multicellular animal, a tadpole.

In their experiments, they had used nuclei from cells from morula and early blastula stage. Many of the transplanted embryos survived to become tadpoles and, when permitted, fully formed frogs. They next decided to see how far along the line of embryonic development they could go and still get nuclei from cells that gave rise to tadpoles and frogs.

As the embryo progresses from the blastula to the next

stage, called gastrulation, it begins to differentiate. A new kind of tissue, the mesoderm, which will ultimately give rise to muscle, blood, bone, and many other cell types, starts to form. During gastrulation, the oxygen consumption of the embryo rises, the genes turn on, the synthesis of new proteins gets under way. The outer surface of the blastula begins to invaginate, or fold under itself. At this stage the embryo is called a gastrula.

When Briggs and King transplanted nuclei from late blastula and gastrula stage embryos, their success rate fell dramatically. A lesser number of the transplanted embryos went on to become fully formed frogs. The others either failed to divide or divided to form abnormal embryos that the scientists termed "monsters."

When nuclear transplants were taken from even more advanced embryos (called neurulas, because the nervous system is starting to form), the results become even more dismal—a scant few survived. By the time the embryonic tail began to appear, at an even later stage known as tail-bud, no nucleus when transplanted would permit totipotency—the complete development of the embryo into a tadpole and frog. The cells had reached the point of no return.

Meanwhile, across the Atlantic at Oxford University, John Gurdon, a young graduate student, was watching Briggs and King's results with great interest. Tall, lean, with a full mop of sandy-blond hair set against a fine-boned face, Gurdon talks about his work in a manner that is understated, almost self-effacing. Sixteen years ago he moved to the University of Cambridge, whose narrow, winding streets, Gothic chapels, lush lawns that may be walked on only by university Fellows, and quaint pubs have seen a number of revolutions launched by the likes of Newton, Darwin, Watson and Crick.

He had started his graduate career at the University of Oxford with "a relatively mundane project," but when his supervisor, Michail Fischberg, read of Briggs and King's success in transplanting nuclei, he suggested that Gurdon take a crack at it. They would try with a different amphibian, the South African clawed frog, *Xenopus laevis*, which Fischberg felt might give better results than the leopard frog. Like Briggs and King, Gurdon began the nuclear transfer experiments by using cells first from the early embryo and then from later stages of development. Finally he took cells from the intestines of a tadpole that were fully differentiated as could be seen by their brush border, a highly indented surface that allows the cell to trap food particles for the hungry growing animal. After hundreds of nuclear transplant experiments, he was able to get fourteen transplanted embryos to grow to maturity. Even more remarkable, some of these frogs went on to bear young themselves.

Although this paper went on to become a landmark experiment in the field, when he published it in 1962, it touched off an immediate controversy. Here was a young graduate student telling the team that pioneered cloning that they had jumped to the wrong conclusion. As Gurdon tells the story: "Briggs and King were getting results that led them to believe that the genes were in some way altered or something had happened to them which made it in principle impossible to do the thing that we found we could do. My interpretation was the opposite to theirs —that the genes were not altered when the cells differentiated." In other words it looked like the committed state was not a one-way ticket. Cloning said that two-way trips were possible, that the nucleus of a differentiated cell could allow totipotent development.

If nuclei from tadpole cells worked, then why not nuclei from cells of an adult animal? Gurdon tried using adult frog skin cells taken from the webbing between the toes. Other investigators, including England's Audrey Muggleton-Harris and Philadelphia's Marie DiBerardino, used nuclei from the eye lens cell and even the nucleated red blood cells of adult frogs. But so far every attempt at nuclear transplantation using cells from an adult frog has ended up producing a few tadpoles that grow to swimming stage and then mysteriously die. The complete circle of cloning is yet to be closed, even in amphibians. You can use early embryonic or tadpole cells and get an adult organism, or you can use adult cells and get a juvenile organism. But you can't yet get an adult cell to develop into an adult organism.

Still, Gurdon and other experts in the field believe that cloning from an adult animal is theoretically possible. "What we were trying to establish," says Gurdon, "was to answer the question of whether a completely formed cell, like an adult skin cell, can now do something completely different, like make muscle, brain, eyes and so forth. And it did form all these things, so we see the principle as having been established. Someone might say, 'In that case, why didn't those normal tadpoles turn into frogs?' Well, we don't know for sure."

But today, Gurdon and others have an idea. According to developmental biologists, adult differentiated cells and egg cells are on two very different timetables for division. The egg is on the fast track, ready to spring into action about an hour after fertilization, while the far slower differentiated cell is programmed to divide every two days or longer. So when the nucleus of an adult cell is placed into a recipient egg, it is forced to divide before it is ready. Chromosomes get left behind or are torn or pulled apart. The result is that a number of the clones have chromosomal abnormalities and may be genetic "monsters." And, Gurdon speculates, errors in the chromosomes that are needed for the frog to complete development may be the reason why it fails to reach adulthood.

One way that Gurdon has tried to get around this problem is by doing serial transplants, in which nuclei from the cells of a clone in an early embryonic stage are used to start a new clone. This can be done over and over again, each time selecting cells from the embryos that show the most normal development. It is this "selection of the fittest" that, Gurdon believes, allowed him to end up with the two tadpoles that almost made it to adulthood. "By transplanting a reasonably large number, we found that we did get a few that had almost everything the parent cell had," he says. Indeed, he believes that if one were to do enough nuclear transfers, it would be possible to clone an adult today, even given the primitive state of our present knowledge.

"By the nature of the experiment, you select the chromosomes that have divided themselves best. So my view would simply say that if you went on and did hundreds of thousands of transfers, you would eventually find one that by luck has gone through and copied itself, and that one would be okay."

Audrey Muggleton-Harris is a short blond-haired woman with a wonderful English blend of effusiveness and no-nonsense sturdiness. For the moment she has had to put cloning on the back burner, since the Medical Research Council, for which she works in Carshalton just outside of London, decided she should do research with more immediate application to human beings. She agrees with Gurdon that it may be a matter of synchronizing the internal clocks of the egg and its donated nucleus. "If you could get the genome [the complete set of genes in the nucleus] to go back to a time when it was more fluid and get the right recipient egg in the right conditions to give the nucleus the right clues, I really do think it will be possible," she says. In her own cloning research on adult frogs, she used the eye lens cell. While the intestinal cells and skin cells Gurdon used divide in the body, the lens cell, once it is formed, never divides again. And yet she too was able to get normal tadpoles. "I've always had the funny feeling with my tadpoles," she says, "that if I had bothered to hand feed them on a one-to-one basis and do all the right things, that it might have gone through to the germ line [become fertile]. I do think that once it has gone through square one, and gotten itself to replicate again, there is no reason why it can't go through metamorphosis and beyond."

If a human being is ever to be cloned, scientists must first succeed not with a frog, but with a mammal. In 1981, two researchers, Peter Hoppe of Jackson Laboratory in Bar Harbor, Maine and Karl Illmensee of the University of Geneva in Switzerland, created a media sensation when they reported that they had cloned mice. The newspapers and TV had a field day. The same question was on the lips of all the reporters and commentators: Now that a mouse had been cloned, could humans be far behind?

(Earlier work by Hoppe and Illmensee points the way toward a form of cloning that might be easier to achieve and work almost as well—the use of reproductive cells that I alluded to earlier. In this case, the experimenters achieved single parenthood with a vengeance. By removing the nucleus of either the sperm or the egg immediately after fertilization and then chemically stimulating the chromosomes of the remaining sperm or egg to double, they claimed to have created a true homozygous diploid —a fertilized egg containing a full set of chromosomes from only one parent. All the mice born from such eggs were also homozygous diploid, offsprings of single parents. To be used in human beings, this approach would have to be modified. Unlike purebred lab mice, most people carry at least one recessive lethal gene from each parent. Since recessive genes require two to tango, these undesirable traits are rarely expressed. But if allowed to double, these genes would kill the embryo during development. The answer is to make a genetic "mosaic" by fusing three homozgyous diploids at the two-cell stage.

This would ensure an embryo with a more "balanced" set of genes, yet one that contained genes from only one parent. Although not identical to the parent from whom it was derived, the mosaic could still be used as a parts clone for transplantation. Its organs would contain proteins that came only from the one parent and would not be rejected. Unfortunately, however, no one else has tried to reproduce homozygous diploid mice, and these experiments remain shrouded in rumor.)

The cheering stopped when two Philadelphia scientists, James McGrath and Davor Saltor, reported that they were unable to repeat this work. Illmensee and Hoppe had claimed that they had cloned mice using nuclei from four-day-old mouse embryos. When McGrath and Saltor tried this, they found that not only did this not work but they couldn't clone using even earlier stages where the embryo had eight cells and even only four cells. The only time they got normal embryonic development was when they cloned from the two-cell stage, just after fertilized egg had divided for the first time. Their conclusion reverberated throughout the cloning community: "[The results] suggest that the cloning of mammals by simple nuclear transfer is biologically impossible."

There the matter of mammalian cloning might have rested, but by the time this paper appeared in 1984, two scientists, Steen Willadsen in Cambridge, England, and Jim Robl in Madison, Wisconsin, were already engaged in experiments that they had no intention of stopping. Spurred on by the original report of mouse cloning by Hoppe and Illmensee, each thought he was the only one working on something that would have immense implications in the real world—the cloning of a farm animal.

Alta Genetics, in Alberta, Canada, seems the perfect setting for the Brave New World of animal reproduction. Located just outside Calgary, a city whose gleaming, geometric skyscrapers seem to have been thrown up the night before, the biotechnology company, set on rolling farmland against the timeless backdrop of snow-capped Rockies, brings together the past, present, and future. The animal shed here is divided into two sides. On one side are the adults like Sophia, a super cow, who has produced more than twelve tons of milk, along with less illustrious cows that serve as surrogate mothers. On the other side are batches of look-alike offspring produced in ways that would have stunned Old McDonald—calves from embryos that have been frozen and thawed, transferred from one cow to another, split in half or quartered, and, most recently, cloned. It is here that Steen Willadsen has come to put the finishing touches on the work that is the biggest thing to hit animal breeding since Noah first selected animals to go two by two into the ark.

Dressed in a T-shirt and corduroy pants, Willadsen, with his brown bangs, boyish build, and throwaway manner, seems decades younger than his forty-five years. Although born and educated in Denmark, he speaks with a lilting English accent. "I think I am more of an explorer than I am a scientist. I go through the same joys and fears that people do when they walk into darkest Africa. Except," he laughs, "you're unlikely to be attacked by an embryo."

After becoming a veterinarian and getting a Ph.D. in physiology and immunology, Willadsen went to Cambridge, where he began his journey into uncharted territory. "There are very few things that are really truly new," he notes. "There are just different and new ways of looking at things. In my own experience I have made three quite minor discoveries and they have kept me busy for fifteen years." In fact, he says, they allowed him to do "a whole bunch of experiments that other people couldn't even think of doing that had to do with taking embryos apart and putting them back together again."

Working at the Animal Research Station in Cambridge, he was the first to make twins by dividing a two-cell sheep embryo into two cells and placing each cell into the uterus of a surrogate ewe. He and his colleagues were also the first to create a geep, an animal that, like the mythical chimera, is made up of different species, in this case sheep and goat. Pictures of this research now hang on the wall of his laboratory at Alta Genetics—a real-life Cabinet of Dr. Caligari. Animals that look like sheep but with black spots that come from a cow. Geeps that look like they were put together by a mad knitter. Three sets of twins, as closely matched as three pairs of differently patterned socks, formed by splitting three embryos in half. And most peculiar of all, a lamb sprung from a giant embryo made of four embryos put together. Although only three of them actually worked, the animal still ended up with six parents!

But while the results of this research were spectacular, Willadsen knew they had limited application for mass breeding. To get many offspring from a single embryo, he would need to reproduce by cloning. As Gurdon's work on serial transfer in frogs had shown, the sky was the limit. Each new embryo could be used to clone more embryos in the same way a Xeroxed copy can be used to make more copies. Starting with a single embryo, one could theoretically clone a production herd in a year. When the news broke in 1981 that mice had been cloned, Willadsen decided that the time was ripe to try it on sheep.

In their work, Hoppe and Illmensee had taken eggs that had been fertilized in the normal way by sperm, removed the chromosomes that had come from both sperm and egg, and put in a nucleus from the cell of a mouse embryo. Willadsen decided to work with fertilized eggs, even though earlier work with frogs had used unfertilized eggs. After all, he reasoned, mice were mammals and were a lot closer to sheep than frogs were. But no matter how he tried, he couldn't get it to work. The egg with its newly transferred donor nucleus refused to develop.

Meanwhile Jim Robl at the University of Wisconsin in Madison was trying the same thing with the same lack of success. Slender, with brown curly hair and mustache, Robl has the open and engaging manner of an endlessly curious adolescent. Seated in his present office at the University of Massachusetts in Amherst, he talks feelingly about his years of frustration in trying to clone a cow.

In 1983, he had gone to work as a postdoctoral fellow in the laboratory of Neal First, who was being funded by W. R. Grace and Company to do research on cloning. But he had no sooner started when they learned that other researchers were having trouble repeating the Hoppe and Illmensee experiments. Robl and First decided to plunge ahead anyway. But a year later McGrath and Saltor's paper saying that cloning was "biologically impossible" appeared.

"We were devastated," says Robl. Although the Wisconsin team had persevered and were beginning to get some results, he believes that that paper may have had a dampening effect on the entire field. His government grant to do the funding work was turned down, and First, the head of his laboratory, had to fly to New York to reassure executives of W. R. Grace that "this wasn't the end of the story." Robl even had to face derision from his fellow scientists. "When I tried to explain the work I was doing to a visiting speaker, he said to me, 'Why are you even doing this? You know it's not going to succeed.' "

Back in Cambridge, Willadsen had reached a turning point. Having had no luck with fertilized eggs, he decided to try a few unfertilized ones. It was an immediate success. "I did only one experiment, and if it hadn't worked, I might have dropped it and it would have been a long time before I tried it again," he admits. "But I knew then that this was significant, so I changed the whole research program to go after it." He began getting embryos and transferring them to sheep uteruses. Then he heard that the Wisconsin group was about to scoop him, and he rushed off his results to the British journal *Nature,* a favorite publication for announcing breakthroughs. On March 6, 1986, the report appeared of the first farm animals ever to be cloned—three little lambs. Willadsen and then Neal First, who followed up on Robl's work after he left Wisconsin, both produced cloned cows.

Would nuclear transfer work in human beings? The early embryological development of humans is virtually the same as that for sheep and cows. Thus, the capacity to create a body clone for one's yet-unborn children is now at hand. We know that all the other steps required for cloning and bringing a human baby to term are feasible because they have already been done.

On July 26, 1976, Louise Joy Brown was born, ushering in a new era of human reproduction. She was the first baby to be conceived in a laboratory dish. Steptoe, who attended Louise at both her conception and birth, died in 1988, but Robert Edwards, the other half of the famous team, continues his work. "This is the only in vitro fertilization center in a stately hall," says Edwards, who at sixty-two, gray-haired, vigorous, and imposing, is the perfect lord of the manor. Walking through Bourn Hill Clinic, on the outskirts of Cambridge, one would be hard put to find a greater contrast between a building and its use. Housed in a red-brick mansion built during the reign of King James in the early 1600s, it was taken over by Edwards and Steptoe in 1980. Now, in these Jacobean rooms, with their dark wood paneling, crystal chandeliers, and stone mantles emblazoned with royal crests, women lounge on Victorian overstuffed sofas, read, talk, or watch television, while upstairs their babies are being created by the latest twentieth-century methods.

Life was not always so comfortable for Edwards. For more than a decade he and Steptoe faced an uphill battle on many levels, scientific, personal, and ethical.

"Patrick was interested in fertility," he says. "I am a scientist. My life is always doing new things." Long before he met Steptoe, Edwards was studying the reproductive cycle in mice. He would give the animal a hormone needed for ovulation and see how long it took the egg to grow. In this way he learned that the mouse, and later on, twelve other species that he worked on, including humans, had a specific program of ovulation that was so regular that you could practically set your clock by it. In women it was virtually 37 hours after the hormonal injection.

But human eggs proved to be a problem. The only ones he could get were from ovaries that had been removed during hysterectomy. He even tried to fertilize some of these but none of them worked. If his research were to progress, he decided, he must have "fresh" eggs taken directly from a woman at the time of ovulation.

"I looked everywhere for a gynecologist who could get eggs out easily," he says. "All my colleagues said it was impossible." He still remembers the day in 1968 when he sat in the library at Cambridge University reading a paper by Patrick Steptoe on a new technique for extracting eggs from the ovary using a laparoscope, a narrow tube with a built-in optical fiber light for viewing. "It was a lovely little paper," he says. "I called him up and he said that, yes, you could use laparoscopy for getting in and out very easily and quickly." Like Edwards, Steptoe had been reviled for daring to intervene in human conception. Edwards was told by a doctor in Cambridge that he should stay away from Steptoe, that the gynecologist was a madman and laparoscopy was dangerous. At a meeting of the British Medical Association in which Steptoe demonstrated the technique, he was treated as a pariah. "They thought he was crazy," says Edwards, "and they left him to sit by himself."

Now that he had fresh eggs to work with, he could begin fertilizing them with donated sperm. For three hectic years he repeatedly drove the 200 miles from Cambridge to Manchester, knowing that if he did not get there on time, he might lose the eggs. "We had blastocysts [early embryos], we knew how they grew, we knew how to orchestrate it. It was an unbelievable time. Looking back on it, I wouldn't change a minute of it."

Then in 1972 came an even bigger hurdle, placing the embryos back into the woman's uterus. "Nineteen things can be right," says Edwards, "but if only one thing was wrong, it was a failure." After giving the woman hormones to superovulate (produce extra eggs), fertilizing the eggs in the lab dish, and replacing the embryos in the uterus, all the embryos died. Later, they found out the very hormones they were giving were destroying the pregnancies. Finally, in 1978, when Steptoe was 65 and about to retire, they switched back to the natural cycle, "and bingo! It worked," says Edwards.

They had labored for ten years, enduring the cancellation of grants, the censure of colleagues, their denunciation from pulpits. The only funds they received throughout the 1970s were from an American millionairess. Among the people who castigated them was Leon Kass, a molecular biologist and bioethicist at St. John's College in Annapolis, who declared that infertility was not a disease and should not be treated. "If a woman is infertile, she should live infertile." By the same reasoning, says Edwards, people should be deprived of "false teeth, spectacles, and heart transplants." The attacks on them were vicious and intense, he says, "but we always felt, Patrick felt, that the work was going to break through."

And with the birth of Louise Brown they did prevail.

"We passed a thousand babies born before Christmas last year," says Edwards. "It was a very nice present for Patrick to have before he died." About sixty of these infants came from embryos that had been frozen in liquid nitrogen before they were thawed and placed into the mother. The techniques that are now used in in vitro fertilization clinics around the world are all based on the ones that made that first birth possible. But the ethical and legal reverberations of their work are still being felt in the continuing skirmishes about the rights of unborn frozen embryos, the fate of spare embryos, the rent-a-uterus custody fights. And the most earth-shaking effect has yet to come: By combining the techniques for nuclear transfer in mammals with that of Steptoe and Edwards in extracting eggs from a woman's ovary, growing an embryo in the laboratory dish, and transferring it to the womb, the technology for cloning human embryos is now on line.

But chances are that in the future we'll go far beyond the embryo stage. "We are going to see what the limit is in animals," says Robl, who has his own biotech company, Gentran. The original cloned sheep came from 8-cell embryos. Now cloning of 16-cell and 32-cell embryos is routine and Willadsen has already gotten animals from the blastocyst stage containing about 120 cells. Could a clone be grown from an advanced embryonic or fetal cell? Could we go all the way to a juvenile or an adult cell? The answers to these questions are not yet known. But given the pace of biology, especially in genetic engineering, the techniques with which to examine these questions may soon be here. This effort may be accelerated if the government or private industry decides to fund a Manhattan Project–type proposal to map and decode the entire human genetic archive carried in every living human cell. Spin-offs from this project may reveal the growth factors and the hormones that play crucial roles in the development of a fertilized egg into a fully formed organism.

Most likely, the breakthroughs in cloning will come not from research on humans but from the multimillion-dollar farm animal industry. Armed with tools created by a new generation of genetic engineers, cloning may soon become a goal of commercial ventures seeking a means of mass-producing custom-designed animals. These are animals in whom the genes for desired traits are spliced into the DNA at the time of fertilization. Dr. Katherine Gordon and her colleagues at Integrated Genetics of Framingham, Massachusetts, have already produced "transgenic" animals, such as mice that make large quantities of a human heart drug in their milk. Manmade animals are costly and difficult to produce and reproduce. If cloning were available, biotech companies could turn out thousands of copies of one transgenic animal, just as they now make thousands of copies of genes for growth hormone or insulin using bacteria or yeast. They could go from one animal to a production herd of ten thousand in one year.

Think about the possibilities: cows producing buckets of interferon or human growth hormone in their milk. We could bring home the bacon without the fats and cholesterol. From the luxurious to the practical, from the preventive to the pharmaceutical, products will be provided that are beyond today's comprehension. But the most important application will be to give a new lease to the human life span. Cloning can provide skin for burn victims, kidneys for those that fail, bones for ones that are smashed in accidents or corroded by osteoporosis. Hearts, lungs, livers, pancreases, any and every organ of the body, including parts of the brain, could be clonally derived from the cells of those who need them and transplanted back.

Seventy-year-olds transformed into nineteen-year-olds. The aging surgeon's dexterity, the athlete's wind, the construction worker's muscles, the fashion model's face

—all restored. Complexions smooth as a baby's, joints and tendons spry as a teenager's, hearts and lungs of an adult in prime. Bones to withstand an octogenarian's high jumps, new endocrines to tune the chorus of cloned cells, tissues, and organs, and maintain their perfect harmony. Bodies and minds, once muted by the winter of aging, will sing with the youthful electricity of clonal rebirth.

What would the creation of a body clone entail? Let us return to the aging model, Xanthia, at the beginning of this chapter. In his office, Dr. Blake removes a tiny slip of skin from under her arm. He then places the tissue in a laboratory dish and bathes it with a solution that dissolves the "cement" binding the cells together. Like beads torn from a fabric, the tissues break up into millions of component parts. Using a stereomicroscope so that he can follow his own movements, the doctor draws up a single skin cell into a hollow glass needle called a micropipette.

The tip of the needle is so fine that it actually breaks the single skin cell as it is drawn up. By turning a knob on the end of the micropipette, Dr. Blake can expel unneeded pieces of cell into the fluid of the dish below. He retains only the globelike nucleus, which is about one-third the size of the cell from which it was taken, and injects it into a much larger, rounded cell waiting receptively in another laboratory dish. This is a human egg cell minus its nucleus. Primed with genetically engineered DNA to spring into action when the new nucleus is introduced, the egg starts to divide.

Over the next few days, the sinewy chromosomes perform their ancient dance of division, a dance as old as the dawn of life. Two, four, eight, sixteen, on and on. At this point, the tiny embryo, which is still an undifferentiated cluster of cells, must leave its glass house and take up residence in a uterus.

Where will that uterus come from? One possibility is a solution already used for endangered species of animals. Some years ago, biologists at the Cincinnati Zoo came up with a unique way to rescue the bongo, a rare species of antelope, from the brink of extinction. In captivity the animal could not reproduce fast enough to ensure a margin of safety. It was decided to isolate eggs from the females, fertilize them with sperm from the males, and then implant the embryos in the uteri of a related but less endangered species of antelope, the eland. The elands made good foster mothers, and the bongo embryos were brought to term. Similar techniques are now being used in other zoos to preserve rare species.

Could such cross-species gestation be applied to human beings? There are three genuses of Great Apes that are related to us: the chimpanzee, the gorilla, and the orangutan. Theoretically, human clones might be cultured in the wombs of such primates and then delivered by Caesarean section.

A second possibility is ectogenesis, bringing babies to term outside the uterus, perhaps in wombs of glass. Scientists have grown rat embryos in glass dishes to the point where their hearts are beating, but when the placenta forms, they die. Recent ground-breaking research indicates yet another means that may be a lot closer to fruition—a machine-assisted uterus. In this report, the first of its kind, a group of Italian researchers took a human embryo that had been fertilized in the test tube and got it to implant into a uterus that had been removed during a hysterectomy. Although they were only able to keep the uterus functioning for 52 hours, they believe that advances in organ preservation techniques will allow them to keep the uterus and its implanted embryo going for a much longer time. In fact, they say, "future complete ectogenesis should not be ruled out."

Using another pipette, Dr. Blake sucks up the tiny embryo from the glass dish, shoots it through the cervix of a sedated chimpanzee into the waiting uterus, where it will ultimately embed itself in the rich, hormonally prepared wall.

After six weeks, the physician removes the embryo from the uterus and, with a fine scalpel and a microscope, excises a minute area at the front end of the embryo's head. This is the telencephalon, a collection of small, rounded, primitive cells at the front end of the embryonic area that will eventually develop into the higher brain. At this point they are still a group of unconnected cells that have none of the distinguishing features of the normal cells they will become. They have not even the most rudimentary capacity for conveying thoughts or feeling. They no more constitute an active human brain than does a dish of skin cells dividing in tissue culture.

Of course, if left in place, these embryonic neuronal cells of the telencephalon would multiply into the billions, forming attachments to one another, creating a network of elongated, interconnected nerve fibers. In several months, they would organize into the cerebral cortex of the fetus, eventually becoming the infant's higher thought center. This is why Dr. Blake removes the telencephalon before it has a chance to develop. First, so that a feeling, thinking human being never develops. And, second, so that these embryonic brain cells can be stored for future use when Xanthia's own start to fail.

After bathing the severed bit of tissue in a solution of glycerine and other chemicals, he places it in a sealed glass container and freezes it down to the temperature of liquid nitrogen. He then returns the rest of the embryo intact to the surrogate uterus. What is left can never be more than a human-looking vegetable. (Very occasionally one out of many thousands of babies is born whose telencephalon never developed. Such infants are known as anen-cephalics, "babies without a brain." They generally do not survive much past birth. The recent decision by Loma Linda University heart transplant surgeon Leonard Bailey to transplant organs of anencephalic babies received much publicity, but this was done several years earlier with far less fanfare in West Germany. There, doctors trans-planted the kidneys of a brain-absent newborn into a four-year-old child and a nine-year-old child. In an even more spectacular case, they transplanted both kidneys from an anencephalic newborn into a twenty-five-year-old man with kidney failure. Experiments on animals had re-vealed that the kidneys would grow and mature after trans-plantation. Indeed, two and a half years later, the German doctors report, the kidneys are functioning well and the patient is healthy.)

The body clone comes to term. It is delivered by Cae-sarean section and fed by stomach tube. To accelerate its growth and maturation, the doctor injects it with hor-mones. From time to time, technicians electrically stimu-late the clone's muscles and bones so that they do not atrophy. After a year or two, the body clone is ready to be disassembled so that its cells, tissues, and organs can restore Xanthia's youth, beauty, and glowing health.

At the time this body clone was created, a second copy was also made. This clone was treated exactly as the first, but instead of being parted out, it was placed in cryonic suspension. Here it will dwell in timeless frozen sleep, backup heart, liver, kidneys, lungs, spleen, or skin to be used when those of the first clone are lost to injury or disease.

Research science can make this projection a reality. Cloning can be used for the Xanthias of this world as well as for the burned and mutilated child, the aging parent, the husband or wife with terminal organ disease. It can trans-form civilization and culture in the same way that the advent of vaccines and antibiotics did in previous generations. It can snatch victory from the jaws of defeat, life from the stranglehold of death.

And yet, how gruesome, you may think as you read all this. How unnatural, how against the grain of everything that our civilization and our culture hold dear. Brainless babies conceived in a test tube, incubated in an ape, and then literally torn limb from limb may strike you as too high a price a pay. But is it?

Recently the national news media carried the story of a seven-year-old boy, Ronnie DeSillers, who died while awaiting his fourth liver transplant. He had rejected the first two, and his mother claimed that the third organ, which failed to save her son, had earlier been turned down by three other centers. In fact, she was now withholding the balance of the payment of the hospital bill for $424,302 until her questions were answered about the quality of her son's treatment. Commenting on the fact that efforts had been made to find four livers for the same patient, John A. Robertson, a law professor on the Federal Task Force on Organ Transplantation, said, "It pits our desire not to abandon that one child against our desire to use every liver in the way most likely to achieve good results. With each retransplant, the likelihood of success diminishes, and there's an argument to be made that no one should get more than two livers as long as there are waiting lists full of people dying for want of a liver."

This story encapsulates the plight of organ transplantation today. Children and adults die for the want of an organ. Rejection of an organ continues to be a terrible problem, with acceptance becoming even less likely the next time around. The cost of the procedure is prohibitive. In this case the hospital would not have accepted the DeSillers child unless the mother had agreed to pay in full. And, most chilling of all is the suggestion that no one should get a crack at more than two livers, thus removing from a patient whose chances are already poor any chance whatsoever.

Just for one moment, think what it would be like to be the parent of a child with terminal liver disease, to wait for an organ to become available while your child slowly turns orange and finally green when the blood is no longer capable of removing the red cell breakdown products. Imagine your feeling of utter helplessness and rage when you can do nothing to stop the relentless course of pain, sickness, and disability. Then imagine the joy of actually getting a liver for transplantation only to be filled with despair when your child's body rejects the foreign organ. Imagine going through it a second time, and being told if that liver should fail, that it's all over, that your only choice is to watch your child die. If you were such a parent, and the technology were available to give your child an organ that would function as well as the old one did, and would never be rejected, would you jump at the chance or would you turn it down because of the way that organ was created?

Or what about the parent of a child with kidney disease, who spends hours each week on dialysis, waiting for a transplant? Think of what it means to be a parent of such a child, to know intimately the pain and suffering he or she goes through. Even after transplantation, the "miracle" antirejection drug CY-A (cyclosporin A) can be toxic to the recipient kidneys and greatly increase the risk of certain cancers such as lymphoma. In a few cases, you can even get a kind of nonviral AIDS due to the action of immunosuppressant. Would such a parent welcome a new kidney that was an exact tissue match? Would the parents of a once-strapping athletic son now wasting away from leukemia welcome a bone marrow transplant that was 100 percent safe and effective? Would the parents of a young girl suffering from progressive cardiac failure welcome a new heart perfect in every respect? Or would these parents turn these organs down on philosophical grounds? (In Chapter 8, I will address these and other ethical issues in greater depth.)

What about the son or daughter of an aging parent who has fallen ill? Would they be willing to watch without taking action as Parkinson's, Alzheimer's, cancer, or kidney, liver, lung, or heart disease slowly wrests away their mother's or father's strength, well-being, and dignity? Would you? What if you, yourself, were suffering from one of these diseases? Would you be so certain in your support of a morality that forbids you to act in your own or your parent's interest, even though no sentient being capable of any human activity or emotion was hurt in the process?

Right now older people do not qualify for most kinds of organ transplantation. After contributing to society for many years, they are told they are too old for such an operation. Organs must be reserved for those who still have many more years ahead of them. This is understandable if we are in a situation where there are not enough organs to go around. But with cloning, the need for this kind of battlefield triage would be unnecessary. There would be organs for all, and society would not have to choose between young and old.

The attitude toward cloning that will prevail, I think, is prefigured in the current debates on the use of tissue from aborted fetuses for medical purposes. In a recent article in *The New York Times*, doctors, medical researchers, experts in bioethics, right-to-lifers, pro-choice advocates, and feminists represented practically every shade of opinion and every moral position. But the bottom line was stated most clearly by Frank Williams, national director of the American Parkinson Disease Association: "The majority of people with the disease could care less about the ethical questions—they just want something that works."

Actually, acceptance for the various pieces of cloning that are already here is starting to fall into place, although not without widespread debate on the ethical issues involved. In vitro fertilization clinics that can culture and even freeze human embryos have now been set up in many parts of the world. A number of state legislatures in this country are now trying to sort out the legal problems involved in surrogate parenting. The chances are that the creation of test-tube babies will be regulated rather than eliminated.

The transplantation of fetal brain cells into the brains of people with Parkinson's disease has already been carried out in Mexico and clinical trials should soon be under way in Sweden. In Mexico, the surgeon used tissue only from fetuses that had been spontaneously aborted in order to forestall debate about the ethical issues involved. But if the technique should prove beneficial in Parkinson's as well as other degenerative diseases of the brain, doctors will surely have to use fetal tissue from elective abortions. The demand for such tissue will put great pressure on legislatures around the world to legalize its use.

Finally, there is already a precedent for the use of a brain-absent organ donor, which is what the body clone will be, in the anencephalic babies in Germany, Canada, and the United States. In these cases, the parents fully consented to the use of their child in this way. In fact, it eased the pain in their minds to know that their baby, who was beyond all hope, could save the life of another human being. Again, the potential for a gross misuse of human tissue exists. Safeguards will have to be built in. As Dr. Wolfgang Holzgreve and the other members of the German team wrote in a *New England Journal of Medicine* report, "We object, however, to relaxing the protection of fetuses or newborns with anomalies less devastating than anencephaly and also to offering any financial gains for parents who might allow their anencephalic infants to be born as organ donors."

The way in which these issues are resolved will pave the way for the acceptance of the body clone. If it becomes legal to use fetal nerve cells to save lives, it may then be possible to use the rest of the fetus as well. If an anencephalic baby could be considered legally brain dead, then its parts could be transplanted like that of any other organ donor. This is what happened in West Germany, when the courts ruled that the anencephalic fetus has never been alive despite the presence of a heartbeat and therefore any pregnancy involving such a "brain-absent" fetus can be terminated at any stage. This "nonperson" status of the anencephalic fetus facilitated its use as an organ donor. And at this writing, the Loma Linda University Medical Center in Southern California has become the first hospital in the United States to approve the use of anencephalic babies as organ donors once brain death has been determined.

As beneficial as fetal tissue and organs are to those receiving them, they are not the final answer. Rejection remains a formidable obstacle although new antirejection approaches are being explored. These include treating the transplanted organ, rather than the recipient, by removing the antigenic proteins on the organ's surface that stimulate the recipient's antibody response. Although this might be feasible for small amounts of tissue, such as the pancreatic islet cells that secrete insulin, it would be a Herculean task in a highly antigenic organ such as the liver. Fetal nerve tissue implanted into the brain presents less of a problem. The brain is immunologically privileged—that is, it appears to accept foreign tissue much more readily than other organ systems. But there is some evidence that, over time, the brain may reject the fetal grafts and the Alzheimer's or Parkinson's or other brain disease process may reemerge.

Then there is the problem of supply. Where are all these organs going to come from? Currently there is a terrible shortage. People wait years for kidneys to become available, while they survive on renal dialysis, which severely impairs their quality of life and has many dangerous side effects. But they are the lucky ones compared to those who wait for hearts, livers, or lungs. The terrible truth is that many of these people die before an organ becomes available. Even if fetal organs are added to the pool of available transplantable organs, this will be a drop in the bucket. (Anencephalic babies, fortunately, are a rarity. And most fetuses with the condition are aborted long before they have reached the stage where their organs can be used.) The prospect of women breeding fetuses for commercial use—what one commentator called the commodification of human tissue—is far more repugnant, I believe, than the alternative—cloning your own tissue for future use, the way you can now bank your blood for transfusions in elective surgery.

As embryonic nerve tissue from aborted fetuses and organ grafts from anencephalic donors become accepted medical practice, so will the body clone. The benefits to mankind will be so obvious, so ubiquitous, and so life-transforming that, I believe, they will eventually sweep away all objections before them.

The battle will not be won without a protracted fight. The pope has declared that the Roman Catholic Church stands firmly opposed to any interventions in the normal course of embryonic development, including in vitro fertilization. It was alleged pressure from the Vatican more than two decades ago that brought to a halt the work of Daniele Petrucci, an Italian researcher, who was reported to have fertilized a human egg in a laboratory dish and kept it alive for twenty-nine days, when its heart could be heard beating. For many years research on cloning has been minimal. Only in recent times, with the advent of

genetic engineering, has it picked up again, stimulated by
the profit potential of "designer" animals for commercial
purposes, such as the recently patented mouse for researching cancer in animals.

Since human cloning may be the major vehicle for the
ultimate conquest for death and aging, let us look now at
some of the objections that are raised. (As we said previously, we will also consider these questions more broadly
in Chapter 8 as part of the overall impact of life extension.)

What about the economic costs to the individual and
to society at large? Won't such high-tech measures as
growing and storing clones be excessively expensive?
Would this technology threaten to bankrupt an already
overburdened public health care system? Who would decide who is to have clones and who isn't?

It might be that cloning will start out a high-price medical option at private clinics. In that case, it will be only
for the wealthy and privileged. This was what happened
when cars and televisions were first introduced. As the
automobile and electronics industries developed, the
price came down and more and more people could afford
them. Now most Americans have both cars and television
sets, and many have several of each.

Since cloning has commercial applications in cattle
breeding and phamaceutical manufacturing, there will be a
great incentive to get costs down quickly. Biotech companies will compete with one another, as they now do in
the race for new products. The ones that find the most
cost-effective ways to do the job will be the ones that
make the biggest profits and get the best contracts with
the large drug companies, which will do the distributing,
marketing, and advertising.

In the long run, cloning will be a cheap way to save
lives. It will be much cheaper to provide patients with
cloned kidneys than to support them on dialysis for five

to twenty years. It will be cheaper to provide lungs for emphysema patients than to have nurses around the clock to suction out their tracheotomies or put them into breathing bags. It will be dirt cheap compared to the cost of treating recurrent bouts of leukemia or maintaining a patient with Parkinson's or some other degenerative nerve disease who might be helped by cloned brain cells. Cloning will repay its cost to society many times over as it puts people back on their feet and allows them to contribute to rather than drain off the nation's economic resources.

If it is only necessary to grow a clone to the same fetal stage as the anencephalic fetal donors used by the West German doctors, this would even further reduce costs. Mass storage of such fetuses in huge liquid nitrogen–filled facilities could be very inexpensive on an individual basis. The cost of owning several, as I will show later, could be substantially less than that of owning several cars—and a lot more beneficial.

But what about the deeply ethical questions, the ones that go the very heart of all the concepts we cherish? Cloning challenges our very idea of what is human. It appears to make a mockery of conception, pregnancy, birth, and motherhood. If we accept cloning, are we not setting down a slippery path that will erode the very sanctity of human life? Haven't we already been down that road before with the ideas of the Third Reich and the sinister brand of "medical research" practiced by Joseph Mengele?

Let us look first at the issue of motherhood. Many women will object to cloning as a violation of their deepest feelings about having a child. The idea of conceiving in a test tube, of relegating the bearing of a baby, which for most women is one of life's greatest joys, to an ape, a machine, or an instrumented body part is for many unthinkable.

Furthermore, the concept of creating infants for the purpose of being dissected into a myriad of parts and pieces constitutes another violation of the dream of motherhood: the delivery of a happy, healthy baby, who is then lovingly cared for until adulthood. There are strong, ingrained religious and social taboos against such violations of the unborn fetus or infant. Witness the sizable, vocal, and politically powerful right-to-life minority among women themselves, who would deprive themselves and others of the right to interrupt a pregnancy for whatever reason.

But far from making a mockery of motherhood, I believe that cloning will provide the ultimate protection to our children as they grow up. Rather than an assault on parenthood, it will become a major factor in insuring its success. Combined with other areas of the life extension sciences, such as cryonics and resuscitation, cloning will make certain that organs and tissues of exactly the right kind are there should our child need them. Cloning can extend these guarantees to their parents as well, so that children do not have to grow up in the care of relatives or strangers.

The goal of parenthood is bringing healthy, happy children through wonderful childhood years into the full bloom of adulthood, with bodies and minds fully prepared for the great life adventures that await them. As a father, I am very familiar with these ideas and feelings, and hold them as a most cherished inheritance from our past. When they are violated, such as under conditions of warfare, poverty, or ignorance, I am horrified. When a child is compromised by illness, injury, or deformity, or is lost due to accident or disease, it is a tragedy of major scope. When a child loses a loving parent and has to make his or her way in the world without the aid of this natural benefactor, I am saddened.

I believe that cloning will enhance rather than erode

the sanctity of life. Some people have told me that the creation of body clones smacks of Nazi experimentation on human beings. To invoke this comparison is totally specious. The Nazis preyed on conscious human beings. A clone is nothing more than a collection of cells, a way to grow hearts, lungs, and livers the way technicians now grow epidermal cells into sheets of skin. Nor is the Nazi idea of creating a master race, while eliminating inferior races, applicable. The body clone is not a subhuman race, in the way Huxley envisioned. As any neuroanatomist can tell you, in the absence of a cortex, it is not an individual or a person in any sense of the word. It never develops a brain capable of anything more than secreting hormones and commanding the most basic vegetative bodily functions. It never perceives and never has the opportunity to feel pain and love. It can never exhibit the slightest form of creativity or any of the emotions that characterize human life. It is less developed than most pregnancies now terminated during legal abortion. Without any portion of a higher brain that processes information, it is less human than the fish that graces our dinner table.

Instead of focusing on the dissection of the body clone, we should concentrate on how it can provide our children with the certainty that they can grow up whole. Should they need a transplant, they would have rejection-free organs readily available. Since cloned organs derive from the instructions in the body's own genes, they would comfortably blend in with the rest of the organs of the host and perform as if they were custom-made—which they would be.

The law ultimately reflects the will of the populace. As in every campaign of major social change, there will have to be the necessary landmark ruling, with courageous lawyers investing long hours, often with little or no pay. There will be organized lobbies on both sides to pressure lawmakers both in the state legislatures and in Congress.

There will be bitter opposition, with all the usual charges and countercharges, demonstrations pro and con, and possibly even clinics wrecked and buildings bombed. In the end, that which promotes human happiness will most likely prevail, as it usually does, with the result that the world will be an infinitely better place in which to live and grow.

Religions, for the most part, will also adapt. Some will never accept the new ways, but many of their members will ignore these rulings, just as they now do those on birth control, abortion, diet, and church attendance, while still believing that they are adhering to the spirit of their faith. Other religions will, undoubtedly, come to embrace these advances for their lifesaving benefits to humanity. They will extol cloning as yet another way in which God has empowered human beings with His gift of knowledge and science so that we might rise to a higher plane of existence.

As the real human benefits of cloning far outweigh its philosophical difficulties, one family after another will avail itself of its promise and become an example to the rest of us. There will be an exponential wave of acceptance. Cloning (and its advantages and spin-offs) will become a part of our way of life as has every other medical advance before it.

In the future, we will learn rapid ways of reading and writing the genetic information encoded in the chromosomes of our cells. In fact someday we will learn how to bioengineer chromosomes and insert them into human eggs. These embryos with their built-in designer genes would then develop into body clones. In this way, we could program in any improvement that we wanted. People with sickle cell anemia could have clones whose bone marrow produces normal hemoglobin. Diabetics could have clones whose islet cells make insulin, and so on.

Today a wide variety of tests are under development

that can identify genes predisposing us to certain illnesses. Some of these provoke our cholesterol levels to surge past safe limits, others make us more susceptible to AIDS, still others invite cancer and Alzheimer's disease in later life. We may wish to program body clones so that we and our children inherit wanted genes while weeding out the unwanted.

Of course, some of these traits may be mixed blessings. Cloning will give us the understanding of human genetics that represents great power over our biological selves. Such knowledge will bring the potential for abuse. People will want to go beyond mending to amending, manipulating their DNA molecules to get bigger breasts or muscles, violet or aqua eyes, curly, straight, or even no hair, depending on the latest rage. Some may change sex or race as they now change clothes. In an open society, as ours is, these variations within wide limits will have to be tolerated, and even protected.

All this will alter the world as we know it in ways that are not now even imaginable. But the world is always changing. The electric light, the telephone, the airplane, television, nuclear power, all have had a revolutionary impact on the way we live. New technology forces us to think in ways that we never have before. Values are transformed and deepened as we glimpse possibilities that once seemed unattainable. The morality of the sixteenth century will not serve us well in the twenty-first.

Survival in evolutionary terms depends on the ability to adapt. Often the most deeply held beliefs and philosophy must be changed in the face of present technology. The price of failing to do so can be disastrous. Societies that cling too stubbornly to the rituals of the past may, like the tribal cultures in today's world, face privation, subjugation, and, finally, extinction. Successful acclimation demands that instead of simply transposing values from the past to the present and future, we extract the essence of truth and beauty from these values and then judiciously apply it so as to enhance our lives rather than hinder them.

Of course, there will be some who, like the right-to-lifers, insist that children who are severely burned or dying from cancer or organ disease go to their graves as countless others have done in the past, and therefore to the salvation that they assure us waits beyond. They have a right to their views. Many others will shun such remedies.

I believe that each of us should have the opportunity to make these decisions for ourselves, rather than have stoical philosophies imposed from without. I predict that ultimately all children will have body clones and that doctors will have the right to use these clones to save the lives of those children, just as now they can legally overcome parents' religious objections to giving their children life-saving medical interventions, such as blood transfusions.

Cloning is the linchpin of the life extension sciences. When reversible cryonics is a reality, when resuscitation science can bring back a long-dead person the way we now routinely revive people whose hearts have stopped, when the techniques of regeneration and transplantation allow us to reconnect the spinal cord and nerves, a clone created from our cells in our lifetime and then cryogenically preserved will provide the raw materials—the flesh, blood, and bone—to put us back together. We will literally be born again.

5

LIFE AFTER
DEATH:
RESUSCITATION AND
REGENERATION

*Pursuing these reflections, I thought that if I could
bestow animation on lifeless matter, I might in the
process of time (although I now found it impossible)
renew life where death had apparently devoted the
body to corruption.*

—Mary Wollstonecraft Shelley, *Frankenstein: Or the
Modern Prometheus,* 1818

A rainy night. Brakes screech, tires skid, the car careens
off the road and into a concrete embankment. A
scream fills the air. Then silence. Sirens wail as the state
troopers arrive.

The two troopers pull the young woman from the
wreckage. No breath, no discernible pulse. They begin
mouth-to-mouth resuscitation and massage her heart
with strong, rhythmic thrusts. A few minutes later, another
bleating of sirens as the ambulance pulls up. A team of
EMS [emergency medical service] paramedics runs over
with a stretcher.

"It's no use," says one of the troopers. "She's dead."

"Never say dead," says a paramedic as they rush the body back to the ambulance.

Inside the ambulance, a positive air flow creates a sterile environment and a gowned and gloved intern is waiting. The paramedics wheel over the electronic heart defibrillator. Three times they deliver large jolts of electricity that make the patient's chest lurch violently, but to no avail. The intern looks at his watch. "It's over four minutes. We can't go for closed chest anymore. I'm going in." Using an electric saw, he splits the victim's breastbone and begins squeezing her heart with his hand. The heart takes up the beat on its own. A mechanical ventilator gets her breathing again. A paramedic picks up the arm of the still unconscious patient, finds a vein, and begins dripping in a drug to counteract brain swelling.

At the hospital, they are joined by orderlies, who hoist the patient onto a gurney and rush her to the emergency room. The ER team of doctors and nurses takes over. Like actors running through a well-rehearsed script, they place her on a heart-lung bypass machine, pump in a blood-thinning solution, and induce a slight hypothermia, in the hope that they can reverse the process of death.

A few years ago, a scene like this would have ended with the ambulance and its occupant headed straight for a one-way trip to the morgue. Now a new kind of emergency care is dawning, with rescue teams and physicians who believe that their work starts, rather than ends, with cardiac arrest. Although the above depiction is hypothetical, it is not futuristic. All these elements exist, and some are already being put into practice.

Can the dead live again? Can people whose hearts and brains have been stilled for more than a few minutes be brought back? Is there a limit to which research science can go to restore life? If so, what is that limit? Is death the final defeat, the point at which there is no longer hope, no need to proceed further? Or will the grave yield its secrets, the deathbed its occupants? What do we know now and what does the future hold?

Seconds and minutes count when the heart stops beating and the brain is deprived of oxygen. Until very recently, it was thought that three to five minutes was the outer limit that the brain could survive without oxygen. After that complete recovery was impossible. Even if the heartbeat was restored, the patient would be left with brain damage that ranged from permanent loss of memory to vegetative coma.

Right now about the best place in the U.S. to be stricken with a fatal heart attack is Pittsburgh. There physicians ride the rescue vans, and there is where Peter Safar, director of the University of Pittsburgh's resuscitation research center, carries out the studies that have made him a world leader in reanimatology, the art and science of bringing people back from the dead. For the last decade, he has headed up worldwide clinical trials involving twelve hospitals in the United States and eight abroad to test promising resuscitation techniques that have first been worked out in animals. A tall, rangy, elegant man who still retains a courtly Viennese charm after decades in the U.S., Safar says that "the opinion of clinicians still is that if at normal temperatures the heart stops longer than five minutes you have no chance is not true at all." In fact, as he wrote in a review article in the medical journal *Circulation,* "The concept of the five-minute limit of reversible cardiac arrest in patients is obsolete."

Safar believes that a person whose heart has stopped beating and whose brain was deprived of blood could be brought back good as new even after twenty minutes. Two people estimated to be dead for twenty minutes have already been fully revived using state-of-the-art techniques devised by Safar and others, while several others have recovered after an estimated period of between six and fifteen minutes of pulselessness. By the year 2000, he thinks we will have worked out the steps that will allow a person to be routinely revived after twenty minutes of clinical death, or prolonged heart stoppage. There is also evidence that some neurons can tolerate up to sixty minutes without blood flow at normal temperature, indicating that a person might be brought back to life after one hour. And in the future, he says, "we may be able to use suspended animation as a means of postponing resuscitation in people who are dying but not yet clinically dead in order to gain time to transport, fix up, and then resuscitate under controlled conditions."

Science is now revealing that death, despite its seeming absoluteness, is just as relative a state as most other phenomena of nature. It has a logic, a chemistry, and is knowable. It is also reversible. Indeed, modern law has had to change the very definition of death to take this reversibility into account.

"Death is a protracted pathophysiologic process, not a moment," Safar points out. It doesn't happen all at once. When the heart stops beating, the brain rapidly depletes its oxygen stores. The patient loses consciousness in fifteen seconds. Five minutes later, the brain's glucose stores and energy charge goes. Chemical balances within the cells shift and the brain begins to swell. Tiny arteries called arterioles, which supply the brain's nerve cells with energy-consuming molecules and oxygen and allow for the removal of wastes, snap shut, cutting off the neurons from the circulation. Eventually the isolated, oxygen-starved neurons die one by one, like lights going out. Twenty minutes to an hour elapse before the individual nerve cells of the brain begin to self-destruct, and only several hours after that do the skin cells follow suit.

Why then has a mere three to five minutes without

blood flow to the brain been so devastating? Before the advent of CPR (cardiopulmonary resuscitation), that question couldn't even have been asked. The heart stopped beating, the doctor put away his stethoscope and closed the patient's eyes.

As a young medical student in Vienna during World War II, Safar decided he would not accept such a procedure. He began training in surgery, but he soon realized that "while the cutting was done pretty well, what surgeons really needed was life support. "He switched to anesthesiology, which, he believes, still provides the best training for reviving the dead.

In the 1950s Safar conducted an extraordinary series of resuscitation experiments at the Baltimore City Hospital on volunteer medical students and doctors, whose faith in his restorative powers allowed them to literally put their lives in his hands. By drugging the subjects with curare, which paralyzed every muscle in their body, including those involved in breathing, he developed the techniques of airway control (holding the head and jaw so that the airway is open) and mouth-to-mouth breathing. So effective were these measures in reviving people in certain situations, such as drowning, that in one year they replaced artificial respiration all over the world.

Now that he had steps A (airway) and B (breathing) of resuscitation, Safar decided to go after step C (circulation)—restarting the heart after it stopped beating. In 1958, while Safar was doing this work, a young engineering postdoctoral student in a lab across town at Johns Hopkins was doing experiments on defribillation. One day, while pushing on the chest of a dog that had practically no pulse, he noticed that the blood presure of the animal went up at the same time. This chance observation became the basis of the C step and together steps A, B, and C made up what is now known as CPR (cardiopulmonary resuscitation).

Boy Scouts, housewives, high school students trained in CPR began to do what would have seemed only decades earlier like magic to the most skilled physician: bring dead people back to life.

But there was one major snag. Resuscitation had to begin immediately or very soon after cardiac arrest. If the heartbeat did not return within a few minutes, the patient suffered irreversible brain damage. Sometimes it happened that a patient's heart could be brought back, but his brain activity was gone. Was that patient dead? The classical definition of death, going back to ancient times, was simply that the heart had stopped beating. Here was a situation where the heart had ceased, but the brain was alive. Then the heart was brought back, but the brain was no longer functional. At what point could the person be considered dead?

Obviously the definition of death had to be changed. It could no longer be simply cessation of heartbeat. It had to be the cessation of brain activity, or "brain death." The paradox was that now a person's heart could still be beating, but if his brain indicated extensive irreversible damage as shown by loss of certain specific reflexes, a flat EEG, and no viable pattern of cerebral blood flow, he was dead. The doctor could sign the death certificate, turn off the respirator, and, given the necessary permission, distribute the organs for transplantation.

In 1970, with the success of CPR well established, Dr. Safar and his colleagues wondered if they could not push the boundary of clinical death back further than five minutes. He and his colleagues initiated an animal research program to get at the mechanism of brain death after cardiac arrest. They would also investigate various methods of restoring brain activity after it had ceased. The question was: Could CPCR (cardiopulmonary-cerebral resuscitation) perform the resurrection miracle for the brain that CPR had done for the heart?

Almost two decades have passed since this research was begun in animals and since the first evaluations of CPCR were carried out in human beings. Some of the methods have been so promising that Safar is now heading a coordinated comprehensive study in hospital emergency rooms around the world to test their effectiveness. Even he has yet to pinpoint a therapy that will consistently revive people after short periods of death and ensure a complete recovery. Overcoming the five-minute barrier has, in his words, "proven extremely difficult to achieve."

The reason for the difficulty is that the mechanisms for cerebral injury are highly complex and still something of a mystery. Basically, there are two completely opposite stages after cardiac arrest. One is the absence of blood flow in the brain and the other is its sudden return after resuscitation. The first of these states is extremely damaging at normal temperature. And physicians are increasingly worried about the second.

When the heart stops and the oxygen supply to the brain is interrupted, a series of reactions occurs that cuts the brain cells off from the rest of the body. The microcirculation—the tiny rivulets of blood that ferry food and oxygen to the neurons and carry off wastes from the cells —is lost. This is known as the "no-reflow" response.

There are a number of different factors that appear to play a role in the damming up of this vital blood supply and different scientists have different hypotheses. One major cause appears to be that the tiny roadways of the brain, the arterioles, become constricted, so that the blood can't get to the nerve cells. Some experts think that white blood cells moving into the area cause a traffic jam. Others hold that highly reactive oxygen particles, called free radicals (a class of atoms and molecules that are missing one electron and, like a gang on the rampage, will grab whatever they need from their neighbors, in this case, other electrons), attack and injure the blood cell walls, causing them to become blocked or snap shut. Still others blame the astrocytes, surface-covering cells that surround brain capillaries. When oxygen is scarce, they believe, the astrocytes swell, squeezing off the blood vessels like a physician's cuff during a blood pressure measurement. Whatever the cause or causes, once the no-reflow phenomenon occurs, the brain cells begin to die one by one over a period of minutes to hours.

Some researchers feel that restoring the blood flow after three to five minutes brings with it a whole new set of problems—a state they have named reperfusion injury. They think that the return of oxygen-rich blood triggers the formation of deadly superoxide particles (superoxide is a free radical). They create new electron-seeking free radicals, and in this way, the free radical gang turns into a mob, wreaking havoc wherever it goes. The free radical riot is particularly damaging to cells and cell walls. So far these lethal chemical reactions have been shown in cells in the test tube and in some cases even organs outside the brain, but not yet in the brain itself. Still, some scientists are so concerned that there are destructive secondary changes that they have been termed a syndrome in themselves—postresuscitation disease.

Can tissue injury be prevented, stopped in its tracks, or even reversed? A few years ago a "dead" twenty-one-year-old gang leader was brought to the ER at Detroit Receiving Hospital. He had been stabbed in the heart and had bled for nearly an hour. Dr. Blaine C. White, another pioneer in resuscitation science, opened the young man's chest, repaired his wounds, and put him on coronary bypass, which circulated oxygenated blood and salt solutions to his tissues. This was more or less standard emergency treatment. What wasn't standard was Dr. White's use of high doses of steroids and magnesium sulfate, one of a new class of drugs called calcium channel blockers. The patient regained consciousness, and after a few weeks he was discharged, the only sign of his ordeal a slight twitch in one hand that later disappeared.

White has now used calcium channel blockers to save a number of patients who would have otherwise died. When the heart stops and the oxygen supply is cut off, vast amounts of calcium flood into the walls of the blood vessels of the body and brain, causing the cerebral circulation to shut down—the no-reflow response. By blocking the initial flood of calcium into the walls of the blood vessels, calcium channel blockers help prevent the no-reflow state following oxygen deprivation and, thus, help maintain the vital blood supply to the billions of brain cells upon which our life and consciousness depend.

Unfortunately, they don't always work. Lidoflazine, a new calcium blocker now being investigated, has successfully brought back dogs after death from ventricular fibrillation, but not from asphyxiation. Safar is not surprised. Although in both cases the heartbeat ceased, the physical effects on the body from fibrillation are less punishing than those caused by choking.

Nonetheless, the results of various studies, including his own, using calcium channel blockers have been so provocative that they are now being used in worldwide trials. Results should be available in the near future.

A second approach to the war on death is being advanced on several fronts. This is the use of compounds called free radical scavengers to mop up, or neutralize, the deadly particles that are thought to arise during no reflow and reperfusion. One of these is superoxide dismutase (SOD), which is the body's own defense against the superoxide radical. While some have observed that SOD protects animals from free radical injury after cardiac arrest, the substance has yet to make a difference in the recovery of brain cells after the cerebral blood flow has been restored, according to Safar. And SOD has a built-in disadvantage in that it is too large to pass through the blood-brain barrier—the gateway that protects the brain against toxic substances flowing in from the body.

At least one pharmaceutical company, Upjohn, is pinning its hopes on a new class of compounds it optimistically calls lazeroids. These death-defying drugs have three things going for them: They are free radical scavengers, they can penetrate cell membranes that are particularly vulnerable to free radical attack, and they can cross the blood-brain barrier. The company hopes to begin clinical testing soon.

A third approach that I find highly promising is bypass combining heart lung/blood substitution, hyperbaric oxygen, and hypothermia. In studies conducted on dogs from 1981 to 1985, Safar found that emergency cardiopulmonary bypass increased the number of animals who awoke after cardiac arrest. He now believes that the procedure should be tried on people who have suffered cardiac arrest and fail to respond to state-of-the-art life-support techniques.

By delivering not just ordinary oxygen, but hyperbaric, or high-pressure, oxygen, I believe we could save many more people from the deadly or damaging effects of cerebral ischemia (lack of blood flow to the brain). Hyperbaric oxygen (HbO) has been used surgically to reach areas of the body that have been cut off from the oxygen flow, as, for instance, in gangrene. The procedure made the news recently when it was used in an attempt to save the foot of tiny Jessica McClure, the eighteen-month-old child who was trapped in a well for fifty-eight hours in Texas. In that case, the doctors were able to restore the circulation to all but two toes.

The idea would be to combine cardiopulmonary oxygen, HbO, and the kind of chilled bloodless surgery we did on Miles. Working in a high-pressure chamber, the doctors would place a patient with cerebral ischemia on a heart-lung bypass machine, replace the blood with a blood substitute, and reduce the body temperature. Through the cardiopulmonary bypass oxygenator, they would deliver oxygen at two to three times the normal atmospheric pressure. The advantage of this treatment is that it would remove the blood cells so that they could no longer "clump" together when the temperature goes down and block access to other vessels. They could also add soluble substances such as starches or sugar to the blood substitute, which could counteract brain swelling. Under hyperbaric pressure, the oxygen-carrying capacity of the blood substitute could approach, and even exceed, that of blood, thus making its way through the traffic jam of blocked vessels. At the same time, reduced temperature would slow down metabolic processes that might be harmful.

The doctors could add other ingredients to the blood substitute cocktail—blood-clot-destroying enzymes (if these could be designed to function at reduced temperatures) and drugs such as calcium channel blockers, steroids, and antioxidants to keep the blood vessels open. When the brain was well oxygenated again and the circulation unblocked, the doctors would transfuse blood back into the patient and rewarm him. This treatment could be repeated, if necessary, to speed recovery.

Of course, until such techniques have been fully explored first on animals, and then on people, their use remains highly speculative. But a modification of this approach is now being used for an entirely different purpose —to enhance radiation treatment for cancer. In clinical trials being conducted in South Africa, scientists are combining high-pressure oxygen, lowered temperatures, and hemodilution, or partial blood substitution, along with X rays to destroy mouth tumors. In these studies, the patient is anesthetized, given intravenous fluids, and chilled. Working in a high-pressure chamber, the investigators respirate the patient with oxygen at three times normal atmospheric pressure for about fifty minutes and then bombard the tumors with X rays. The hyperbaric treatment delivers oxygen to the tumors, which makes them more susceptible to the lethal effects of radiation.

After therapy, they depressurize the patient, in much the same way that a diver is brought up from the lower depths, remove the person from the chamber, and rewarm him in a bath of warm water. Over a one-year to two-year trial period, the techniques appear to have succeeded in destroying about half of the presumably lethal tumors.

We are just beginning to scratch the surface of resuscitation medicine. As our knowledge of the mechanics of death increases, we will begin to pinpoint the drugs and techniques that singly or in combination can revive us even after a considerable period of clinical death. As successful approaches are identified in clinical trials, such as those being coordinated by Safar, these measures will become the standard protocol at emergency rooms everywhere. Eventually much of this rescue armamentarium will be carried in ambulances and rescue vehicles so that paramedics arriving at a scene like the one that opened this chapter can start reviving the heart and brain directly, greatly increasing our chances of survival under now fatal conditions.

Once again the boundary of clinical death will be pushed back and the definition of death will have to be redefined. Right now society has become comfortable with the notion of brain death, having forgotten all the ethical arguments that were advanced against it at the time it was first proposed. As provided by law, brain death is a state in which those functions that define our humanity, such as thinking, feeling, perceiving, communicating, and loving, are no longer possible. It is the loss of these higher-order abilities that we have decided to call death rather than the ones involved in the basic task of maintaining the integrity of our body.

In essence, death has become defined by the *number* of brain cells that have died before the cerebral circulation is reestablished. If a small number of neurons die, the victim recovers fully or with minimal neurological damage. A larger number may mean that the person is left with a cerebral disability such as seizures, paralysis on one side, difficulty speaking or remembering. More cell death can spell more severe brain damage, patients whose memory or thinking apparatus or motor function is so impaired that they can no longer care for themselves. Finally, if enough cells die, consciousness itself is lost and the person has become an empty shell, where the heart beats but nobody is home.

What percentage of the cells in the brain must die before an individual can be considered irreversibly lost? Are there special brain areas that are more important than others? Is it worse to lose cells in the portions of the brain connected with memory than in those areas governing breathing? Using the revolutionary technique of nerve cell transplantation, we may soon be able to answer these puzzling questions.

As mentioned in earlier chapters, scientists are now developing techniques of replacing brain cells with those harvested from embryos. This was done for the first time in Mexico using brain tissue from a fetus that had been spontaneously aborted. The overwhelming evidence from earlier animal studies is that many of these transplanted embryonic nerve cells are incorporated into the injured brain, where they then function in ways similar to the lost cells.

In the future we may be able to mend critical areas of the brain with embryonic nerve cell patches, replacing nerve tissue lost from a number of different areas of the brain. If enough vital bodily and brain functions can be maintained mechanically and/or with drugs until the embryonic nerve cells can take over the job, it may be possible to revive people after an hour or more of clinical death.

Brain cell transplants may also reverse death in those cases where nerve death is due to injury, such as a sharp blow to the back of the neck. In this case, groups of nerve cells in the lower "vegetative" areas of the brain controlling respiration are knocked out and the patient dies because breathing is no longer possible. (While respirators can be used to sustain such people, the quality of life would obviously be markedly impaired.) Similarly, injury to certain areas of the brain can cause loss of blood pressure and flow to the cerebral hemispheres, leaving permanent destruction in its wake.

What happens to the definition of death when new brain cells can take the place of ones that have been destroyed and damaged? Will it be when the number of cells lost is so great and the renovation necessary is so extensive that our original identity, the "I," is lost? And at what percentage of replacement will this occur? Twenty? Forty? Ninety? Ninety-nine? Although this question cannot now be answered, it is clear that attempting to define death as a simple physiological state beyond which intervention is impossible is inadequate.

If, instead of constantly redefining death, we simply accept its existence when the classic criteria of cessation of heartbeat and loss of reflexes appear, then we can go on to apply all the miracles of modern medicine to its defeat. This does not mean giving up on the patient. On the contrary, death will no longer be synonymous with finality. It will simply be another obstacle to overcome. Although this may sound farfetched, bear in mind that physicians now routinely revive people who a generation ago would have been given up for dead. In the future we will be even better at reviving people who have died. It is this reality that gives the irreversibility of death its temporal dependency. Simply put: Dead today isn't necessarily dead tomorrow.

As the life extension sciences progress, I believe we will move away from the idea that there is a cutoff point called death beyond which medical intervention is no longer possible. Instead we will define cases as "terminal." Once this definition has been applied, the patient will be given the choice of death followed by burial or cremation, treatment by methods designed to reverse the terminal process, or cryonic suspension in the hope of future revival.

Some people have already signed "living will" documents that indicate their desire to suspend all but supportive treatment once they become irreversibly incapacitated. In Holland, there has been a growing campaign to decriminalize the medical practice of helping people die once a panel of experts has decided that the person choosing death cannot be expected to live longer than six months. Public opinion in favor of this kind of "mercy killing," or euthanasia, is also gaining ground in the United States.

At the point at which death appears inevitable, those who wish to "die with dignity" will be allowed to do so, perhaps even be helped along, if there is a change in the law. When their heart stops, their attending physician will sign their death certificate and their organs may be distributed for transplantation. Any death benefits will be paid to their beneficiaries at that time.

Other people will insist that everything possible be done for them. When their heart stops, rescue teams will attempt to restart it. If that fails to work, they will be placed on bypass and cooled. At ice point temperatures, doctors will have hours to repair damage that is normally fatal in minutes. By circulating a chilled blood substitute containing a "cocktail" of drugs that reduce brain swelling, slow acid production, mop up free radicals, and decrease the energy demand of cells, they will slow the death process. Buying time in this way will also let them carry out complex operations such as finely tuned nerve cell transplants into all the injured areas of the brain.

If necessary, some people may be stored for one or two days at the ice point and maintained on a heart-lung machine. Their blood would be replaced with an artificial solution oxygenated under pressure and they would remain this way until the appropriate surgery could be carried out. Others may be partially frozen, like frogs in the leaf cover, for a month or longer while a search for suitable transplantable organs can be completed. Still others will be frozen in liquid nitrogen to await future revival when a cure is available. Death benefits will also be paid off at that time, although these people will probably retain their organs unless they have opted to preserve only the head. Shorter-term suspended animation would be covered by health insurance policies, except instead of hospital space, the patient would take up space in the freezer. The point is that the traditional view of death would be replaced by a gradient, a gradual slope, along which, at each step of the way, a person would decide how far he or she is willing to allow, or not allow, medical science to proceed in the business of keeping him or her alive.

I have already discussed the work being done to delay, arrest, and reverse aging. Most people who die today are old. Often heroic measures to reverse their terminal conditions are not implemented. Sometimes their charts are marked with the ominous letters NTBR—"Not To Be Resuscitated." As senescence becomes more reversible and as cloning provides youthful tissues and organs for those lost through aging, disease, and injury, more vigorous attempts will be made to rescue old people from the jaws of death. These attempts will be stepped up as the potential life span of seniors approaches that of younger people. The death sentence that now looms so large in the lives of the elderly will be first appealed, and finally dismissed.

Resuscitation will become a very important area of geriatrics. The current practice of expecting old people to die (and even in some cases encouraging it) will seem a barbaric relic of a primitive past. The right to die, now so fiercely fought for, will be gladly relinquished by many people when a healthy life is the alternative.

Resuscitation medicine will develop hand in hand with yet another of the life extension sciences, regeneration. Where resuscitation is aimed at bringing the dead back to life, regeneration is directed at creating new life at the cellular level. Scientists have already begun using growth factors, substances extracted from our own body, to regenerate tissue and cure disease.

So far about thirty growth factors that stimulate or guide the development of new cells have been discovered. Nerve growth factor is being explored for its healing potential in everything from Alzheimer's disease to reattaching severed limbs. Skin growth factors have halved the time it takes wounds to heal, grown skin in the laboratory for burn victims, helped corneal transplants "take," cured ulcers, and even bolstered sperm production. Blood growth factors have restored the extremely low white blood cell count of AIDS patients to normal levels, generated new red blood cells in patients with severe anemia, and rescued the bone marrow of cancer patients from the lethal effects of chemotherapy.

The use of growth factors, which play a major role in the development of a fetus from a fertilized egg, is making it possible for doctors to do what they have never done before: unlock the body's regenerative powers. The question is how far can we extend these powers? There are secrets hidden deep within our evolutionary past that may help us achieve this goal. Perhaps we can learn from our primitive ancestors how to restore decaying tissue, grow new body parts from old, regenerate organs, replace the rigidity of age with the plasticity of youth.

The ability of some lower life forms to regrow themselves is almost legendary. Like the hydra-headed monster of Greek mythology who grew two heads for every one lopped off, some animals can regenerate their entire bodies from small bits of tissue. Perhaps the most notorious of these animals is the starfish. Some years ago, the fishermen of Chesapeake Bay hit upon a plan for ridding the bay of the starfish that were preying on the shellfish that were their livelihood. They caught the starfish, cut them up into small pieces, and threw them back into the sea. Little did they know that their solution literally multiplied the problem, because for every starfish they quartered, four new ones would spring up.

Another virtuoso regenerator is the tiny flatworm called planaria. Cut a planaria in half and its head end will generate a tail; its tail will grow a new head. Bisect the head lengthwise down the middle and the animal will grow two heads.

Interestingly, some species of frogs can regenerate their limbs, while others cannot. What makes the difference? A critical element appears to be the influence of nerve cells on the regenerating regions. Those frogs capable of limb regrowth have large nerve fibers growing into their limbs. In one species the hind legs can regenerate but not the forelegs. However, if you reroute the nerves from the hind limb to the forelimb, severed forelegs *can* grow back.

Generally, as you move up the evolutionary ladder, a kind of law of diminishing returns appears to operate in regard to these global regenerative powers. But one class of animals, the amphibia, is a striking exception to this rule. The star of this class is the salamander. Should a predator grasp the tail of a salamander, it may find itself with just that as the animal darts off to safety. A few weeks later the salamander is sporting a new tail. This remarkable amphibian can replace its limbs, grow back part of its vital organs, and even repair a broken heart. (Scientists have surgically removed portions of the heart, and the remaining cells shift around, making the organ whole again.)

By the time you work your way up the evolutionary ladder to mammals, regenerating limbs and organs has become virtually a lost art, except among the very young. Working with the opossum, a marsupial animal low down on the evolutionary ladder of mammals, researchers have gotten the severed hind limbs of pouch-dwelling infants to reform. They did this by implanting pieces of the animal's brain into the limb stumps. Mice whose foretoes are amputated early in life will grow them back. Even humans share in this ability to some extent: children under the age of ten can regenerate their fingertips if the severed part is above the third joint and if the wound is not sewn shut.

Even into adult life, some of our organs can partly regenerate under certain conditions. A damaged liver can grow back after as much as three quarters of it has been destroyed, though the regenerated tissue never functions as well as the original. And while we can't replace whole organs as the starfish can, we do know one trick of our own, called compensatory hypertrophy, the overgrowth of a body part to make up for lost tissue. This is seen, for instance, when one kidney is removed and the remaining one enlarges to handle the increased load.

At first glance the brain seems a most unlikely candidate for regeneration. It is believed that we are born with all the brain cells we will ever have. It is like a savings account from which there are only withdrawals, never deposits. But even here there appears to be a hidden reserve fund.

If, for instance, a nerve cell or group of nerve cells in a given area of the brain is damaged, nearby neurons will send out projections to take the place of the lost tissue. For this reason, a very high percentage of nerves in a given region of the brain must be destroyed before any real loss of brain function occurs.

Sometimes drugs can enhance this process of neuronal compensation. There is a group of cells in the brain of all mammals, including humans, called the substantia nigra, or "black substance." This area coordinates rhythmic movements such as those used in walking or dancing. With age, the number of functional cells in this region declines. This is believed to cause the tremor seen in the hands of aged individuals. The loss of cells in the substantia nigra has to be drastic—almost 80 percent—before the patient is visibly affected. During the flu epidemic of 1918, many people were infected with a flu virus thought to cause destruction of this brain area. With their reserve fund cut, the withdrawals of neurons with age cut even more deeply into their savings account than normally. The result was that when more than three quarters of this brain region were depleted, the dreaded Parkinson's disease appeared. The drug L-DOPA, which stimulates the ability of neighboring nerve cells to replace those that were lost to virus and aging, helped relieve the symptoms.

The brain has shown remarkable recuperative powers even under severe brain damage such as from a sharp blow, gunshot wound, or brutal vehicle accident. Here the major survival factor seems to be that excessive bleeding from a large cerebral blood vessel or damage to vital brain centers, such as those that control respiration or blood pressure, does not take place.

In the last few decades, a number of factors have been isolated that seem to accelerate the growth of nerve cells. One of these is nerve growth factor, which encourages the proliferation of one particular kind of nerve cell. Other factors promote other types of nerve cells. Eventually, scientists believe they will be able to concoct a "cocktail" of factors that will stimulate the growth of nerve processes into the injured areas.

One of the most exciting areas in regeneration research, with profound implications for the conquest of death and aging, is the work now going on in rejoining severed nerves. Advances in surgery have now made it possible to rejoin fingers, and even whole limbs, that have been sliced off in industrial accidents, car collisions, or violent trauma.

The real challenge lies not in the more tractable peripheral nerves of the arms and legs, but in the central nervous system of the neck and spine. Right now a severed spinal cord is forever. And no injury is more devastating than a diving accident or car crash that leaves its spine-injured victim, who is usually young and athletic, paralyzed for life. In an attempt to do something about this hopeless situation, the American Paralysis Association, known for its support of innovative research, is sponsoring studies in the reconnection of the spinal cord in animals.

In a pioneering study, neuroanatomist Jack de la Torre of the University of Ottawa in Canada found that severed spinal cords can be made to reconnect at least in part. This kind of nerve regeneration, he says, may one day allow people paralyzed by automobile or diving injuries to walk again, Alzheimer patients to regain their memories, and people with brain damage caused by aging, disease, or the removal of cerebral tumors to have their mental and physical function restored.

"We are working with the notion that [nerve] regeneration is possible," says de la Torre. When he and his colleague, neurosurgeon Harry Goldsmith of Boston University Medical School, completely severed the spinal cords of cats, there was absolutely no regrowth in the severed spines. But when they used a special technique that they had devised to rejoin the cut ends, they got an estimated 8 percent of the spinal nerve fibers to reconnect and grow back into the brain from where they originate. While the animals still had no function in their lower bodies, the researchers were able to transmit electrical signals across the severed spines into the brain. "We have never seen such robust regeneration, regardless of the technique tried," says de la Torre.

The team combined two techniques that had been used previously to treat brain and spinal cord problems in both animals and people. One involves using liquid collagen to fill the gap that forms when the spinal cord is cut in two. For the nerve fibers to bridge this gap "is like jumping the Grand Canyon," says de la Torre. The collagen, which gels at the temperature of body heat, is chemically inert and not rejected by the body. The other technique, pioneered by Goldsmith, uses the omentum, a membranous sac that hangs from the stomach and drapes over the intestines. By stretching out the omentum like a rope and bringing it through a tunnel under the skin to the back, Goldsmith places it over the spinal cord and collagen bridge. The omentum, the researchers speculate, may promote nerve regrowth in two ways. It increases the blood flow to the spinal cord, and it contains certain brain chemicals that may nourish nerve tissue. Whatever the reason, the combined collagen-omentum technique was far more effective in getting fibers to grow back than the collagen bridge alone. Goldsmith and others are now using the omentum technique by itself to increase the blood flow to the brain of stroke patients and the spinal cord of accident victims.

The next step of course, says de la Torre, is to increase the number of nerve fibers that grow back. If this could be done, then function could be restored. In rats only 1 to 2 percent of their nerve fibers are needed to walk. No one knows what the amount would be in humans, but he suspects it would be something more than 10 percent.

Among their ideas for getting the number of fibers up are to add various agents to the collagen, such as nerve growth factor, or put fetal cells in the omentum, which may naturally contain factors that help nerves grow. Any techniques that prove successful will be tried first on large animals, then on people. "With the collagen, with the increased blood flow from the omentum, with nerve growth factors, we may *bribe* the nerve fibers into making their contacts," he says. "This is one of the biggest biomedical challenges in the world today. But I am convinced that regeneration—functional regeneration—is possible."

Another dramatic breakthrough made the front page of *The New York Times* when scientists actually restored nerve function in rats after the spinal cord had been crushed, although not severed. In this case, the researchers, Dr. Jerry Silver of Case Western Reserve University in Cleveland and Dr. Michael Kliot of Columbia Presbyterian Hospital in New York City constructed an ingenious "living bridge" of fetal cells across which the damaged nerve fibers could grow.

In their experiments, they injured a network of nerves in rats that conveyed the signals for sensation from the spinal cord to several toes. As a result the animals lost all feeling in the affected toes. Then, using a paperlike material to support nerve cells taken from fetal rats, they got the injured nerve fibers to grow back into the rats' spinal cords. In seven out of fifteen rats, reaction tests showed that the feeling in the toes returned. According to the team, this was the first study that had gotten injured nerves to reconnect into the spinal cord and function again. Exactly what role the fetal cells played in this regeneration is not known, but some scientists believe that they released certain "survival" factors that enabled the nerve cells to grow again.

The successful restoration of the spinal cord and brain

cells will be necessary if we are ever to attain the goal of letting the dead live again. The brain is the command center of the individual. In its two small hemispheres are contained the memories, the personality, the unique identity that make each of us who we are. If that is lost, then it doesn't matter what else is retained. If that stays reasonably intact, it doesn't matter what else is lost, because everything else can be reconstructed or cloned. All that remains is to reestablish the connection through the spinal cord.

So the absolutely crucial question to answer is, Can the brain survive death and freezing? While the answer is still not known, there is much reason for optimism. First of all, the brain is remarkably resilient when it comes to storing memory. People have retained complete access to their memories even after massive damage to the cerebral hemispheres. Deficits in brain regions controlling motor or sensory function may leave people unable to communicate, while completely sparing their ability to think, feel, and reason. The reason for this, neurobiologists believe, may be that memory is banked in the highly redundant fashion, so that if one portion of the brain is lost, memory can be reconstructed from the parts of the brain that remain untouched.

The implications of this redundancy for human life extension are obvious. As scientific progress continues, our techniques for restoring function to a damaged brain will also improve. The irreversible brain damage of today may be reparable with techniques available fifty or one hundred years in the future. It is for this reason that we still consider people who are dead after a period of an hour or more candidates for cryonic suspension, even though it is apparent that their brain function has been terribly compromised. Even the freezing damage done to a brain by the current relatively primitive cryonics technology, which no doubt adds insult to the injury caused by the patient's condition and the cerebral ischemia following cardiac arrest, may be fixable by the techniques of future science. As long as the fundamental substratum of brain tissue that defines the individual and a significant portion of the memory remain, there is hope that the cryonically suspended person might someday be repaired to the point where he or she can resume living as before.

The percentage of the brain that may be lost before we can declare the individual hopelessly destroyed, along with exactly what constitutes the neurological basis of identity and memory, is yet to be determined. But the recent progress in the regeneration of nerve tissue suggests that we will see some startling changes in our perception of what we now term irreparable brain damage in the very near future.

Advances in embryonic nerve transplantation, fetal cell living bridges, growth factor isolation and applications, and bionic junctions in which nerve cells are connected to each other via computer microchip circuitry, will pave the way for what may be the ultimate in life extension technology—the total-body transplant. We will examine this possibility in the following chapter.

Can the dead live again? The answer is a resounding yes. It is already happening. So many people have been brought back from cardiac arrest that an entire literature on near-death experiences has grown up. As we push back the point of no return further and further, as bringing back the dead becomes a daily routine, we will see death for what it really is. We will grasp that death and life are not polar opposites but a continuum. Just as the understanding of genetics and molecular biology destroyed the principle of vitalism—the idea that a life force somehow distinct from chemistry and physics permeated all living organisms—so, too, will we give up the idea that death is something other than a loss of specific organization of physicochemical matter. If that order can be restored, or replaced, with the techniques of resuscitation, regeneration, and cloning, then death will surely be undone.

6

CHANGE OF HEART:
TRANSPLANTABLE
AND ARTIFICIAL
ORGANS

I'd like a can of beer.

—William Schroeder, November 17, 1984, after
receiving an artificial heart

In the 1970s millions thrilled to the television exploits of the Bionic Man and the Bionic Woman. Part flesh, part machine, these superbeings combined the best of both worlds—human intellect and emotions with extrahuman capabilities such as telescopic vision, long-distance hearing, and gravity-defying leaps. Although the TV programs hinted at secrets possessed by the government that made such technology possible, the truth was that we had not as yet come anywhere near a machine-man interface.

At that time, replacing a body part with a machine that performed the same function, let alone one with superpowers, was still the stuff of science fiction. Even transplanting human organs, while under way in several centers, was a hit-or-miss affair, and, especially with hearts, more often miss than hit.

Now, just a decade later, bionic replacement is on the verge of being realized. While the totally implantable heart is still more than a heartbeat away, artificial hearts are keeping people alive until a transplant replacement is available. Organ transplantation, the most fully developed of the life extension sciences, has given second—and, in some cases, third and fourth—chances at life to tens of thousands of people around the world. So successful has this program been that now the big question is not Will it work? but Where will all the organs come from?

In the foreseeable future, people will run on battery-operated, totally implantable hearts, kidneys, livers, and lungs the way they now function on pacemakers. The first generation of synthetic parts will be designed to be as close to nature as our technology will allow. But just as the home computer evolved from a kind of toy into a number-crunching, document-processing, graphics-generating, data-collecting, information-sharing tool, so will the manmade organs gradually improve upon the original. The Shakespearean seventh stage of man—"sans teeth, sans eyes, sans taste, sans everything"—will give way to the man who lacks nothing, having received everything he needs from the organ bank or factory. And all this will merely set the stage for what's to come—the reconstruction of the individual after cryonic suspension.

Barney Clark never really knew what he started. Then again, maybe he did. Although he only survived for 114 days, he began an era as surely as the Wright Brothers did at Kitty Hawk. In both cases life would never be the same again. As surely as that historic three-minute flight led to the moon's conquest, Barney Clark's ordeal will lead to the day when ageless polycentenarians are equipped with internal machinery that will make today's artificial heart look like a Tinkertoy.

Following Clark's courageous experiment, which shocked an entire world and still divides the medical, surgical, and bioethical communities, Drs. William De Vries and Robert Jarvik moved their research program from the academic sanctuary of the University of Utah to Louisville's Humana Hospital. Fortified with a generous research contract and the go-for-it attitude of a billion-dollar hospital chain, they received a green light for their scheme of trading plastic and steel for mortal flesh.

Unfortunately, as is the case with most experimental programs, the problems the two men encountered were more than they had bargained for. Subsequent implants proved that a long-term total artificial heart was yet to be designed. And the program left in its wake four more victims, who, although they had all had their lives extended (in one case for more than a year), suffered such debilitating strokes that some family members questioned whether the time gained was worth the suffering entailed.

From another perspective the project was a great success. While Jarvik, De Vries, and others are now trying to devise synthetic hearts that will avoid the strokes that plagued the initial design, artificial hearts as well as other cardiac-assist devices in clinics around the world are being used as a bridge to sustain people until a human organ is available. And hearts are not the only hardware for sale at the biomedical trading post. Many tens of thousands of people throughout the industrialized world owe their lives to the bionic kidney—the renal dialysis machine. Although most patients with end-stage renal disease are tethered to the artificial kidney for many grueling hours per week, a lucky few can temporarily switch to a portable alternative, the WAK (or Wearable Artificial Kidney).

This, too, has its downside. WAK users have a high

likelihood of serious peritoneal infection, and so much scarlike tissue can form at the site of implantation in the abdominal cavity that the device often becomes unusable after eighteen months. But this implantable machine is clearly the wave of the future, and with advances in bioengineering it will become safer, more sophisticated, and longer-lasting.

In the years to come, we should see an explosion of such devices. Designs already exist for totally implantable hearts and lungs as well as heart-lung units, with implantable livers just beyond the immediate horizon. Synthetic guts aren't yet here, but the technology of total parenteral nutrition (TPN)—where the equivalent of whole meals is delivered by IV directly to the bloodstream—has kept people entirely lacking in functional intestines alive for years. Prototypes of artificial eyes consisting of a grid of numerous light-sensitive elements, each connected with a separate point on the surface of the brain, have already been tested, and similar devices are being explored for bringing hearing to deaf people.

These are just the beginning. On the drawing board are implantable synthetic glands that will provide regulated doses of genetically engineered hormones such as human insulin. This approach is already benefiting some diabetics. Artificial brain devices in the form of electronic computer-assisted machinery will increase the firing range of neurons so that they can once again trigger movement in people with severed spines, allowing them to put aside their wheelchairs forever. Even artificial uteruses, which could be used to nurture body clones as they develop into genetically compatible banks of organs and tissues, are being developed.

Potentially, the most important lifesaving man-machine hookup is a pump oxygenator, better known as the heart-lung machine. By taking over the blood-pumping and oxygen-delivery functions of the heart and lungs, the pump oxygenator allows the surgeon to carry out procedures that were unthinkable previously: cardiac bypass operations, removing tumors from large arteries, even the highly publicized operation where doctors at Johns Hopkins University Medical Center separated Siamese twins whose circulatory systems were intertwined at birth. Indeed, the entire field of low-temperature medicine, including the chilled-blood-replacement operation we performed on Miles, could not be done without the pump oxygenator.

Where the pump oxygenator will fulfill its greatest life-extending possibilities will be in resuscitation, the reversal of the dying process. As outlined in the previous chapter, it can be used to introduce lifesaving drugs and chemicals directly into the circulation to reawaken the heart and brain after the blood flow to these vital organs has ceased. It can carry solutions that reverse swelling, remove lethal toxins, and unclog arteries. It can circulate blood substitutes that are better engineered than our own blood to deliver oxygen to tissues and cells that are dying for the lack of it and, combined with hyperbaric oxygen and low temperature, it could be used to load the tissues with oxygen in cases of stroke or heart attack. Finally, it is the means by which biological antifreeze agents are pumped to the cells to protect the body during its extended frozen sleep.

As microtechnology and nanotechnology (from *nanos*, Greek for "dwarf," and designating one billionth of a given unit) develop, the possibilities for man-machine interface will become truly mind-boggling. It may be possible, for instance, to replace groups of lost or damaged nerve cells in the brain with microchip (and later nanochip) circuitry. Ultimately, such bionic "brain assist" devices might even allow direct "on-line" cerebrum-computer communication. Imagine what it will do to the idea of intelligence and education when we can literally call to mind whole data banks of information, "learn" a language, cross-check an obscure reference, solve a difficult mathematical problem, research the various ramifications of a particular fact, all within a matter of minutes.

The line between inanimate and animate will become ever more blurred. Already, experiments have been going on in creating implantable manmade membrane-covered compartments containing living cells from the islets of the pancreas. These half-organic, half-synthetic implants would provide vital hormones for people who need them, but, at the same time, they would be protected by the membranes from rejection by the recipient's body.

Working together, the materials scientist and the biological engineer are fabricating an array of biosynthetic parts and pieces to patch people up good as new—things such as artificial joints, simulated skin to stabilize burn victims, synthetic shafts for lost bone, and mesh plates to cover damaged portions of the skull. Materials now being developed will be longer lasting, more reliable, and allow us to avoid the pitfalls of using today's substances, such as the overgrowth of pannus—scarlike, collagenous material that often coats implants such as heart valves or the wearable artificial kidney, rendering them totally useless.

As biotechnology progresses, the Bionic Man and Bionic Woman will go from being television superheroes to ordinary, everyday humans. Until that time, and until cloning is available, the best organs will literally be manmade, gifts from others who no longer need them.

In the late sixties, two events took place on opposite sides of the globe that shook the world. In the United States, scientists launched a rocket that carried men to the moon; in South Africa, surgeons performed the first human heart transplant. A few years earlier, Dr. Christiaan Barnard removed the diseased heart of his patient, Louis Washansky, and replaced it with the healthy heart of an accident victim who had been declared brain dead; that was also in its own way "one small step for man, one giant leap for mankind."

The world was hooked on technology, both in medicine and space. The new heroes were the scientists, astronauts, and technicians who were breaking the barriers of existence in both time and space. But with new knowledge came new problems. Heart transplantation meant getting around what Nobel Prize–winning immunologist Peter Medawar called "the uniqueness of the individual"—the biochemical differences between us that make it impossible for one person to accept an organ or tissue from another.

Barnard administered huge doses of synthetic steroids to neutralize the immune response—recognition that the new heart was not made of the stuff of "self," but was "foreign." But steroids are a doubled-edged sword. While they suppressed Washansky's body from rejecting his borrowed heart, they also suppressed his ability to fight off a myriad of infectious diseases, such as pneumonia, that rarely threaten a person with an intact immune system. Moreover, the drugs cause unpleasant side effects such as a characteristic moon-faced swelling, weakening of the bone, and an alteration of body salts that can trigger mood swings and extreme depression.

In the early 1970s other surgeons, particularly in this country, began heart transplantation programs. The results were not too different from those obtained a decade later with the artificial heart. Although people were often rescued from the brink of death, they were so debilitated, the complications were so numerous, and the overall quality of life achieved was so poor that, except in a few cases, most people felt it was almost a toss-up as to whether the extra time was worth it.

By the late 1970s heart transplantation had all but ceased. Then a remarkable breakthrough occurred that single-handedly turned the situation around. J. F. Borel, a scientist at Sandoz, Inc., the huge Swiss multinational pharmaceutical house that years earlier had given birth to the controversial mind-altering drug LSD, was to develop another product that would change our perception of the world, this time in matters of life and death.

Sandoz had instructed its scientists to scoop up a handful of soil whenever they visited another country and to bring it back to the laboratory. When Borel examined a sample of earth collected from Hardanger Vidda, a high treeless plateau in southern Norway, he found it contained an unusual mold. He put it through a series of tests to see what kind of biological effects it might have and, much to his surprise, stumbled on something everyone was looking for—a substance that inactivated the part of the immune system primarily responsible for attacking transplanted organs. That substance became the basis of cyclosporin-A (CyA), the first drug that suppressed the rejection response without greatly compromising the body's ability to resist disease. Although it, too, had serious drawbacks, such as toxicity to the kidneys and increased risk of leukemia, it was far less debilitating than high doses of steroids.

The field of organ transplantation started to boom. Kidneys, livers, hearts, lungs, heart-lung combinations, pancreases, and bone marrow all became transplantable, with first-year survival rates zooming to above 90 percent for some organs. Today, corneas are transplanted at the rate of one every twenty-two minutes; kidneys, one every seventy-five minutes; and hearts, almost daily. CyA has more than quadrupled the survival rates and cut the weakness associated with organ transplantation so remarkably that recipients of second hearts now compete in marathons.

An even more bullish future awaits the field of organ transplants. Research is now going on to find more effective and less toxic ways to knock out the body's rejection response. Antibodies are the shock troops of the immune defense system, useful when they are turned against foreign invaders such as viruses and bacteria, but counterproductive when they attack a foreign graft. To knock out these unwanted antibodies, scientists are creating monoclonal antibodies, or mass-produced antibodies cloned from a single cell, that can go after a specific target. Their hope is that when these missiles are launched they will home in on the rejection antibodies and leave everything else intact, thereby protecting the graft or transplant without impairing the recipient's ability to fight off disease. Another approach is to improve the techniques of matching up the tissue types between donor and recipient. Studies have shown the best ten-year survival of transplanted kidneys occurred in those patients who received organs from donors whose tissue matched their own as closely as possible.

Advances will only serve to intensify the most pressing problem in transplantation—where will the organs come from? At this point demand has so exceeded supply that tens of thousands of potential recipients are in line, waiting for a second chance at life. Some desperate individuals carry their appeals for an organ for themselves or a family member to the media, hoping to jump out of line and receive a transplant before it's too late. Others, with the help of make-do technology such as cardiac-assist devices and kidney dialysis, play a waiting game, trying to survive long enough to rate a high-priority number but not deteriorate so rapidly that they are out of the race altogether. France has reversed the traditional practice of leaving the disposal of a dead body to the family by considering the deceased person an organ donor unless there are objections by the family.

The availability of organs, like the availability of food in a famine-stricken country, may be partly a matter of storage and distribution. Human organs are eminently perishable, deteriorating within a few hours after removal, and the lack of an adequate means of preservation causes an estimated 60 percent of the hearts and 90 percent of the livers that are transplantable to end up in the waste basket.

This is where the work in low temperature I described earlier may make an enormous contribution. In a striking example of how developments in one branch of the life extension sciences can fuel developments in another, the same techniques we used on Miles—total-body washout, replacing his blood with a blood substitute, and bringing the body down to near-freezing temperatures—are now being explored as a means of preserving organs for transplantation for up to twenty-four hours or longer. Chilled blood substitution could be used to lower the temperature of the donor to the ice point in order to avoid damaging the organs by exposing them to periods of bloodlessness while the body is still warm. The transplantation team would have more time to remove the organs and could harvest the organs in the order they are needed. Right now, the heart, which is needed to pump oxygenated blood to the body, must be removed after the liver, kidneys, or any other potentially transplantable organ.

Ice-cold blood substitution should also greatly extend the storage time for organs. Since dogs have recovered intact after as much as eight hours of bloodless cold, one can assume that their hearts, livers, kidneys, lungs, pancreases, bone marrow, and other organs have successfully survived this ordeal as well. Extra preservation time would allow transplant donors to be transported to a central region, where their organs could be distributed all over the country rather than be limited to one geographical area as is now the case. Other technology could extend the shelf life of ice-cold blood-substituted organs even further. For instance, hyperbaric oxygen in which pure oxygen is compressed to three times normal atmospheric pressure may give the organs twenty-four or more hours of storage time.

Eventually we may even be able to store organ donors on ice by partially freezing them at the moderate subzero range used by overwintering frogs. In a recent article in the British scientific journal *Cryoletters*, Dr. Kenneth Storey, who does research on the frogs' survival strategy, exhorted scientists to use the knowledge gained from studying these animals to learn how to preserve organs for days or weeks. Such knowledge could be applied to putting not only the transplant donor on hold, but the recipient as well. In this way, surgery could be delayed until the replacement organs with the closest tissue match became available.

Unfortunately, all of these are just stopgap measures. The demand for organs will always outpace the supply, especially as more and more people live to the ages at which their organs inevitably fail. The ultimate solution is obvious—cloning, the science of growing your own.

As described earlier, we are making landmark strides in the area of nuclear transplantation in mammals. Although only a handful of laboratories are now involved, as the biotech industry turns its attention to cloning animals the pace of progress will pick up. At the same time, research is going forward in the technology of rejoining severed spines. When the fruits of these two powerful life extension sciences are brought together, the most radical transplant of all, the total-body, or head, transplant, will become possible.

In a series of extraordinary experiments, Dr. Robert White at the Case Western Reserve University School of Medicine in Cleveland actually transplanted the brains and heads of dogs and monkeys onto the intact bodies of other dogs and monkeys. In some cases these two-headed or two-brained animals survived for days. Although White was able to hook up the circulation of the blood of one animal so that it flowed to the head of the other animal, he could not establish a nervous system connection between the two. The result was that the grafted-on head could not direct the movements of the body. But both the original head and the transplant were fully conscious —able to see, hear, taste, eat, and react when threatened —proving at the very least that a host body could keep a transplanted head alive.

While White's experiments seem ghoulish and bizarre, they were designed to increase our understanding of basic neuroanatomy and neurophysiology. What he showed was that the brain could survive in isolation cut off from all its sensory inputs with just a few circulatory connections intact. This finding has implications for diagnosing and treating devastating conditions where the connection between the brain and body has been damaged, such as stroke, loss of particular brain areas due to disease or accident, and spinal injury.

But the most far-reaching implications of White's work, from a cryonicist's perspective, is that it raises the possibility that a human head could really be frozen, thawed, and placed on another body. While decapitation followed by whole body transplant is not something that I personally favor, there are a number of individuals in the cryonics movement who believe that this is the way to go. They argue that it is easier to rapidly perfuse a head with cryoprotectants and freeze it rather than an entire body and that reversing cryonic suspension of just the head should be an easier task in the future. Second, since the technology for growing cloned bodies should be on line by the time reversible cryonics is possible, there would be no reason to preserve the original body, especially if the patient was already old or in a deteriorated condition at the time of freezing. Finally, from a strictly economic point of view, storing a frozen head is substantially cheaper than storing a whole body. White's studies suggest that one could experiment with preserving isolated monkey heads by various freezing or vitrifying techniques and then, upon rewarming, graft them onto host bodies and test for viability. Such a system might allow for the rapid development of a reversible head-freezing protocol. While the idea has obvious scientific merit, the bizarre nature of the procedure will no doubt keep it from becoming widely accepted.

With advancements in the science of regeneration, we may learn to rejoin severed spines and reestablish the nervous connection between the brain and the rest of the body. At that point total body replacement will become a reality. And the argument for neuro-preservation, as cryonicists call it, becomes more credible. Although their logic is persuasive, there are arguments to be made on the other side. We may find that certain tissues of the body are better sources of nuclei for cloning than that available from the head. Second, the whole body may contain clues to what orginally caused death, leading to an earlier and more complete revival. Whether or not it makes more sense to preserve just one's head or the whole body is certainly not clear at this point. I, for one, would rather not discard my body so fast, whatever its faults, until the arguments for doing so become overwhelming.

What should be clear at this point is that everything is starting to come together—the antiaging regimens, the low temperature technology, the breakthroughs that will lead to cloning, resuscitation after clinical death, regeneration, and the progress in organ transplantation and artificial organs that will extend our life spans beyond anything we have dreamed of. All this will serve us in the final battle of the war against death and aging: reawakening the frozen dead.

7

CRYONICS:

WHEN ONCE IS

NOT ENOUGH

And when he thus had spoken, he cried with a loud voice, Lazarus, come forth.

And he that was dead came forth, bound hand and foot with grave clothes; and his face was bound about with a napkin. Jesus saith unto them, "Loose him, and let him go."

—John 11:43–44

"It's all over," said Dr. Hartley, turning off the screen on which a flat line traced an endless horizon.

"Oh, my God," said Allison Campbell, instinctively clutching her dead husband's hand. "Is that it? Is that all you can do?"

"We did everything we could. But your husband did not respond to the resuscitation protocol."

"But what about a transplant, an artificial heart? What about the new experimental lazeroid I just read about in the papers?"

The young doctor put her arm around Mrs. Campbell's shoulder. "I'm afraid it's too late for any of that. After all, Richard is a hundred and two years old. What's the sense of imprisoning him in that century-old body, even if many of his

155

*organs have been replaced? No, there's only one thing that
makes any sense now."*

*"Cryonic suspension," said Allison, the tears forming in
her eyes in spite of herself.*

*"Come now, Allison. There's nothing to cry about. You'll
have him back very soon. And"—the doctor winked at the
woman, who was old enough to be her grandmother but who
looked as young as herself—"he'll be better than new."*

*"I know I'm being irrational, but freezing sounds so . . .
so . . ."*

"Cold?" They both laughed in spite of themselves.

"It just gives me the chills." They laughed again.

*"You know, Allison, your reaction is typical. Even though
we've been freezing and thawing people now for twenty years,
there is something about cryonics that seems unnatural. But
it's not. It's actually nature's way of preserving life. There are
several life-forms, such as some species of North Country
frogs, that make it through the winter in a semifrozen state.
All science has done is learn to capitalize on the life-preserving
qualities of ice."*

*She looked at her watch. "Later we'll sit down in my office
and I'll explain to you everything that is involved in a freezing.
But right now I suggest that we call in the suspension team
and let them get started before any more of Richard's brain
cells die. And we'll get his clone ready at the same time."*

*"Oh, of course. Of course." Allison kissed her husband
tenderly on the lips. "See you soon, my darling."*

*Six weeks later Allison sat at the bedside, tense with anxi-
ety and excitement. With a flourish, as if unveiling a painting,
Dr. Hartley drew back the curtain that surrounded the bed.
There he was, looking younger and handsomer than she could
ever remember. But what would happen when he saw her?
Would his mind be as sharp and quick as before? Would he
even know who she was?*

Richard opened his eyes, which were the china blue of his

youth, stretched his sinewy arms, and smiled like a child wak-
ing up from a nap. "Hi, Allie. I'm starved. What's for dinner?"
*   "This," said Allie, as she held up the chocolate layer cake*
with one candle in the middle. "Happy rebirthday, darling."

What are the odds that any one of us will live to see a
rebirthday? Only one group of researchers so far has revived a live mammal from a *partially* frozen state—Audrey
Smith and her colleagues at the Mill Hill research laboratory in England more than thirty years ago. Not only did
Smith revive hamsters that had half their body water frozen, but one of these animals went on to live for nearly
eighteen hours after being thawed. When we revived Miles,
it was with a technique that killed most of our hamsters
in less than eighteen hours. Today, more than two years
later, Miles has shown not a single sign of his brief stay at
ice point temperatures.

There are those, even among cryonics scientists, who
argue that Smith's hamsters were not completely frozen.
That is true even for the frogs in the leaf cover that revive
each winter from their partially frozen sleep. No veter-
brate, they point out, has ever come back after being frozen solid.

Two recent developments should change that situation dramatically. Indeed, I believe we have entered a new
era in the history of cryonics. The first is the success,
small though it is, of the first signs of life in a mammal
whose body temperature was brought down so low that
its tissues were largely a solid block of ice. Using synthetic
cryoprotectants that mimic the kind of cold-protecting
agents found in overwintering frogs, we chilled blood-
substituted hamsters to temperatures as low as -20 degrees centigrade (-4 degrees Fahrenheit) and kept them
there overnight. Although we could not revive the animals
after thawing, we were able to detect small amounts of

low-amplitude, coordinated electrical activity in their hearts, indicating that there were a number of intact heart cells that were beating in concert. Other researchers have observed the return of beats in isolated rat hearts brought down to similar temperatures. Because of our long experience in chilling and rewarming animals, which went from detection of a heartbeat to full recovery, we are confident that as our techniques improve we will see the same progression at subzero temperatures. Most important from a scientific point of view, the experiment demonstrated that with the hamster we now have a small animal model that can be used to test the evolving cryonics technology.

The second recent development is the conversion of cryonics from a largely armchair science carried out by part-timers, volunteers, and amateurs to a business with commercial spin-offs that have attracted Wall Street investors and large investment banking houses. It could not have come at a more opportune time. We now have the personnel, techniques, and small animal models to make reversible cryonics a reality. All that has been lacking is money, the kind of money that built a high-tech, uniquely American industry from the discovery thirty-five years ago of the nature and structure of the genetic material DNA.

From the beginning, geneticists were able to take advantage of model systems for the manipulation of DNA in such life-forms as intestinal bacteria, with its simple chromosomes and rapid reproduction time, and the common fruit fly, with its larger and hence more visible chromosomes. Then, with the discovery that a small extracellular piece of bacterial DNA, called a plasmid, could be inserted like extra tape on a cassette, gene splicing was born. Now any gene from any species can be introduced into the DNA of bacteria or yeast, where it can be grown with assembly line rapidity.

Dr. Herbert Boyer, the discoverer with Stanley Cohen of the first gene-splicing machine—a genetically engineered plasmid that successfully transferred antibacterial resistance to a strain of intestinal bacteria—formed the first genetic engineering company, Genentech, with $500. Another $500 was put up by a venture capitalist, Robert Swanson, who became president of the company. After that came Cetus and other San Francisco Bay Area biotech giants, as well as their counterparts in the Boston and New York areas. Investors bought into these new companies to the tune of hundreds of millions of dollars; they were followed by large drug companies who, armed with billions, swept into the smaller biotechs like kings annexing the territories of lesser lords.

Fueled by working capital, the industry developed gene libraries of DNA sequences, sophisticated viral probes, and complex molecular decoders and sequencers that could read large molecules the way a stockbroker reads the AMEX listings. The first fruits of that partnership between business and science are now reaching the marketplace with products that are saving people threatened with heart disease, supplying diabetics with human insulin, and permitting abnormally short children to grow normally. This billion-dollar industry is now financing the research and development of new drugs that will have an impact on virtually every aspect of human health and disease. Currently a move is afoot, spearheaded by Nobel Prizewinning scientist Walter Gilbert, founder of yet another firm, Biogen, to decode every gene in the human body and put that information on a computer. With this kind of information, scientists will be able to tackle the mysteries of the human body, including aging, in ways that were inconceivable before.

Could this kind of explosive growth happen in cryonics? My feeling is that nothing can stop it.

Robert Ettinger first thought of the idea of cryonics back in the thirties when he read a science fiction story in which an astronaut left to die in the deep cold of space was revived by an alien civilization. Years later while lying in the hospital recovering from battlefield wounds during the Second World War, Ettinger heard about experiments in cryobiology indicating that tissues could be revived after thawing. What if someone were to freeze a person after he died, instead of burying him? he thought. Could that person be brought back to life at a later date, when the technology existed to thaw him and fix whatever damage freezing and dying had done to his body? He was determined to explore the possibility.

After his recovery, Ettinger went on to become a professor of physics at a community college in Highland Park, Michigan. During his study of physics he had learned of the promise of cryogenics, the realm of the ultracold, where gases such as oxygen, nitrogen, and even helium changed into liquids that poured like water. Once something was frozen to such temperatures, it virtually turned to stone for an eternity. Time itself came to a standstill as motion halted and change ceased.

He also read of advances in a new science, cryobiology, the science of cooling and freezing living tissue and organisms. At subzero temperatures, ice formed within cells, disrupting their structure. But, he learned, you could add substances such as glycerol and dimethylsulfoxide (DMSO) to cells and tissues before freezing that allowed them to withstand the rigors of ultralow temperatures. In the presence of these water-binding cryoprotectants, the cells actually shrank and then froze in such a way as to survive. Later, by placing them in a balanced salt solution and washing away the cryoprotective agents, you could rewarm the cells and bring them back to life.

Ettinger realized that if cells could be treated in such a way, so could human beings. Theoretically, if you chilled people rapidly at the point of death, their cells could endure the removal of their blood and its replacement with blood substitutes containing these cryoprotective agents.

For someone in this frozen state—for a day, a year, a century, or ten millennia—time would stand still, while humanity moved on.

On to the conquest of death and aging. On to the knowledge of restoring life in those from whom life has departed. On to the reconstruction of lost organs and limbs. On to the repair of minds, aided, perhaps, by tireless robot surgeons repairing each damaged cell, one by one, until a brain, once dead and frozen, danced with the electricity of life generated by its ten billion cells. Ettinger could not contain himself. He had to tell the world.

His book *The Prospect of Immortality* received immediate attention worldwide when it was published in 1964. Societies such as the Life Extension Society in Washington, D.C., sprang up in response to Ettinger's call for a war against death. Their members, people drawn from all walks of life, had only one thing in common: a desire to rid the planet once and for all of what they considered humanity's greatest foe—death itself.

Suddenly cryonics was in the news. Magazines such as *Playboy* carried articles about Ettinger's book. Television talk show hosts such as Johnny Carson invited him for interviews. I was still a student when I read the *Playboy* article titled "Intimations of Immortality" by science fiction writer Frederik Pohl. Of course, I thought, if one had to go, cryonics was obviously the way.

It was not so obvious to others. Ettinger never could understand why so many people resisted, indeed were repelled, by an idea that to him was so persuasive. Neither could most immortalists, as adherents to cryonics became known. But Ettinger was no diplomat. He grew impatient with the feelings of those who had accepted philosophies and religions that were designed to accommodate death and aging, aspects of life that have been with us since the beginning of time. When people who did not share his perspective objected to what he was saying, he didn't mince words even on television. He even quoted scriptures to support his case. Once alluding to the Bible's description of raising Lazarus from the dead, he recalled that Jesus said, "Greater things than I have done, so shall you do."

Cryonics began to lose its appeal. Scientists who had once embraced it in the hope of receiving grant money for cryobiological research now rushed to distance themselves, fearing that the association with cryonics would damage their careers. They perceived that those who held the power and purse strings in society sensed in cryonics a severe challenge to the status quo—on which, of course, rested their social dominance. Cryonics became an object of ridicule, the purview of the eccentric. It was impolite, at best; a dark science at worst—perhaps the closest thing to witchcraft in an age of scientific miracles.

But Ettinger inspired a following. A twenty-six-year-old beach boy turned science writer; a mathematics student who would drop out of graduate school to form a body-freezing company; a lawyer who gave up law to lead a cryonics organization; an engineer who turned to the study of biophysics to figure out better techniques for freezing living things; a high school student who became a cryobiologist; a logician who took over the Bay Area Cryonics Society and converted it into an operating entity; engineers from NASA and Pasadena's Jet Propulsion Laboratory. And, of course, there were others—taxi drivers, businessmen, housewives, artists, and hundreds more who just wanted to say no to death and aging.

I was among them. Some people, on hearing about Ettinger's world-shaking idea, were immediately sold. But when they tried to make this idea a reality by spreading the gospel among friends, seeking jobs or careers in research science, or attempting to recruit others, they encountered criticism and skepticism, often from the people they cared

most about—their parents, spouses, and lovers. The result was that many of these converts abandoned their
newfound cause and went on with their lives. Others, like
myself, realized that the conquest of death and aging
could not be done by individuals working independently.
It required teamwork—support from others. I decided to
join a cryonics society. After all, I had seen Professor
Ettinger on television, where he told the chilling truth
about cryonics. Either you join a cryonics society or you
do not get frozen when you die. Nobody freezes themselves. If the legal and financial arrangements are not
made, you do not get frozen. Period.

The reason is that a cryonic suspension costs money,
lots of it. Most people cannot afford that kind of expense.
It must be financed through prepayment, either by some
other person, an insurance policy, or an estate. There are
forms that must be signed ensuring that your body will be
cared for by a cryonics society. If these forms are not in
force at the time of death, your estate, and even your
body, can become the property of relatives who may decide that they have better uses for your wealth than maintaining you in a cryocapsule for the next century or two.

After Ettinger received my letter asking if I could join
his society, he suggested that I get in touch with Saul Kent,
who was forming a society in New York. Saul and I met
for lunch, and when I saw that he was as motivated as I
was, I was sold. I joined the Cryonics Society of New York
and met Curtis Henderson, a lawyer who was the president
of CSNY. Well versed in history, and especially knowledgeable about humanity's favorite occupation—warfare—
Curtis had become a survivalist. He had actually built a
bomb shelter in his home on eastern Long Island that he
thought might withstand an atomic attack on New York
City. This was not as outlandish as it seems when you
consider that he built it at the time of the Cuban missile

crisis, when the United States and the Soviet Union stood toe to toe with both hands on the triggers of their formidable nuclear weapons.

In the spring of 1968, Saul arranged a conference, which was attended by a number of distinguished guests, including scientists and science fiction writers, at the New York Academy of Sciences. At one point during the discussion someone asked, Could the aging process be halted? Having become involved with nutritional restriction by this time, I answered yes and gave my reasons why. After the session was over, a member of the audience sought me out. He was Alan Harrington, a writer who was working on a book for Random House; his book was called *The Immortalist.* I volunteered to act as a consultant and was ecstatic when he accepted. We saw each other periodically, often joined by my friend and colleague Harry Waitz, as well as by Alan's lovely wife, Peggy.

By the time I met him, Alan had already written a number of notable works of fiction and nonfiction, including *Life in the Crystal Palace*—which told how he turned his back on a job as an advertising executive with a well-known oil company in favor of a literary career. He was not just a writer; he had lived, studied, and even befriended some of the literary giants of the Beat Generation, including Jack Kerouac and Allen Ginsberg. Harvard educated, as a young reporter he had been at the scene of the first atomic bomb explosion in the South Pacific. His experiences had given him an unusual degree of sophistication, sensitivity, and insight.

Harrington intended *The Immortalist* to be his major work, which indeed it was. While never a best-seller, it brought the immortalist concept home with such force and was written with such style and depth that it even impressed the book reviewer for *The New York Times.* Unlike Ettinger's book, which was a presentation of the optimistic thoughts of a brilliant college professor thirty years ahead of his time, *The Immortalist* could not be lightly dismissed.

"Death is an imposition on the human race," wrote Harringon, "and no longer acceptable." He demanded that life extension be taken seriously. And it was.

In 1968, some months before Random House released *The Immortalist,* the Cryonics Society of New York did its first freezing. This was not the first publicized cryonics suspension. That occurred in 1967, when a small group in Los Angeles, headed by Robert Nelson, an electronics technician, suspended a former psychology professor from a California state university. Nelson described the experience in his book *We Froze the First Man. Life* magazine also wrote about it, but just as its presses had run off slightly more than one million copies of that issue, an explosion killed three American astronauts. *Life* stopped the presses and substituted the story of the accident in place of the first reported freezing of a human being.

One evening during the memorable summer of 1968, when students and radicals were battling the police in Chicago's streets in the Days of Rage, I was hosting a rather wild party in my Lindenhurst, Long Island, home. The next morning, guests were sleeping all over the place, and the house was strewn with debris from the night before. While I was still asleep, Curtis Henderson and Saul Kent came charging up the stairs. "If I was the enemy," Curt screamed, "you would have all been dead! Get up, we've got a freezing."

Suddenly everyone was in action. Someone went for the dry ice. I made the blood-substitute solutions. Saul and Curtis called the mortuary to tell Fred Horn, the proprietor, that we would need him that day. Then Saul, Curtis, and Fred went in Fred's station wagon for the body of Steven Mandell, a young college student who died of abdominal infection. Saul-Paul Sirag, now a mathematical physicist, stayed at the house to man the telephone.

They packed Steven's body in ice and brought it back to the mortuary. There we removed his blood and replaced it with a blood substitute, copying the ingredients from solutions that had been used to freeze cells and tissues. Then we packed him in a Zigler case, a metal box used by morticians to transport bodies, filled it with dry ice, and placed the box into a regular coffin. Later we would remove the body from the dry ice and place it in a large, liquid nitrogen–filled cryocapsule. At the funeral, only the rabbi, Steve's mother and aunt, and the cryonicists knew what had gone on. The rest of the friends and relatives saw only a traditional Jewish funeral, never noticing the small amount of moisture that was condensing on the side of the coffin due to its frozen contents.

Throughout the services, I had the giddy feeling that we were all being swept along in a furious rush of history. Events were happening that I knew were greater than anything I could fully understand. I felt the way I do on a roller coaster ride—out of control, thrilled, scared, excited. I remember thinking that we had nothing to lose. Without cryonics, without this scenario that we were enacting, we were all headed in the same direction. I knew I didn't want to go there. Later, everyone talked about how young we were. Saul was not yet thirty, Frosty was twenty-seven, and I was twenty-six. It seemed to me that what had taken place was a preview of a movie yet to be released, a glimpse of a world yet to be.

The press conference that followed was a rowdy affair. There was a great deal of laughter as reporters referred to it as a "fish fry." At first, it struck them that all we had done was put bodies on ice, like "freezing fish at the Fulton Fish Market," as one said. But as we talked about the scientific basis behind cryonics, cloning, the fact that the brain might not be totally eradicated following death, and all the possibilities of the future, they started listening. When it was over, one by one the reporters came up to me and shook my hand, saying things like "I never knew there was a science here. This is serious stuff. I thought it was a joke." In the days that followed, various newspaper accounts of the freezing appeared. Although there was a good deal of skepticism, and no one quite knew what to make of it, we were being taken seriously.

Public exposure to cryonics started to grow. Saul Kent and I were invited to talk on several radio shows, and together with science fiction writer Frederik Pohl we appeared on a show with the late-night talk show host Long John Nebel. At about this time a talented young artist, Vaughan Bode, joined our ranks, and his cartoons began to grace the pages of *Cryonics Reports*, CSNY's monthly newsletter published by Saul Kent. Distributed at an inexpensive subscription rate to CSNY members, this small journal chronicled our developing approach to life extension, described actual cryonic suspensions as they occurred, and carried reports on our meetings and conferences. It was given free to certain select people, including Nobel laureates and Hollywood stars. Among them was Woody Allen. I would like to think that this little journal, with its accounts of freezing Steven Mandell and others and its discussions of how cloning could be used to develop spare parts, helped inspire Allen's hilarious movie *Sleeper.*

Over the years there have been other freezings. Not all of them went smoothly. We got a call from a woman in upstate New York who wanted to freeze her middle-aged husband, who had just died of a heart attack. Fred Horn and I drove to Binghamton. We packed the woman's husband in ice and made the long trip back to the funeral home on Long Island. As we prepared to perfuse him with the blood substitute, the wife grabbed me by the arm. "Please promise you will have him back to me in ten years," she pleaded. I was stunned. She did not understand cryonics at all. I told Curtis, who had come over to help, that we should not continue unless she clearly understood what was involved and he agreed. "I can't promise to revive your husband in a hundred years, much less ten," I told her. "In fact, I can't make any promises at all." If she had any expectations of our reviving her husband any time soon, we would stop what we were doing and not take any of her money, we said. Her husband was buried a few days later.

We froze the wife of a New York policeman. On Palm Sunday, a priest came and placed palm leaves on her capsule. Although many lay people were nervous that we were doing something sacrilegious, most of the clergy we met were fascinated. Their feelings can be best described by a Jesuit priest, an expert on cryobiology, who appeared with me on the *Phil Donahue Show*. He said, "God works through human means." He thought it would be a wonderful thing to learn how to revive a person frozen at death, despite the fact that he believed that cryonics, at this stage, was a shot in the dark and thus a poor choice for the allocation of scarce resources. Although he did not favor its being carried out on a large scale, he saw its potential in specific human medical situations and was strongly in favor of continuing research in the field.

The priest's view is not surprising. The theoretical foundation of cryobiology, and therefore cryonics, was laid down by a Jesuit monk named Basile Luyet, who taught at St. Louis University and founded his own cryobiological institute in Madison, Wisconsin. Father Luyet studied the effects of low temperatures for years, experimenting with the freezing of embryonic organs of animals. He had frozen and thawed embryonic frog hearts, filming the beating heart afterward. His book, *Life and Death at Low Temperatures*, launched cryobiology. He also trained dozens of young scientists in the field, many of whom now hold university positions and have made their contributions to this area.

Unfortunately, some of these early freezings were not to last. Robert Nelson convinced the relatives of the people we had frozen that his cryonics group could do a better job of caring for them. Although we tried to persuade them not to do so, they transferred the care of the bodies to him. Several years later it was discovered that the bodies in his charge had not been kept frozen as promised. In the ensuing scandal, the relatives successfully sued Nelson and his associates for a large sum of money. But the damage had already been done: The bodies had long ago thawed.

At about this time, 1971, I decided to relocate to Berkeley. I felt that in New York I did not have the support to develop the kind of approach to life extension that I needed and felt I would have at Berkeley. My hunch was justified. It was in Berkeley that cryonics became both a science and a business.

During my final days as a graduate student at New York University I met a woman who insisted that I look up a friend of hers who lived in Berkeley. His name was Art Quaife. A straight-A mathematics graduate student at the University of California at Berkeley, he had dropped out after finishing his courses to start Trans Time, Inc., a company set up to do cryonics suspensions.

That did it. Not only did Berkeley have a physiology Ph.D. program in gerontology headed by an accomplished researcher with an interest in aging, there was a cryonics company in the area as well. Within a year, Frosty and I were living in Berkeley, doing research on our Ph.D.s at the university, and working with Trans Time. It was not long after that that Trans Time was also freezing people.

A judge from the Midwest had us freeze both of his parents within a period of a few years. An engineer from Maryland had his parents frozen, but then died unexpectedly in an auto wreck. He had made no provision to freeze himself or maintain his parents in suspension. Fortunately, a group of Southern Californians raised enough money to keep his parents frozen and we had the bodies transported to Los Angeles.

Perhaps the most notable freezing we carried out was that of Luna Wilson, the fifteen-year-old daughter of renowned science fiction writer Robert Anton Wilson, known for his *Illuminatus!* trilogy. Luna was a charming teenager who liked to spend her time on Berkeley's bustling Telegraph Avenue. She had volunteered to close up a friend's clothing store on a Friday evening in the mid-1970s when a deranged man entered the store and delivered a lethal blow to her head with a heavy metal plate used to imprint charge cards. Her body was not discovered until the following day. The word of her death spread through Berkeley like a shock wave.

I had grown quite close to the Wilsons over the years. They were wonderful people who loved to entertain all sorts of interesting folks who would gather in their living room to share their experiences, plans, ideas, and dreams. When I heard the tragic news, I called the Wilson home to see if it was true and if there was anything I could do as a friend to assist the family. Michael, the fiancé of Luna's sister, confirmed the horrible story; he also told me that Bob and his wife, Arlan, wanted Trans Time to do whatever was necessary to place their daughter in cryonic suspension.

There was no time to lose. One of my housemates, Carl Abrams, called our lawyer, Ron Barkin, who immediately persuaded the Oakland medical examiner not to do an invasive autopsy on Luna's brain. Since so many hours had elapsed since the time of death, we felt that little would be gained by doing a cryoprotective perfusion of the entire body. Instead we opted to freeze only the brain, which had been removed and studied to determine the exact cause of death. In this way we could save the parents much of the considerable cost associated with cryonics suspension, for which they had made no prior arrangements. Luckily, the body had been refrigerated since it had been discovered.

A taxi-driving friend rushed my wife, Judy, and me to the medical examiner's office. We handed a dry-ice-filled container to the medical examiner, who was friendly and did as we asked—placed Luna's brain in our container. We closed the lid and took it to Trans Time, where it was immersed in its liquid nitrogen home.

During the 1970s, interest in cryonics increased. One television station after another made its way to Trans Time, often from other countries, including France, Britain, Australia, Japan, and Italy. Bruce J. Friedman, the celebrated humorist, planned to write a satirical piece about us for *Playboy.* But after meeting us, he, too, decided that cryonics was no joke. The story that ran, "Frozen Guys," was a lighthearted, good-natured account. The next year, a man who wrote for the German edition of *Playboy,* and had seen the American article, decided that a serious manuscript was in order and he wrote one.

By this time our work on low temperatures in animals had advanced to the point where we were able to give demonstrations on film for television reporters who wanted to see cryonics at work. For one Japanese TV group, we inserted electrodes through the skull of a rat and attached them to the membranes covering the surface of the brain. We then chilled the rat to the ice point and revived it. The camera captured on film first the brain waves failing, then respiration ceasing, finally the heartbeat stopping. Then it showed, on revival, each function returning in the opposite order. This demonstration was shown several times on Japanese national television.

By the 1980s we had begun surgical research, and in 1982 we revived our first hamster after ice-cold total-body washout. Two years later we presented our results at a meeting of the Cryobiology Society, the professional organization of scientists who study the effect of cold on living tissue. Many of the society's leaders were on record as being opposed to cryonics, and the members sat in silence during the presentations. During the discussion, only one question was asked: Of what possible use was it to do such things? I told them: performing bloodless surgery, protecting patients during chemotherapy, facilitating multiorgan retrieval for transplantation, freezing wholebody transplant donors, keeping transplant recipients on ice until an organ became available. I even spoke about suspended animation as the cornerstone of space medicine. Even though I never mentioned the primary purpose of these experiments—to perfect cryonic suspension so that it is totally reversible and medically acceptable—the only response was a deafening silence. The chairman of the session returned to the microphone, commenting that it looked as if Orwell's 1984 was really here, and he was not so sure he liked it.

The next year, cryonics researchers from northern and southern California presented their findings on ice-cold blood substitution at the 1985 Cryobiology Society meeting held at the University of Wisconsin at Madison. The southern Californians told of their work on dogs; we reported our results with hamsters. Although many of the society members were friendly and helpful, the leaders kept their distance. Cryonics was still a dark science.

Normally, abstracts of presentations at such a conference are published in an issue of the society's journal, *Cryobiology*, following the conference. But when the conference issue of *Cryobiology* appeared, all the abstracts submitted by the cryonics groups had been left out. Any decision to omit our abstracts could not have been made on their scientific merit. There had been absolutely no discussion of either presentation and no one claimed that there was any scientific irregularity. It was our impression that the abstracts were not published because some of the authors, myself included, advocated and publicly supported cryonics and that that was not acceptable to the leadership of the society. We were never informed of any reason for our work's exclusion. We never asked. We felt that any group of scientific administrators that would stoop to such conduct was not worthy of our time. We had more important concerns ahead of us.

Our ultimate goal, the reason we became cryonics researchers in the first place, was, of course, to perfect ways of freezing and thawing people. With the ice-cold blood-substitution experiments in hamsters, we had developed a model system that we believed would serve us well in our continued search. Hamsters were small, cheap, and could be frozen quickly with small quantities of dry ice and rapidly rewarmed. But many people in cryonics questioned whether the knowledge gained in research on hamsters would be applicable to human beings. They suggested using a larger animal such as the dog, as some of the other cryonics researchers had done.

While we were certain that our hamster work would be useful in developing cryonics techniques, we needed to prove it. The successful revival of Miles vindicated our belief that the low-temperature methods worked out on hamsters could be applied to nonhibernating larger animals. Now we could proceed with confidence to the true heart of our research: freezing.

Up to this point, we had recovered significant EKG signals in hamsters from temperatures that were only a few degrees below the freezing point of water. We had done this by perfusing the animals with a solution containing a quantity of glycerol similar to that which keeps some North Country frogs alive in their partially frozen state during the winter. But, we learned, these quantities of cryoprotectant were not sufficient to bring back animals from even deeper cold.

Hal Sternberg, a dedicated biochemist who had been

interested in cryonics and life extension research since childhood, had been intensively studying solutions that cryobiologists used to protect frozen cells and tissues. He insisted that we needed more concentrated solutions of cryoprotective agents if we were to explore the icy lower depths. We decided to use concentrations of glycerol that were several times that commonly found in nature, and we also added some synthetic compounds. We then brought the hamsters down to a frigid − 20 degrees centigrade and kept them at this temperature overnight. At the time of this writing we have not been able to get strong, clear-cut, and persistent heart activity back after freezing to this degree using these high-powered solutions. But we can get the blood substitute flow started up again, so that we can wash out what we put in, showing a degree of intactness in the circulatory system. We have also seen the first hint of coordinated electrical activity.

One thing was obvious to us from these experiments. We now had a animal model with which to study cryonics suspension techniques. But there was still a major problem—how to pay for this research. Throughout the mid-1980s we were able to get donations from small private foundations interested in financing life extension research. By cutting back on our personal expenses, we could survive on tiny salaries, with enough left over to buy the necessary animals and equipment to do the experiments.

Then, just as it looked like we were on the way to developing a reversible cryonics suspension technique, our supply of research money began drying up. Luckily, Miles bailed us out. Thanks to the dramatic publicity surrouding his successful revival, investment in Trans Time started to soar. Membership in the San Francisco–based American Cryonics Society (formerly the Bay Area Cryonics Society) also zoomed. H. Jackson Zinn, the forward-thinking president of ACS, released enough funds to allow some basic research to continue. Trans Time matched these funds from the sale of its stock, which rose 50 percent in value despite Black Monday (while the biotech companies crashed through the basement).

Media interest continued. Television, radio, newspapers, and magazines from places around the country and the world besieged us for interviews. The publicity even reached New Zealand, where a brilliant computer scientist–businessman who had successfully developed programs for computerized foreign language translation heard one of our interviews on a radio program. He sent a research contribution and engaged us in a project to set up a cryonics center in New Zealand. A group of entrepreneurs and investment bankers offered to finance a subsidiary of Trans Time to develop medical products from spin-offs of cryonics research. I was invited to participate in campus debates as an advocate of biotechnology in opposition to Jeremy Rifkin, the noted opponent of genetic engineering. A department head of a prestigious midwestern university hospital made arrangements with his colleagues to test our blood substitute in a series of liver transplantation experiments. The research-and-development director of a major medical supply firm toured our facilities and spent the day discussing whether his company should enter the area of cryoprotective fluid development.

Suddenly cryonics has become a hot topic, and its future looks brighter than ever. Twenty years ago, when we were starting out, cryonics suspension took place in funeral homes, and the societies were run out of bedrooms of tiny bachelor apartments. Today we use sophisticated surgical facilities with state-of-the-art cardiopulmonary bypass technology.

Tomorrow, mobile units, either vans or helicopters equipped with portable high-pressure oxygen chambers and computer-controlled bypass circuits to provide rapid, oxygenated, and chilled perfusions, will rush to the deathbed. Blood substitutes containing highly effective cold-protecting molecules will defend tissues against freezing damage to a far greater extent than is possible today. New methods of solid state storage, such as vitrification, may be available. Medical-imaging apparatuses, with the aid of a contrast medium that has been added to the cold-protecting solution, will detect the areas of the body that have not been adequately cryoprotected and these will then be selectively perfused. As cryonics progresses to the point where it is fully reversible, it will be increasingly applied before death, rather than afterward.

I also believe that the closer we get to achieving reversible cryonics the more people who oppose the idea of freezing bodies after death will speak out against it. Like Bernie in *Cocoon*, there will be those who are committed to playing out the hand that nature dealt them. Unlike Bernie, many of them will try in every way they know to force others to play the game by their rules.

Ultimately, the decision will be made in the marketplace. In a free-enterprise society, like ours, dollars usually cast the deciding vote. No amount of bureaucracy, legislation, or back room agreement among influential scientific and university administrators can stop such forces. If there are enough people out there with the money who want cryonics, cryonics they will get. (In the next chapter I will deal with the ethical, moral, social, political, and economic issues involved in this kind of radical life extension.)

When I first began my study of the aging process, more than two decades ago, I was often ridiculed and attacked for trying to accomplish what most scientists at that time thought was impossible and even immoral. Now, intervention in aging is a popular theme for staid scientific volumes. Tens of millions of tax dollars are going to fund interventive aging experiments that will characterize what happens to rodents that are age-delayed by nutritional restriction. Prominent individuals have formed groups such as the Alliance for Aging Research, which lobbies Congress to support life-extending technology.

While many scientists continue to feel threatened by cryonics, there are compelling reasons for such people to reexamine their views on the subject. These reasons range from the future burden of sustaining millions of people as they linger in a progressively deteriorating state from AIDS, Alzheimer's, and intractable cancer, to the under-supply of vital organs for transplantation, to the need for suspended animation in the coming era of space trans-portation.

The history of science shows that most new ideas are greeted at first with derision, suspicion, and skepticism. Usually in the beginning only a handful of people are will-ing to gamble their reputations and careers on an enter-prise that seems to have so little chance of success. As they begin to make some modest progress, they may at-tract a small following. At the same time, traditional sci-entists, who feel threatened by this work, may organize in opposition. But if the pioneers are on the right track, their experiments become more and more convincing. They begin to have breakthroughs that convince others that their goals may be attainable. More scientists join in the effort, accelerating the pace of research. At some point, men and women who have already made their name in science become interested, and as they add their repu-tation to the effort, the new field becomes more and more acceptable. This is what happened in the field of aging, where until recently most scientists declared that nothing could be done to change the basic rate of aging or extend the maximum life span. Now it is common to see promi-nent scientists declare that an understanding of the mechanisms underlying aging is close at hand and that this understanding should be used to give us longer, happier, and more productive lives.

So it will be with cryonics. In spite of the opposition that will surely be ranged against it, especially if a backlash develops in response to its growing acceptance, the science of cryonics will continue to progress. Even if it were to be suppressed and cryonics services banished from the country, people would go elsewhere to get it, because cryonics speaks to our deepest nature: Most of us want to live and not to die. Because life is sweet and we want it to go on. Because we want to continue to eat and drink and make love and talk to our friends and spend time with our children and grandchildren and walk on the beach or in the woods or on the city streets and work and play at the things we love. Because if it is worth doing once, it is worth doing again. Here today and here tomorrow.

8

PANDORA'S

ICEBOX

Pandora hastened to replace the lid, but alas! the whole contents of the jar had escaped, one thing only excepted, which lay at the bottom, and that was hope.

—Thomas Bulfinch, *The Age of Fable*, 1855

On January 7, 1988, an army of police, investigators, and other officials converged on the Alcor Life Extension facility in Riverside, California. As the president of the organization and a number of volunteer workers were led away in handcuffs, local authorities nervously searched the building. The object of their search was the frozen head of Dora Kent.

Saul Kent, president of the Life Extension Foundation, author, financier and promoter of life extension research, and the person who introduced me to cryonics, had had his eighty-three-year-old mother's head frozen by Alcor members. According to newspaper and television accounts, Mrs. Kent had been ailing for some time and was in the advanced stages of organic brain disease. Her son had ordered the feeding tube that was sustaining her to be withdrawn and removed her from the nursing home where she had been maintained.

Apparently the coroner did not recognize the name of the physician who appeared on the death certificate and became suspicious. During his investigation, he learned that the physician had not been present at the exact time of death, that a cryonics suspension had taken place, and that only the head had been frozen. There was also a question as to whether she had been decapitated prior to death, which would make her son and those who helped him liable to a murder charge. The incident made national news, drawing even more attention when the search of Alcor's storage vault failed to turn up Mrs. Kent's head.

The coroner threatened to autopsy Dora Kent's head when it was found, as well as all the other heads stored in Alcor's Riverside laboratory. The lawyer for Saul Kent and Alcor moved to obtain an injunction blocking any attempt by the coroner to autopsy the cryonically preserved heads. He succeeded at a court hearing, which included testimony gathered from scientists all over the country stating that cryonic suspension was a scientifically valid endeavor and should not be lightly interfered with. The location of Mrs. Kent's head has never been determined.

The case brought into sharp focus some of the issues we may face as cryonic suspensions become more common. First was the public reaction to the incident, which was divided. Many people recoiled in horror at the ghoulish son willing to desecrate his mother's body by decapitating her. Others saw it as a heroic effort by a son to preserve his mother's consciousness for a future day when he and she might be reunited in health and youth.

Then there was the terrible dilemma that faced Saul Kent, who is a dedicated cryonicist: He could allow his mother to be artificially sustained in a vegetative state, while her incurable, progressive organic brain disease inexorably destroyed her higher mental function, turning her into a member of the living dead, with no personality, consciousness, memory, ability to recognize friends or relatives, or any other vestige of what we call human. Or he could withdraw her external life support, thereby hastening her death, so that she could be frozen with at least some of her higher brain still intact. How much would persist, he had no way of knowing. But at least he would have done something that added hope to a hopeless situation.

What about the fact that there was no physician present at the time of death? Since a freezing is best done starting immediately after death, should Saul have hired a physician to sit by his mother's side twenty-four hours a day until she died? Although dreadfully expensive, that would have avoided the furor that now surrounds her suspension. What if the physician had insisted on waiting until all the vital signs had ceased? Could this wait have further compromised the integrity of his mother's deteriorating brain? And did his realization of a conflict between the need of the physician to satisfy the legal requirements of certifying death and his own need to start cryopreservation without delay once her heart had failed contribute to his reluctance to hire an attending physician?

At that point he would have three alternatives. He could keep the feeding tube in and allow the brain to disintegrate further. Or he could remove it, thus letting her starve to death, not a pleasant prospect. The third alternative is to anesthetize and chill her using the same procedures that are now done in certain forms of open-heart surgery, and then proceed to cryonically suspend her. While this practice is currently illegal, could one really blame Saul had he chosen the third alternative, considering that his goal was to freeze his mother and that this would offer the best possible preservation? I think not.

The case has tremendous implications for public policy. What if it was accepted that there were overriding reasons for ending the life of a terminally ill person whose brain was deteriorating so that one could attempt to cryo-preserve what was left? If it was to become permissible to terminate an individual's life prior to the loss of all the vital signs specified in the legal definition of death, how could society protect those patients who might recover if given high-quality medical attention? Should the family of the patient be allowed to make that decision in view of the fact that such care may be extremely expensive? And how could one ensure that hospitals did not prematurely discontinue care for nonpaying indigents who might otherwise have a chance to survive?

Finally, there is the question of cryonics itself. Is cryonics a ripoff by unscrupulous individuals who prey on the fears and grief of those who can't face the finality of death? Or is it a reasonable alternative to burial or cremation, from which there is no hope at all of ever returning? If the latter is true, shouldn't society be obli-gated to do its best to guarantee each citizen his or her place in the frozen casket, or should such recourse belong only to the well off? Considering the difficulties, it is little wonder that government officials have been reluctant to press the issues involved in cryonics.

Although the questions raised by this case may seem bizarre, they are the same ones that society has been grap-pling with since the advent of high-tech care several de-cades ago; only the context has changed. There is the same question of the quality of life versus an almost meaningless existence; the same question of two systems of health care—one for those who can pay for it and another for those who can't; the same question of how far one should go in artificially sustaining life when the body can no longer do the job; the same question of whose life is it anyway? The individual's who can no longer make the decision? The closest family member's? Or the hospital's?

It is important that we begin to anticipate as much as possible the various questions that will arise in the context of the coming technology, because the foundations for it are already being laid. Many of the things described in this book took place just in the year that it has taken me to write it: the implantation of human fetal nerve cells into the brains of sufferers of Parkinson's disease, the harvesting of organs from an anencephalic baby born in Canada, the use of lazeroids to resurrect people after clinical death, and the first transmission of nerve impulses across the crushed spine of a rat using a bridge of living fetal cells. In my own laboratory we achieved the first signs of life in hamsters that had actually been frozen and thawed. At this writing there are 125 clinics worldwide set up to do in vitro fertilization, and, for the first time, women are starting to donate eggs for implantation to other women in the same way that men have long contributed sperm for use in artificial insemination. And a Nobel Prize winner has announced the formation of a company to carry out the complete mapping and DNA sequencing of all human genes. In addition, there are all the unforeseen breakthroughs that occur serendipitously, or through the workings of a highly original mind, that suddenly catapult us into a new understanding that opens up a world of possibilities. As UCLA gerontologist Roy Walford points out, scientists as a group make lousy forecasters. Einstein, Neils Bohr, and Ernest Rutherford, the fathers of atomic physics, each predicted that we would never get power out of the atom. And in 1937 an elite corps of specialists reporting to President Franklin Roosevelt on future technological developments overlooked the following events that would revolutionize society: the discovery of nuclear power, jet propulsion, aviation as mass transit, and the transistor. Let us not make their mistake.

The life extension revolution, like no other in human history, touches on every aspect of our lives. It literally hits us where we live.

As a frequent campus lecturer and guest on radio and television talk shows, one of the questions I am asked repeatedly is: Why would anybody want to live forever, even if they were to remain young and healthy? To me, this has always seemed self-evident, but obviously it is not to everybody.

On San Francisco's KCBS radio, talk show personality Lila Peterson said to me during an interview, "Well, Dr. Segall, this is all very interesting. But when I think about life extension and all it implies, I get this feeling deep in the pit of my stomach that something is wrong."

A friend of mine, while I was still in college, remarked that if he found out that I had just discovered a treatment to prevent or arrest aging he would shoot me.

Over the years, as I have become familiar with reactions such as these, I have come to realize that some people find the very idea of life extension upsetting. Since life extension has such vast implications, it is not surprising that many react with confusion, anxiety, and even hostility. In fact, these intense reactions probably lie at the heart of the resistance to the "immortalist philosophy," as it has become known since the publication of Harrington's notable dissertation. While these are off-the-cuff remarks that should not be taken at face value—my former college classmate, for instance, would never consider carrying out his threat—the feelings they express may well shed light on some of the gloomier aspects of the human soul.

Why should anyone take offense to the proposition of extended life and youth, especially their own? These feelings could not stem from a belief that it will never happen, because people would then just dismiss the whole idea, rather than get upset about it. For some people, I think that their underlying antagonistic attitude toward life prolongation comes from the feeling that it will take place, and that they, for whatever reason, will miss out on it. If they can't have it, why should others? In other words, it is a case of sour grapes in advance.

I believe that many of those who resent the immortalist position are jealous of the idea that someone may possibly achieve such a coveted goal. The conquest of death and aging is difficult enough if one spends one's entire life in its pursuit (just ask any of us who have). But if one rejects it at the outset and refuses even to accept it as a legitimate goal, then surely he doesn't have to worry if the effort fails.

But what if someone devoted his life to such a goal and *succeeded*? Wouldn't it be the best of all possible successes? Shouldn't everyone have lived this way? And then, haven't those who chose not to, who rejected life extension, really missed the boat? No one wants to feel like that.

Another personal objection I hear all the time is that life itself is not all that it's cracked up to be: day-to-day existence is boring; work is unsatisfying; marriage, love life, family life, or lack thereof are trying; friends and relatives are hard to deal with; daily problems are unending. Many people feel that they are obliged to go on for the sake of others who are dependent on them or to meet society's goals. To them, aging and retirement look like an escape hatch, a parachute from the humdrum.

Once we are old, daily life is often filled with medical problems, pain, loneliness from the loss of friends and family members, a feeling of uselessness from lack of work. Time hangs heavy on our hands. Immortalism, from this perspective, seems only a way to prolong the pain, suffering, and hopelessness.

Although I can respect and appreciate these kinds of feelings (who among us has not had them from time to time?), I can't help thinking that those who believe that aging is a comfort and death is the answer would be better off doing something about the life they have. Perhaps they should explore professional counseling, get involved with a support group, try changing their occupation, or introduce some kind of variation into their daily routine to make their life more exciting, interesting, and worth living. In this modern world, so many choices are open to most of us that before giving up one should seek some kind of alternative, to create a world not simply bearable but rewarding and stimulating.

Putting our feelings aside for the time being, what about all the social, political, economic, philosophical, and ethical implications of the coming war against death and aging? What about all those questions that people ask me all the time that reveal just how uncertain they are about the entire enterprise?

What are we going to do with all the people?

Could we still have babies?

Doesn't the finitude of life provide its meaning?

Wouldn't we get bored?

Are we trying to play God?

Won't life extension undermine religion?

Won't God get mad?

Won't it be only the rich who get to have life prolonged?

Is it fair to spend hundreds of billions on extending life when a quarter of the world doesn't have enough money for food?

Won't the quest to achieve these things lead to even greater competition for money and resources, thus increasing the tensions among the nations of the world?

What would life extension do to Social Security, which is already strained?

Would one have to live with the same partner for centuries rather than decades?

What about coming back after centuries of cryonics suspension to find everyone you know has gone and there are no friends or family to help you adjust to a world that has changed beyond recognition?

How would you fit in? Would you just be in the way? Could you contribute?

What if you were revived with brain damage—who would pay your medical bills and support you?

The questions are endless.

Let's begin with the issues of morality, because if life extension is immoral, then how could we go forward with it? Is life extension a worthy goal? Is it right? What about the means-end relationship implicit in a democratic society? If the goal is a worthy one, should an individual be allowed to pursue it even if the means required grossly offends our sensibility? What if the means involves decapitation for the purpose of cryonically preserving only the head? Or removing the higher brain of a fetus so that it never develops into a thinking, feeling individual? Or gestating this brainless baby in the womb of a chimpanzee and then dismembering it in order to harvest its parts for transplantation?

I am certain that there are many people, including professional moralists, who would argue that we should disavow these options because, despite their medical value, they violate the basic sense of humanity that underlies the fabric of our society. They would invoke images of Nazis performing inhuman acts and claim that by producing brain-absent clones we were creating a subhuman species that existed only to serve our own selfish purposes. But, as I pointed out earlier, a clone is not a human being, nor, for that matter, a member of any species. (This is true even of anencephalic infants, who are considered "brain-absent" under West German law.) It is nothing more than a collection of living cells, tissues, and organs, with no consciousness to guide its actions, sense pain, or provide an identity. As for decapitation, is that any more a desecration of the body than autopsy, in which the corpse is eviserated like a cow at a butcher's shop? Where does our sense of humanity, decency, and morality lie? In needlessly extending the suffering of human beings or in making available techniques that would greatly enhance health and longevity, while not harming another sentient being?

How would someone who rejects cryonics on moral grounds justify his position to a grieving son who begs for a second chance for his recently departed mother? What if that son believes that neuropreservation is the most effective way to rapidly chill, freeze, and store the consciousness of a person whose body has been ravaged by aging and illness? Although I, myself, have my reasons for not favoring neuropreservation, I can see the logic behind it.

And how would someone tell the desperate parents of a child dying from the lack of a liver, kidney, or heart that although obtaining an organ from a genetically identical brain-absent body clone grown in a chimpanzee surrogate mother is possible, the use of this technology is unethical? Would it really be so easy to convince the parents that they must use donated organs that would subject their child to a lifetime of immunosuppressant drugs capable of promoting cancer and possibly even a form of AIDS? Could that individual in all conscience deny these parents a technology that would provide an organ as biologically compatible as the child's own?

When asked what he would do if it were his own child, a philosopher who specializes in bioethics answered that he would rather let his daughter, whom he loved dearly, die than use a technology that he believed was unethical. His reason was based on the Kantian Categorical Imperative, which exhorts us to act in ways that we would have everyone act. That is his choice and one he would have to live with. (Although, if the use of cloned parts became standard practice, he might not be able to deny it to his minor child in the same way that Christian Scientists and Jehovah's Witnesses have been forced to allow their children to accept medical procedures that violate their own religious ethics.) But few of us, I suspect, would forgo lifesaving technology for our children, our parents, our spouses or partners, or ourselves for the sake of an abstract philosophical principle. I daresay we would also be acting in a way we believe that others should act. Decent, law-abiding, moral people can differ over what is or is not ethical. Those who call themselves pro-choice and those who are pro-life both claim that theirs is the correct moral stance. If there were a gold standard of morality to which everyone adhered, we would not have debates on such issues as the use of fetal tissue for medical purposes and the right to die. In the recent case of the use of an anencephalic baby as a transplant donor, while hospital after hospital turned down the offer of this baby's organs on moral grounds, the people closest to the child, its parents, believed that the highest moral purposes were served by using their brain-absent infant to save the lives of other children who would otherwise be doomed.

In the end, morality is about drawing the line. There are no absolutes. We say that it is immoral for one person to take the life of another but then make exceptions for wartime, self-defense, extenuating circumstances. In the same way, as new technologies bring with them new possibilities as well as new problems, people are forced to rethink questions they believed they had already resolved, and the line shifts again. So, for instance, when in vitro fertilization first became available, doctors were often in the position of having to destroy excess embryos that were not needed for implantation. Later it became possible to freeze the extra embryos for use at a future date (reversible cryonics!). Now you have this situation, as recently reported on the front page of *The New York Times*: "Quietly, and with virtually no publicity, a number of doctors have begun offering a way out for women who are pregnant with more fetuses than they want or can carry safely: They are aborting some of the fetuses while allowing the rest to proceed to birth."

We are not talking about ordinary abortions to interrupt pregnancies that were unplanned or were the result of rape. These are pregnancies that occurred in women who have often spent years of effort and a great deal of money trying to have a baby. The techniques they tried, such as fertility drugs or embryo implantation, have resulted in more live fetuses than they wished to bear. At first their only choice was to abort all the fetuses and start again or to have multiple births of anywhere from twins to sextuplets. Now, using ultrasound to locate the fetuses in utero and lethal injections of potassium chloride to destroy selected fetuses, they have a new option: pregnancy reduction. Once again, the line between what is considered morally acceptable in terms of abortion is being redrawn. While some physicians and bioethicists are against this new form of abortion, others support it. Says one bioethicist, Dr. John C. Fletcher, who is also an Episcopal priest, pregnancy reduction to save the lives of babies who might otherwise not survive, or have serious medical problems, satisfies the ethical principle of "least harm for the most potential good." One could say the same for cloning, cryonics, and the other life-extending technologies.

What about religious objections? Religion by its nature is the most conservative of our institutions and is slow to change. The Catholics and Orthodox Jews have long forbade birth control and abortion. The pope has spoken out against in vitro fertilization, egg donation, and surrogate motherhood. One cannot expect that he will look with favor on body clones anytime soon. Jehovah's Witnesses may not approve of a procedure, like ice-cold bloodless cancer chemotherapy, that requires blood transfusions from others. (One may not want to reuse a patient's own blood for medical reasons such as fear of reestablishing the cancer from a vagrant malignant cell that has escaped into the bloodstream.) Some groups of Orthodox Jews might not approve of the cryocapsule as the correct means of disposing of the faithful at death, since the manner of burial they use is rigorously proscribed by law set down several millennia ago.

But because of the human value of each life-extending technology, I believe that most, if not all, faiths will come around to some degree. This will not happen right away. There will be adaptations, regulations, and special dispensations as they learn to accommodate each innovation. As the lives of their congregations are enhanced by this technology, as an aged parent recovers from cancer, or a small boy walks on a perfectly restored limb, or even a middle-aged woman rejoices in the restoration of her youthful beauty, clerics closest to these people will begin to rethink their attitudes. When it becomes clear that these innovations protect life and promote human happiness, there will be compromises in practice, if not teaching, just as there now are with regard to contraception, abortion, and many of the other practices of modern society.

The promotion of human health and longevity is consistent with the teachings of all the major religions. Has not every great spiritual leader talked of treating our bodies as temples? The wisdom of Jewish and Moslem lore in proscribing pork has been confirmed in our century by the discovery of microscopic parasites that cause the devastating disease trichinosis. The meditation practiced by Hindus and Buddhists has been approved by cardiologists as a means of coping with high blood pressure and stress. The Catholic Church teaches reverence for human life and forbids the taking of our own life (or that of another) even under conditions of unbearable pain and grief. Seventh-Day Adventists and Mormons who follow the strict requirements of their Churches not to smoke, drink alcohol, or use other products that can endanger health enjoy a longer-than-average life span.

The notions of extreme longevity and resuscitation after death even find their way into the Bible. In the Old Testament, Methuselah lives nine hundred years, while Lazarus rises from the dead in the New Testament. It is said that God made man in his image. If this is true, then doesn't it follow that the ability to do research, to discern the workings of nature, to build on the findings of others, and to make discoveries that will enhance, extend, or restore life after prolonged periods of extended death, is God-given? I daresay few knowledgeable clerics would dispute this.

Priests have blessed cryocapsules. Rabbis have presided over frozen funeral caskets. Ministers have become cryonics society members, and there even existed Theologia 21, a Christian cryonics organization. I have taught courses on gerontology containing life extension sections at Holy Names College in Oakland, California, a campus run by a scholarly order of Roman Catholic sisters. During one semester I even taught a course attended only by clergy.

Rather than harsh criticism, I encountered the most stimulating queries from people who have dedicated their lives to the pursuit of knowledge, teaching, and public service. I have lectured on life extension at synagogues and have been warmly received by both the rabbis and the congregations. Ministers and priests with whom I have shared the microphone on television programs featuring life extension have insisted, even in the face of hostile lay people, that life extension is welcomed by their faiths so long as it does not presume to answer questions pertaining to absolute truth and the infinite, which it does not.

What about physical immortality? Isn't this quest in and of itself a sacrilege? Despite the term *immortalist*, life extension never really addresses questions of the infinite. Forever is a very long time indeed. When religions first evolved, the human perception of time and distance was very limited. No one traveled to the other side of the earth, let alone the next city, in a single day. No one could perceive of a prehistorical process taking billions of years. No one knew of far-flung galaxies millions of light-years away. Only recently has civilization become acquainted with such magnitudes. Now we know that even a million light-years or a million millennia are mere drops in the bucket on the scale of the infinite. Even if our life span were to be extended by one thousand or ten thousand or a hundred thousand years, which would seem to us in today's terms to be life everlasting, it would only be a drop in the ocean of eternity.

Perhaps the greatest accomplishment of religion has been its staying power. According to one survey, 95 percent of Americans say they believe in a Supreme Being. Thus, discoveries of a universe billions of years old and so vast that light itself may not cross it in this time, has not shaken this belief. Instead, the appeal of religion in this age of scientific miracles has grown even stronger. In a world where one out of two marriages ends in divorce, where people uproot themselves every few years, where single-parent families (and singlehood in general) are becoming the norm, the hunger for community and stability has grown more intense. This is precisely what religion has to offer.

Indeed, the constancy of religion may be its greatest

gift to those participating in the life extension revolution. Alert cryonics society members could not fail to see the advantage of a special relationship between their organization and one that has survived through time, sometimes only by dint of the most fanatic devotion of a small group of people. The preserved bodies of popes have remained in state for several centuries in the basement of the Vatican. Temples and churches have stood for thousands of years, while the secular structures around them crumbled. The organization and customs of churches have prevailed through the darkest periods of suppression.

Who could be better caretakers, guarding the frozen bodies and tending the nitrogen levels for decades or even centuries? While companies and governments have come and gone, and even nations and empires risen and fallen, the religions have endured. Who could better fulfill a promise that may take half a millennium to keep?

And when the long-frozen sleep is over and one at last ventures into the outside world, what better refuge will there be to turn to than the churches, synagogues, and temples, with their timeless message of compassion and love? The Bible, the Talmud, and the Koran will be the same a hundred or a thousand years from now as they were a thousand years ago. What a source of stability and comfort for those emerging from another time.

Let us turn to more worldly concerns. One of the questions I am asked most frequently is: What will we do with all the people? If everybody lived forever, wouldn't the population explosion plunge us into a Malthusian nightmare, where people would compete for food and resources would become so strained that the earth could no longer support human life?

Just to begin with, where would we get the room? Although the world now contains five billion people, we have yet to colonize large unoccupied land masses of our planet. Starting with our own country, in California, the most populous state, almost all of the population lives within the relatively limited boundaries of the San Francisco Bay Area, metropolitan Los Angeles, and San Diego; vast stretches of the state are barely populated at all. As one drives across America, which holds the world's fourth largest population, one sees endless, virtually uninhabited areas of mountain, desert, prairies, and forest. Our next-door neighbor, Canada, one of the largest countries in the world, contains almost all of its population within a few dozen miles of our northern border. In many other countries, similar possibilities exist for harboring increased population. Ultimately, we will find ways to inhabit areas now unthinkable—such as the Sahara Desert, the surface of Antarctica, the upper slopes of the Himalayas, and even the floor of the ocean.

But at what cost? What are the ecological implications of building cities in the desert, carving out a habitat in the jungle, raising skyscrapers out of forests? In many parts of the world, pollution has already reached unacceptably high levels. Will we be setting the stage for more Love Canals, Three Mile Islands, Bhopals, and Chernobyls? Will we destroy the ozone layer and hasten the "greenhouse effect"? These are difficult and complex problems that will require international cooperation and regulation to an unprecedented degree. But we have already begun to address these issues, and the old attitude of progress without limits has increasingly given way to an awareness that everything we produce and consume has an impact on the environment.

A significant increase in life span will intensify that awareness. Now the policymakers, who are in their forties, fifties, and sixties, worry about the kind of planet they will be leaving for their grandchildren. But self-interest is a much stronger motivator than altruism. The knowledge that they will also be around in the future will make them reluctant to put off for tomorrow the improvements they can make today. A society that is forced to inhabit a crowded world for an indefinite period of time will think twice before it permits pollution to build up to threatening levels or strips our resources to exhaustion. Already governments and concerned groups are conferring about how to handle such issues as acid rain, deforestation, the greenhouse effect, and destruction of the ozone layer.

If we are to survive, even at our present rate of growth, we will have to become an ecotechnologically oriented society that lives in harmony with nature. We will have to find ways of renewing our resources rather than depleting them. Our planet is already the beneficiary of energy from the sun. It is this energy, of course, that plants and ultimately animals convert into the foodstuffs that sustain us. Other indirect forms of solar energy, such as its impact on the tides and the winds, are already being tapped in small quantities for human benefit. These will be exploited on a far greater scale. Massive wind farms have already been constructed that supply energy to substantial local populations. Fuel cells and new kinds of solar panels will be used to store far greater amounts of energy than ever before.

Scientists are now turning toward new technologies that promise to release untold amounts of energy with minimal pollution. The recent breakthroughs in superconductivity at temperatures that make it practicable promise to change the way in which we live as dramatically as the advent of electricity did. New forms of nuclear fission using recently discovered subnuclear particles are under intense investigation. We may even achieve the dream of nuclear fusion, duplicating the sun's power on earth, without the buildup of nuclear fission products.

Technology not only puts more power at our disposal, it makes possible ways to use that power more judiciously. Revolutionary developments in the microelectronics and computer industries are already being used to make cars that "know" when to fire four, six, or all eight cylinders, depending on how much power is needed. Many factories and office buildings now employ computer monitoring of their energy usage in order to minimize fuel costs and maximize efficiency of consumption.

But according to author Jeremy Rifkin, with whom I have had the pleasure of debating on college campuses, any time you use power—any time you use or build from extracted, nonrenewable resources such as coal, oil, or minerals—you increase the entropy of our planet. Entropy is a complicated mathematical concept involving the principles of thermodynamics, but the bottom line as Rifkin sees it is that there is a depletion of nonrenewable resources and a buildup of pollution. This is basically true if you consider the planet as a closed system. But we are surrounded by a massive, endless universe. I believe it is ultimately on this "high frontier" that the human future depends.

Long before we are ready to colonize space, won't we find ourselves overwhelmed with the press of people? It is worth noting that the countries which have the highest standard of living, the longest life spans, and are most industrialized, have the lowest birth rates. In fact, right-to-lifers are insisting that no measures be taken to prevent a child from being born, clearly indicating a lack of fear of overpopulation. Many people are worried about the low birth rates that are now occurring in industrialized countries around the world. It is in these countries that life extension is a real possibility. Overpopulation is largely a problem in the poorest countries of the world, where birth control is seldom practiced. The life spans in these areas are about those of the industrialized nations before the advent of modern medicine and sanitation.

For the time being, life extension will probably be restricted to those cultures in which the technology allows for reproductive control. This will prevent its introduction from quickly creating unmanageable population increases. Furthermore, it is precisely these highly technical cultures that can create the innovations necessary to meet the needs of an expanding population without immediately hastening the destruction of the environment. It is also these cultures that have aimed their rockets toward the stars.

Even within the industrial world there will be people who reject life extension. Some will want to experience growing old and even death, in the hope of passing on to a better place. Others will want to live short, action-filled, high-reward lives, preferring to "live fast, die young, make a good-looking corpse." Still others will turn against life extension as they have turned against life. Not everyone, perhaps not even a majority, will embrace each new technological advance as it becomes available. It is, will be, and should be a very personal decision. Thus there will be a substantial number of people dying, possibly giving up precious organs and tissues for those wishing to remain in the fray of human existence.

What about children? Will the price of extending our lives be drastically curtailing the creation of new lives? I think not. Any society as technologically advanced as ours should support the current birth rate. But the increased cost of providing for comprehensive health coverage, including the cost of potential transplantation, cloning, and cryonics, will demand a much higher health insurance premium per family member. Unless some governmental arrangement is made, those who opt to pay for life extension benefits through insurance-related coverage for their entire families will spend a far greater amount of their personal budget for health care than is now the case.

There will be a number of factors that will work to limit population growth. As noted above, many people will reject the life extension option. Others will choose either to have no children or to have only one because of the high cost of insurance premiums. Also, the government may choose to offer incentives to keep population down by providing low-cost abortion on demand or giving tax exemptions for childlessness. Any resulting population increases could then be met by technological advances.

What about the quality of life in such a world? Those who chose to forgo life extension would be spared the expense of carrying high-premium insurance policies and increased health-care costs. With added disposable income, they could afford to have more children, travel, buy a new house or car, or enjoy the delights of a high-tech society. For those who chose an increased life span, there would be other rewards.

They could explore multiple careers and live in many different environments. Eventually they could enjoy space travel, perhaps even to other planets. Even slow learners would have time to acquire new languages, study various sciences, try their hand at one or another art form. How many of us have thought of changing professions or learning a new discipline only to abandon the idea because we thought that by the time we could put the new skill to work we would be too old? But if our lives were significantly extended we could, for instance, take a few college credits each year in a subject of our interest, and after thirty or forty years we would have another profession. Then we could start on a third. Two careers are not unusual at our present life span. Imagine if we lived two hundred years, we could have three or four separate educations, specialties, and careers; some of us could have six or seven.

Technologies now on the drawing board will give new meaning to the term *Global Village.* Space planes, like the one Singapore Airlines has planned for deployment by the year 2000, will carry us to any point on the globe in less than one hour. We will be able to breakfast in New York, lunch in Paris, and dine in Tokyo. People could live on one side of the earth and commute to the other. Vast computer networks will allow electronic visits or conferences with family, friends, and colleagues, either on a one-to-one basis or in groups. The world will become our entertainment center. With the use of simultaneous computerized voice translation, we will be able to understand and converse in Russian, Japanese, Chinese, and any other language. We could watch England's BBC for our evening news, Russian ballet, soccer from Argentina.

Travel will take on new dimensions as people explore exotic regions, from the ocean floor to the Himalayan heights, now tamed for human habitation. Rapid and affordable space transit will allow people to shuttle to giant space stations for dinner or spend romantic weightless weekends at luxurious moonside mountain resorts. If the future is anything like the past, options will open up to us that dwarf our twentieth-century imaginations. Boredom may become so rare that it may be considered a form of entertainment.

What about the financial and economic implications? Will life extension be only for the rich? Can Medicare afford body clones for the regeneration of every older person, and a cryocapsule for each person for whom modern technology is not yet advanced enough?

For the time being, I think that the burden of providing for life extension should remain within the private sector. As with any major economic decision in our lives, we must decide what our priorities are. Those who are not willing or able to carry expensive insurance policies may not be in a position to reap the rewards. But it seems to me that those of us who wish life extension for ourselves should also consider donating money and time in support of charities and foundations that will provide life-extending technology for others who can't afford it. Middle-class and upper-class immortalists could promote fund-raising efforts to provide cloned organs for poor children whose lives are at stake or to subsidize a financially burdened family in the cryonic suspension of a beloved grandparent. If this is not done, and only those who are well-off can benefit, there will be a backlash against life extension. It will come to be perceived as a purely selfish venture rather than a bold step into a future that will eventually encompass everyone.

And that will come to pass. It is a general rule that as new technologies are introduced into a society they first become the province of the well-off and only later become available to practically the entire population. Who, today, lives in a house or apartment without indoor plumbing or a refrigerator—things that were luxuries at one time? Cars, once the toys of the rich, are now considered a necessity by the vast majority of Americans. When I was a child growing up in the late 1940s and early 1950s, few people had televisions. Airplane trips were extremely expensive and usually cost one month's salary, if not much more. Home videotape recorders did not exist, and computers were owned by only the most prestigious universities. Now all this has changed as modern manufacturing techniques and the industrialization of the Third World has improved our standard of living. A mass life extension market will become affordable to almost everyone in the same way that automobiles, TV, air travel, VCRs, home computers, and even many medicines now are.

It will be no more expensive to grow and store a body clone than produce a new car. The modern car, which requires exotic metals and components, depends on products that span the globe—copper from Chile, steel from Korea, aluminum from Jamaica, chrome from Zimbabwe, oil from Saudi Arabia. Clones, on the other hand, will be homegrown affairs, since they require only amino acids, proteins, sugars, starches, vitamins, and minerals, all of which can be provided by domestic food sources or even processed by genetically engineered bacteria, fungi, or animals. Their production will not depend on the importation of foreign resources. Since the life extension technologies are often labor-intensive, they will be a major source of jobs in the future.

Freezing people, right now, is very expensive. This is because much of the equipment is handmade and custom designed. But as more people sign up for cryonic suspension, the equipment will be mass-produced. Cryocapsules and heart-lung bypass units will be turned out on the assembly line and the price will fall to much more affordable levels.

Now let us consider what the cost will be of *not* developing life extension technologies. What if reversible cryonics suspension does not become available? What if cloning cannot provide genetically identical parts for transplantation and embryonic nerve cells for the senile?

By A.D. 2000, we can expect more than three million cases of Alzheimer's disease in the United States. Over only a ten-year period at a low estimated cost of $20,000 per patient annually, the expenditure for caring for these patients will reach $600 billion. Cryonics and cloning could dramatically reduce this. The freezing of patients by reversible means and maintaining the body at liquid nitrogen temperatures will cost a fraction of nursing home care. Even at today's rates, using extremely wasteful individual cryostorage units, maintenance is under $5,000 a year. Effective mass storage could bring the price down many times over.

Perhaps it may seem cruel and heartless to suggest cryonic suspension as an alternative to nursing home care. But if no cure is available to arrest the course of Alzheimer's, what humane purpose is achieved by maintaining patients at the advanced stage of the disease in nursing homes at discomfort to themselves, great cost to their relatives, and a huge emotional burden to people who watch daily or weekly the pitiful descent of someone they once knew and loved into a sorry state? For the children of the Alzheimer's victim there is the terrifying realization and fear that comes with knowing that the disease has an inherited basis and that each day that goes by may be bringing them closer to the fate of their parent. Wouldn't a concerted project by government to develop reversible techniques of cryonic suspension make more sense? The success of such a project would give people the option of choosing cryonics over long-term terminal care—something that could be dealt with in advance by a Living Will—or letting the next of kin make the choice if the patient is not mentally able to do so. And since this would only be done after reversible cryonics had been achieved, it would mean giving a second chance to people before their minds had been irreversibly destroyed.

What about the larger political scene? Will the achievement of life extension drive an irrevocable wedge between the have and have-not nations? Will international tensions increase as a result? What will happen to our relations with foreign governments if we start to pull ahead in the race to conquer aging, to reversibly freeze and thaw people after death, or to clone? How will the Soviets feel about this great challenge as America comes closer and closer to offering its citizens extended youth and indefinite life span, while their own people go to their graves in their mid-sixties? How will the countries of Europe and the technological giants of the Pacific Rim deal with this phenomenon? What will be the reaction of rapidly developing countries such as China and India, with their huge populations, or the countries of Africa, South America, and Southeast Asia, with their impoverished masses?

Will the countries of the world become united in

hatred and jealousy of the United States, perceiving it as stripping the resources of the world in order to pursue the youth and vigor of its own population? Wouldn't these feelings totally undermine international cooperation as each nation engaged in a bloodthirsty race to gain advantages over the others as it tried to acquire life-extending technology?

This scenario need not take place if we are willing to share our knowledge with the rest of the world. Indeed, life extension can help bring the world closer together. Historically, nothing has forged a joining of forces between one country and another more than the provision of medical care. (And nothing is as disruptive of foreign relations as death extension, i.e., war.) When radiation from the Chernobyl disaster destroyed the bone marrow of hundreds of victims, American physicians jetted to Kiev to perform bone marrow transplants. A German pair of Siamese twins joined at the head were flown to the United States for hypothermic surgery. Few international efforts have been as successful as the worldwide eradication of smallpox.

In the same way that the standardization and mass production of life extension technologies will bring the price down within the range of the average person in this country, so, too, will it become affordable to people in the Third World countries. As physicians in these countries become familiar with the techniques, aided by computerized information and video consultation with better-equipped hospitals, they will start to apply this knowledge to their own people. At scientific conferences, researchers (who have long ignored political borders when it comes to talking with their colleagues from other countries) will continue to present and discuss their findings as they always have. Eventually, the combination of reduced costs, trained personnel, and highly motivated health professionals will conspire to bring life extension to even the poorest of areas, just as many medical advances spread through the world earlier.

True, these countries will lag behind us for a long time. But the obvious rewards of life extension will make our way of life, which made possible such progress, seem even more attractive to other cultures. In some ways the medical and biotechnical advances of the West have motivated China, and even the Soviet Union, to greater political cooperation.

What about the threat of nuclear war itself? This is where I believe that life extension may make its most lasting contribution. The people who hold the fate of the world in their hands, whose fingers are on the nuclear buttons, are all middle-aged or older. They, like the rest of us, know that their future is likely to hold cancer, heart disease, senility, osteoporosis—an old age of decrepitude, disability, and pain. As they edge closer to their fate, does nuclear annihilation, a death so quick as to be totally painless, possibly lose some of its terror?

I, personally, would rather have our world's leading senior citizens (they are almost all over fifty) looking forward to centuries of youthful life. How much more loath would they then be to giving this all away by committing a single, irresponsible, socially unjustifiable act? How much more protective would the world leaders be of the environment and of the political climate of the earth if they knew they had to depend on the continuation of life on this planet for hundreds or thousands of years, rather than only for the next twenty or thirty. All in all, I feel that life extension will help to bring the countries of the world closer together rather than drive them apart, as millions of caring, hardworking, and intelligent people everywhere work toward the goal that will benefit all humanity.

Coming closer to home, what will be the impact of life extension on us as individuals? How will we handle the dislocations that will inevitably arise as youth no longer supplants age and the dead come back to life? What about the grandmother who finds herself competing with her granddaughter on the dance floor or even in the bedroom? The grandson bested on the playing field by a rejuvenated grandfather? The father who emerges from cryonic suspension to find his son, twenty years older than himself, running the company that he founded?

Reanimated, rejuvenated men may find themselves in the care of gray-haired daughters who do not wish to be made young again. Wives who remarried after their husbands died may be faced with the prospect of newly resurrected spouses looking younger and healthier than on the day they first met. How would society hold together under these kinds of strains?

Obviously, there are no clear-cut answers. The world is constantly changing and adjustments always have to be made. In the last century, science and technology altered our lives to a greater degree than ever before in all of human history. Inexpensive air travel scattered families to the four corners of the earth. The automobile spawned giant cities where there were once just sleepy towns, while thriving communities of the past languished for the want of a nearby interstate exit.

Social values have also changed. In a country where nice people talked about sex only in the most intimate of circumstances, people now watch seductive actresses cavort naked on nationally broadcast cable television programs. Even the telephone has become an instrument of carnal gratification—"lovers" are available for toll-call conversations that would have been totally unthinkable only a few decades past.

There will be other problems of an economic nature that will have the potential for social upheaval. In the workplace, a company could have the same boss for centuries. A U.S. Supreme Court judge could serve for several hundred years. A senator might be reelected twenty times. The people at the top might tend to stay on top, instead of dying off and being replaced by newer, younger, and possibly brighter workers every generation. Wealth might stay in the hands of the wealthy, instead of being passed on to others, creating an aristocracy never yet seen on the face of the earth. The intergenerational competition for a place in the sun could get ugly.

How could Social Security exist where 90 percent of the population was over sixty-five? Could the life extension option be withheld from a person if he or she was unable to pay for it? Would we choose to make people over sixty-five continue to work, arguing that they were age-retarded and thus capable of supporting themselves?

Certainly one can envision some form of social support to cope with problems of this sort. Older people who were really age-retarded would indeed be capable of working, and with their superior skills and greater experience gained over the years might even outcompete youth. As older people retained their youth and vigor, the laws would probably be changed to allow people who are productive to continue working and, in this way, contribute to Social Security rather than draw from it. Arrangements would probably be made to rotate job responsibilities so that younger people would have a chance to run things, while older people tried their hands at different aspects of the job. As mentioned before, many people, if not most, might want to change careers or take sabbaticals from work in order to travel and learn a new skill.

What would happen to the poor? Would we end up with an institutionalized caste system, in which the same rich stayed rich and the same poor stayed poor for hundreds of years? Would some people live on the dole for centuries? Would there be a permanent underclass of people doomed to centuries of unemployment, forever outside looking in on a world they could never hope to be part of? An unlikely fate in a world technologically advanced enough to conquer death and aging.

Finally, what would happen to our spiritual and moral values? If we devoted so much of our energy to the pursuit of our own physical salvation, would this reduce our concern for other people? Would our narrow focus make us more likely to accept injustice to others if it was likely to benefit us? What about the search for higher truth, the wish to help our fellow man, the ability to sacrifice our own wants for the common good? Would we become so materialistic and so blinded by the scientific miracles of our age that we would turn our backs on the teachings of the great philosophers and religious leaders of the past?

I think rather that life extension will give us a perspective on the world that is not possible in the short time now granted to us. Imagine a world in which youth is no longer wasted on the young, where our strength and vigor don't begin to decline just at the point where we have accumulated the skill and experience to really do what we were trained for, where the wisdom and judgment that come with age are not acquired at the expense of the quick-wittedness and sharp-mindedness of youth.

We could have blue-ribbon commissions composed of our finest minds, whose long perspective would give them valuable insights into complex social problems. A polycentenarian with the mental powers of a young JFK, the physical strength of a tireless George Washington, and the wisdom of Abe Lincoln could provide us with the leadership that could raise the ethical and social level of our entire society.

There is one development at which I have only hinted, which will take place independently but go hand in hand with the movement toward life extension: the colonization of space. We will not only find ways to live on the desert, under the ocean, on mountaintops, and on frozen tundras; we will find ways to duplicate our environment on huge space stations, on the moon, and on other planets. Reversible cryonic suspension will make it possible to put people into suspended animation as they journey to their far-off destinations. Indefinite life spans will allow us to explore the solar system, visit people on other worlds, send and receive messages over vast distances.

In the world of the future, the world of interplanetary travel, supercomputing, robotics, micro- and nanotechnology, suspended animation, and reversible cryonics, wealth should accumulate at rates never before observed. Robot mines will pepper the surface of every approachable planet and moon, extracting and delivering their bounty to waiting servomechanical transporters that will take their precious cargo to space-borne manufacturing sites, perhaps on the outer surfaces of synthetic hollow asteroids. Here, robot supercomputerized factories will convert this matter into products now undreamed of in variety, quantity, and uniqueness. Robot-guided rockets will then deliver these goods to depots scattered throughout the inhabited universe.

People living on space stations, planets, and moons will be able to view this merchandise on three-dimensional-holographic, video monitor catalogs, ordering the items by computer, with the price electronically deducted from their charge accounts. Since all work performed will be magnified many times over by machines, each employed person will become in effect an individual production company turning out alone what previously required an entire work force. And, of course, as our productivity increases, so will our wealth.

I realize that the same technology that could bring untold benefits to billions of people could be used to control, manipulate, and destroy huge segments of the of the population. The computerized systems that facilitate our entertainment, communication, and employment could be used to spy on us, recording our every move. The opportunities to cheat and steal will be magnified to interplanetary proportions. Computerized "intelligent" weapons may be able to reach and kill selectively at the whim of a powerful tyrant, police agent, terrorist, or criminal. No doubt there will be armaments that could obliterate whole continents and even planets. It would be naive to think that basic human nature will change. But the stakes will go up as the power and intelligence at the beck and call of each of us grows accordingly. As each individual has access to greater power, his or her potential for wreaking havoc increases, accordingly.

What about evil uses of cloning and cryonics? Could they give rise to an immortal Hitler, a perennial Stalin, a Khomeini who never grows older but wages a thousand-year war against an equally long-lived foe? This strikes me as an unlikely scenario since it is historical forces, not technology, that allow such people to come to the fore. The history of warfare over the centuries shows that conflict usually arises out of the desperation of a people in severe economic distress. Look at the examples of our own century: Some historians assert that the conflagration of the Second World War was kindled by a depression-ridden Germany seeking to expand its territory in order to invigorate its stifled, landlocked economy. Japan, too, harboring a huge land-poor population, was driven into conflict by its lack of territory and the need to expand into the Eastern markets dominated by Americans and Europeans. The Soviet Union, devastated after the First World War and struggling to protect its borders from the threat of a German invasion, made it easy for a dictator to mobilize the vast impoverished population into one huge monolithic army in order to battle the Nazis, who dominated the most technologically advanced nation the world had ever known.

A future society based on abundance could hopefully avoid the desperate warfare that has for so long marred human history. Perhaps the kind of peaceful competition that we now have with our former foes, Japan and Germany, both economically sound and both solidly democratic, is a harbinger of things to come. Battles will be waged with the equivalent of BMWs, Acuras, and Buicks instead of tanks and bombs, and all the world will be a winner as competing nations place their goods in front of the ultimate dictator—the consumer.

What about the unfortunates of such an era? Will a world in which physical perfection exists accept people who are born with deformities or those who were left irreversibly brain damaged by primitive cryonics techniques? No doubt advances in biotechnology will repair or cure almost everyone with inherited or acquired deficiencies. And, as the universe changes, those who are different may have options that are not open to normal people. For instance, new educational techniques, possibly including direct artificial intelligence links directly to the nervous system, may convert mental defectives into unique masterminds. In short, the future is wide open for those of us who make it there either alive or in the cryocapsule.

What will happen as the as the world we know and love changes beyond recognition? Will interplanetary travel, mines on the moons and asteroids, and the colonization of vast gray regions of the solar system ever stir our hearts like a walk along the beach at night with someone we love, a night out on the town in New York City, or the smell of barbecue with our relatives on a plush lawn in Kentucky? As long as we are human, we will love and cherish this earth and the experiences on it that are unique to our culture and our ways. Will life extension convert us to soulless wanderers among the celestial bodies of the universe, making us forget our origins and our homeland? I think not.

In fact, I suspect that ultimately the whole earth will be zoned nonindustrial, with all manufacturing and polluting processes banished to the surfaces of other planets and their moons and to natural and manmade asteroids. This will create a pollution-free environment in which human beings can live in a more natural relationship with their surroundings. People will move around on the earth in non-polluting vehicles driven by long-lived power sources that have been energized extraterrestrially and delivered for earthside use. Populations of wild animals will return to the restored forests, prairies, and jungles freed from the killing effects of industrial wastes. Fish will reenter the once uninhabitable lakes and streams. Birds will fill the sky, their ranges limited only by other avian competitors. The biology of our world will revert to the patterns established over the timeless eons before the first man made fire or fashioned a spear.

As a child, I read every volume of science fiction I could get my hands on. Of all the writers, Ray Bradbury was my favorite. Perhaps I sensed in the beauty of his stories an inalienable humanness that was always a part of the characters in his dramas whether they were set 100 million years in the past, in the far-flung regions of a distant star system, or in the heartland of America.

I firmly believe that this humanness will prevail, whether we live to seventy-five or to seventy-five thousand. I also agree with Bradbury's published comments that for the spirit of humanity to thrive, we must push back the barriers of space. At the same time, I insist that we win the war against time. When all is said and done, when all the arguments are in, when the pros and the cons have been laid on the table, dissected, and reassembled, I, too, have a voice that cries out from within. Of course we must prevail. Of course death is the enemy. Aging is not a friend: It is an imposition and should be vanquished without quarter. Medicine, when it makes us happier, stronger, and younger, is good. Arteriosclerosis, cancer, heart disease, senility, osteoporosis, and all the nemises of youth and of life are evil, and no person should have to be subjected to their rigors against his or her will.

Let us rise up as a society, as a people, as a nation, all humankind together, and, as we once did with the dreaded disease of smallpox, banish this scourge of involuntary death and aging from every corner of our world. And let us do it now, for all of us, in our time.

9

THE CHANCE OF A
(SECOND) LIFETIME

If I were God, man, everybody would live forever.

—Bob Fosse, *All That Jazz,* 1979

The ultimate test of any philosophy is the effect it has on the lives of its proponents. The philosophy of immortality and life extension has been around for hundreds, even thousands, of years, but to what avail? Where are all those would-be immortals now? Where are all the Ponce de Leons who drank from the fountain of youth, the alchemists with their elixirs of life, the food faddists with their life span–extending diets, the yogurt fanciers, the sheep gland recipients, the sardine eaters, the supplement swallowers, the proponents of one or another method that was supposed to do away with aging and death once and for all? They have all died or grown old right on schedule along with everyone else. The dust will cover them.

So in all fairness, you may ask, as do many members of the audience in television talk shows or lecture halls, "What gives you the certainty, Dr. Segall, that you, too, will not join the ranks of the would-be immortals? What makes your program any different from all the others?"

The answer is that the only thing that is certain is uncertainty. Life extension is a gamble. What are the odds of dramatically extending life? There are no real ways to handicap them, no precedents, no controlled studies, no references. And unbiased, intelligent, well-informed, and sophisticated views are about as rare as hen's teeth. In many ways, you're on your own and so am I. So for me, the answer is to read, consult, listen, proselytize, cajole, convince, join up, and gang up, if necessary, to get on the right track. And, of course, even that might not work.

My gut feeling is that the one thing to avoid is the "true believer" approach. It's hard enough to stay alive being streetwise, critical, skeptical, even knowledgeable. To expect to live an extended lifetime with blinders on, oblivious to all the facts and information around you, is really asking for it. Second, there is just so much that an individual can do on his or her own. We are all in this together, or we are not in it at all.

So, with all these caveats in mind, here are ten rules for how to hang around long enough to be a part of the life extension revolution.

RULE 1. FOLLOW YOUR INSTINCTS.

They have evolved to keep you alive. If you sense a diet isn't working for you, get help. If your exercise program doesn't feel right, stop it and consult an expert. If you feel your doctor isn't helping you, ask questions and get a second or third opinion. Which brings me to . . .

RULE 2. BE INFORMED.

If you want life extension, read about life extension. If you feel your knowledge of biomedical science is too limited, improve your understanding with books and courses designed for the intelligent laymen or student. Attend lectures, conferences, discussions, and debates. Get knowledgeable. Make life extension education part of your life. It makes a difference whom you read and listen to as well as how much.

RULE 3. CONSULT WITH AS MANY EXPERTS AS YOU CAN FIND.

Don't take their word as gospel, but hear what they have to say. Perhaps you can't find two who will agree; don't worry, they never do. Each may say the other is ignorant and uninformed, and they may both be right. The important thing is to take from each what will work for you and ignore the rest.

RULE 4. JOIN UP.

Get together with others who have the same goal. In this way you can share information about diet, exercise, and the latest scientific advances. You can also find out what has worked for others. But be careful. Make sure you're not getting involved with a cult or some sort of misguided operation. Look for the classic signs of such enterprises: the claim that they alone have the answer; a paranoid attitude that society or unspecified individuals are out to get them; an attempt to isolate you or cut you off from other sources of influence. If you feel that the group you are with is tending in that direction, get advice and get out, even for a little while, just to make sure.

RULE 5. INVOLVE THOSE AROUND YOU.

Every sane person wants some aspects of health, longevity, and life extension. Try to convince others that a life-extending program can work for them. Share gourmet, low-cal dinners that are high in the vitamins and nutrients often missing in our meals. Exercise together. Spread your newfound knowledge around.

RULE 6. MAKE LIFE EXTENSION A FAMILY AFFAIR.

Interest your spouse, your children, your parents. Plan family vacations around life extension conferences. Some life extension organizations have social events such as parties and dances. One life extension organization has sponsored balls and conferences at the Beverly Hills Hilton with many of Hollywood's stars attending. Important life extension meetings have been held in resort areas such as Lake Tahoe, California, or at the popular Disneyland Hotel near Los Angeles. The American Cryonics Society has social dinners weekly or monthly in cities with significant membership size, such as San Francisco, Los Angeles, and New York, to which members are encouraged to bring their families, relatives, and friends. Many family-oriented life extension recreational and social events have low or no fees.

RULE 7. FOLLOW A LIFE-EXTENDING LIFE-STYLE.

Seat belts saves lives—use them. Smoking is the single largest life-style factor contributing to disease and death. If you smoke, quit now. Obesity is a major killer—maintain a moderate weight. AIDS kills—practice safe sex.

Drinking and driving is a lethal combination—if you drink, let someone else drive.

Develop a life extension life-style and share it with your family. Members of a family that practices life extension together encourage one another to follow good health habits and break bad ones. It is easier to follow a prudent diet if the whole household eats that way. It is more pleasant to exercise if you have company. It's good to have a wife, or even a child, who tells you to buckle up your seat belt even if you don't want to. And it's good to have someone talk you out of a hot fudge sundae, take the car keys when you've had too much to drink, or throw those cigarettes away.

Be cautious about engaging in overly hazardous work or play. There is a reason that riding motorcycles or piloting small planes carries high insurance premiums. If you want to do these things, learn how best to minimize the dangers. Street drugs can be hazardous to your health. In addition to their well-publicized dangers, they may be prepared and stored in a nonsterile way and contain fungi, bacteria, and viruses that can compromise health or even kill. Using a nonsterile needle—or, even worse, sharing one—to administer any kind of street drug is a form of suicide. Millions of people are slowly dying from this unfortunate sport, with the AIDS virus–positive incidence among such users exceeding 70 percent in some urban communities.

Practice preventive medicine. See your doctor when something is wrong and have annual checkups after age fifty. If you are a woman, your checkup should include a mammogram, breast examination, and Pap smear. How often these are done will depend on your medical history as well as that of your family. Learn the danger signs for cancer and heart disease and act on your suspicions. These and other life-threatening conditions can be nipped in the bud if caught early enough.

RULE 8. HAVE FUN.

Laughter is an antidote to disease, pleasure a painkiller, enjoyment a life extender. Have fun with others in ways that are safe and life-fulfilling. If you're not getting a kick out of your life, change it. Change your job, your friends, your life-style, maybe even your mind about some things. If you can't, get some counseling or professional help to assist you. You owe it to yourself to enjoy life—if you love life, you'll probably live longer.

RULE 9. MAKE MONEY AND MAKE THE PROPER ARRANGEMENTS.

Life extension doesn't come cheap. Good doctors can be expensive. Comprehensive medical coverage is invaluable. Cryonics insurance, especially for a whole family, with benefits that do not diminish with age just when you need them most, or whose premiums do not skyrocket in your advanced years, can be costly. Heroic treatment is not always available for those in financial need. If you want longevity, you will have to make it a budgetary priority. You don't have to be a millionaire to take advantage of most life extension opportunities, but it helps to have a middle-class standard of living. Unless you are wealthy, choosing life extension may mean foregoing certain luxuries.

RULE 10. GANG UP.

Promote life extension at work, in your community, and at large. Educate your elected officials. Let your congressperson and senators know that you want them to support life extension–oriented legislation. If you are religiously observant, tell your priest, minister, or rabbi about it. There is nothing in most religions that can't coexist with life extension principles and practices. Inform your doctors, nurses, and other health-care professionals. Help educate your local school officials, teachers, and social workers as well.

Since this is a highly emotionally charged subject, be discreet, use good taste, and consider the feelings of others. As your own community becomes more oriented toward life extension goals, its support for your plans will grow. No one person by him or herself is going to beat death and aging. Our whole society must eventually become involved if we are to have our way.

At this point you may be asking yourself, "Why bother with all this since the best most of us can do is to live to seventy-five or eighty-five and many of us reach seventy with the worst of health habits?" The answer is that at the rate biomedical science is moving today, living five or ten years longer can make all the difference between life and afterlife. Especially when it comes to cryonics.

If I died today, the technology used to freeze me would be fairly primitive, but better than that used five or ten years ago. Five years ago, our hamster suspension model had not yet developed to the point where we could use it to test the effectiveness of cold-protective agents. Now we can circulate various cryoprotectant blood substitutes through the bloodstream of hamsters and freeze, rewarm, and attempt to revive them. We can study how well their circulation works after freezing and whether they have a heartbeat and can breathe. In this way, we can figure out the best way to freeze as well as thaw these animals and then apply what we have learned to more humanlike animals such as dogs and monkeys.

In order for me to live a dramatically expanded life span, I do not have to survive until I can be frozen and thawed without the slightest damage. I only have to survive until I can be frozen in such a way that relatively small advances need be made in the revival process to bring me back in even better shape than before I died. In other words, I could die, be frozen by a more advanced method than exists today, be stored for ten or twenty years while the life extension sciences progress, and then be revived and rejuvenated. This tactic could leave me healthier, stronger, and even physiologically younger than before, if during the years of my frozen sleep the ability to treat whatever I died of and the technology for reversing aging had been developed.

All of the life extension sciences are in a logarithmically accelerating phase. Resuscitation, cryonics, cloning, and interventive gerontology are making dramatic advances by the day. As the public becomes more aware of their promise, as investigators become more cognizant of the potential health benefits, as a critical data base of knowledge builds up, and as investors realize the market potential for life-extending and age-retarding products, research will move at an even faster pace.

In ten or fifteen years we may partially freeze our first person (like the overwintering frogs) and then revive him. And it may make a big difference whether a person is frozen by advanced technology or by that which is available today. Thus, a person like me, in his mid-forties, who jeopardizes himself by overeating, following a nonnutritious diet, smoking, drinking heavily, or risking his life unnecessarily, might only live ten more years and not the fifteen or twenty years needed to be frozen by a technique that will preserve him until aging can be reversed.

If I can reach my life-table-predicted length of life of approximately seventy-five years, I may even be able to escape the icy casket altogether. With cloning and age-reversal techniques, I will be able to have many more and younger years, perhaps be rebuilt like a classic car. No sane cryonicist truly wants to die and get frozen. It just beats the alternative.

What about people who are already old or who have life-threatening diseases or conditions? What can they do to extend their life spans? I would recommend that they immediately make arrangements for cryonic suspension at death. If they are lucky enough to have reached a position of power, influence, or wealth, I would suggest that they use these commodities to help speed up progress in cryonics technology.

Cryonics researchers are eager for a "crash course" in their discipline. Perhaps those people with incurable disease or older indigents know someone who sits on a board awarding research funds or an official who would be in a position to use public or corporate money to improve cryonics research either to create profit-generating medical spin-offs or to offset public spending for keeping alive terminal patients who would opt for cryonics suspension if they had the choice. Up until now, cryonic research has proceeded with very little financial support. With stronger backing, it could really begin to move.

Even if one did not have the means to be frozen at death, one might be able to raise the money as well as improve freezing technology by taking one's case to the media, as is sometimes done for organ transplantation. A senior citizen or someone with a terminal illness who wished to make the case for cryonics would probably create enormous public interest in the subject.

There are organizations of terminally ill people. Imagine the effect a well-orchestrated effort by such a group might have on a public already eager for extended life and youth. The bottom line is that our culture, which spends hundreds of billions of dollars for destructive weapons of life extinction, could set aside money for life extension and cryonics. In the end cryonics would be cheaper and far more humane than the present system of prolonging the pain and suffering of a hopeless, terminal existence.

What does the immediate future hold for life extension? What are the near-term breakthroughs and benchmarks to be on the lookout for? Some of the most exciting prospects I see in the next five to ten years are:

- the revival of first an organ, and then a whole small mammal, such as a rat or hamster, from a partially frozen state similar to that in overwintering frogs.

- the cloning of a mouse or other mammal from a nucleus taken from an advanced embryonic stage.

- a sophisticated understanding of exactly how nutritional restriction delays aging.

- the routine revival of people who have been clinically dead for as long as twenty minutes, using advanced resuscitation techniques such as combinations of blood-substitution, hyperbaric oxygen, drugs, and hypothermia.

- a permanent, implantable artificial heart that can be worn for years without causing strokes.

- a genetically engineered, immunosuppressant, monoclonal antibody that knocks out specific antibodies that cause rejection and not those that protect against disease.

- ice-cold, bloodless surgery using hyperbaric oxygen that allows heart and brain activity to be suspended for as long as twenty-four hours at the ice point.

- a cancer treatment using bloodless cold that destroys the cancer in a specific organ while protecting the others.

Although we have thoroughly discussed the biological, medical, and physical effects of life extension, perhaps the most important of all might be its psychological benefits. It is legendary among cryonicists that their fellow members, many of whom are in their seventh, eighth, and ninth decades, do not die. Although more than 200 people worldwide have made arrangements to be frozen and the majority are middle-aged and older, Trans Time Inc., the largest and most active cryonics company, has frozen only one person since 1980.

What do these potential suspendees have in common? According to a recent survey of cryonics society members, the distinguishing factor is that they are "death postponers." They would rather fight than give in. Death is even less acceptable to them than it is for the average person because it means the end of new experiences. As Saul Kent says, "Being frozen at death is the second-worst thing that can happen to you."

Of course, if the wish to stay alive were all that was needed to do so, there would be no reason for this book. But to paraphrase the old Roman saying, a young mind in a young body. The psychological value of a youthful outlook on life regardless of one's years may be one of the most important elements in maintaining health and vigor in old age. Just say no to death and aging.

Think young, act young, look young, and be young. A wide range of cosmetics are available today for both men and women to peel years, even decades, off their appearances. Various styles of dress can also help. Look at our perennial Hollywood stars who flit across the silver screen as universally acclaimed symbols of sex and beauty and then go home to their grandchildren.

There is a lot of talk nowadays about accepting aging and flowing with the rhythm of time. My personal feeling is that the rhythm of time, if left to its own, will make short work of us all. I would urge us to work against Mother Nature and Father Time, using all the wiles at our disposal. I can even understand why some people might choose cosmetic surgery, provided they have a highly competent surgeon and there are no major contraindications. But I would advise anyone considering a tummy tuck, face-lift, liposuction, or other procedure to first explore all the possible adverse consequences, both cosmetic and in terms of health, before submitting to surgery. I would also interview a number of customers, particularly those who had their operations five, ten, or fifteen years earlier, to make sure that a stiff toll is not exacted years later.

We are still in the learning stages of how best to maintain health, youth, and vigor. Therefore, any advice contained in this chapter is philosophical rather than promotional in regard to a particular procedure. I look forward to the day when body clones will be available to yield up their genetically identical tissues for both medical and cosmetic purposes. At that point, restoring our bodies to their youthful appearances will be totally safe and convenient.

As I finish, what comes to me more clearly than anything else is what a truly great adventure we are embarked on—to look into death's hollow eyes and challenge it face-to-face. Like any other great adventure, one cannot know the outcome beforehand. As always, there are heroes and villains, wise men and fools, saints and sinners. On some days, everything gleams crystal clear, the right road is obvious, success waits just around the bend. On others, the air hangs thick with peril and uncertainty, and it seems that it will take forever to make the tiniest bit of progress.

None of us, who are actors in this strangest of all plays, life itself, knows how the script will end. And, of course, the biggest reward of all is that, perhaps, it never will.

BIBLIOGRAPHY

1. DEATH, THOU SHALT DIE

Blank, J. P. The baby who came back from the dead. *Reader's Digest,* May 1981, pp. 103–107.

de la Torre, J. C., P. K. Hill, M. Gonzalaz-Caravajal et al. Evaluation of transected spinal cord regeneration in the rat. *Experimental Neurology,* Vol. 84, pp. 188–206, 1984.

Editor. Calcium blockers given after CPR may save brains denied blood up to one hour. *Medical World News,* January 18, 1982, pp. 11–13.

Ettinger, R. C. W. *Prospects of Immortality.* Doubleday, New York, 1964.

Fine, A. Transplantation in the central nervous system. *Scientific American,* Vol. 255, no. 2, pp. 52–58B, August 1986.

Fuller, R. A., and J. J. Rosen, Materials for medicine. *Scientific American,* Vol. 255, no. 4, pp. 118–125, October 1986.

Gan, S. C., P. E. Segall, H. D. Waitz et al. Ice-cold blood-substituted hamsters revive. *Federation Proceedings,* Vol. 44, no. 3, p. 623, 1985.

Gruman, G. J. A history of ideas about the prolongation of life. *Transactions of the American Philosophical Society,* December 1966.

Gurdon, J. B. The developmental capacity of nuclei taken from intestinal epithelium of feeding tadpoles. *Journal of Embryology and Experimental Morphology,* Vol. 10, pp. 622–640, 1962.

————. Transplanted nuclei and cell differentiation. *Scientific American,* Vol. 219, no. 6, pp. 24–35, 1968.

Hayflick, L. On the facts of life. *Executive Health,* Vol. 14, no. 9, June 1978.

Kent, S. *The Life Extension Revolution.* Morrow, New York, 1980.

Newell, J. Drug hope on brain injuries. *Sunday Times* (London), July 12, 1987, p. 29.

Ooka, H., P. E. Segall, and P. S. Timiras. Histology and survival in age-delayed low-tryptophan-fed rats. *Mechanisms of Ageing and Development,* Vol. 43, pp. 79–98, 1988.

Prather, R. S., F. L. Barnes, M. M. Sims et al. Nuclear transplantation in the bovine embryo: Assessment of donor nuclei and recipient oocyte. *Biology of Reproduction*, Vol. 37, pp. 859–866, 1987.

Safar, P. Cerebral resuscitation after cardiac arrest: A review. *Circulation*, Vol. 74 (Suppl. IV), IV 138–IV 153, 1986.

Segall, P. E., and H. Sternberg. Aging: A CNS-endocrine perspective. In A. V. Everitt and J. R. Walton, eds., *Regulation of Neuroendocrine Aging. Interdisciplinary Topics in Gerontology*, Vol. 24, Karger, Basel, pp. 9–20, 1988.

Segall, P. E., and P. S. Timiras. Patho-physiologic findings after chronic tryptophan deficiency in rats: A model for delayed growth and ageing. *Mechanisms of Ageing and Development*, Vol. 5, pp. 109–124, 1976.

Segall, P. E., P. S. Timiras, and J. R. Walton. Low tryptophan diets delay reproductive aging. *Mechanisms of Ageing and Development*, Vol. 23, pp. 245–252, 1983.

Segall, P. E., H. D. Waitz, H. Sternberg et al. Ice-cold bloodless dogs revived using protocol developed in hamsters. *Federation Proceedings*, Vol. 46, no. 4, p. 1338, 1987.

Sternberg, H., P. E. Segall, V. Bellport et al. Glutamic acid decarboxylase activity in discrete hypothalamic nuclei during the development of rats. *Developmental Brain Research*, Vol. 34, pp. 316–317, 1987.

Sternberg, H., P. E. Segall, H. Waitz et al. Interventive gerontology, cloning and cryonics: Relevance to life extension. Annual Spring Symposium on Biochemistry, George Washington University, 1988, manuscript submitted.

Timiras, P. S. An agenda for healthful aging. Life Extension Sciences. Chapter 27 in P. S. Timiras, ed., *Physiological Basis of Aging and Geriatrics*, Macmillan, New York, 1988, pp. 449–455.

———. Definitions: Demographic, comparative and differential aging. Chapter 2 in P. S. Timiras, ed., *Physiological Basis of Aging and Geriatrics*, Macmillan, New York, 1988, pp. 7–26.

Waitz, H. D., H. Yee, S. Gann et al. Reviving hamsters after hypothermic asanguinous perfusion. *Cryobiology*, Vol. 21, p. 699, 1984.

Willadsen, S. M. Nuclear transplantation in sheep embryos. *Nature*, Vol. 320, pp. 63–65, 1986.

2. FOREVER YOUNG: THE SECRET OF THE MICE

Bellport, V., R. Steinberg, G. W. Young et al. Maturational changes in regional hypothalamic neurochemistry of tryptophan-restricted rats. *Federation Proceedings,* Vol. 46, no. 3, p. 435, 1987.

Farah, A. P. Hair and now. *Health,* Vol. 19, April 1987, p. 12 + .

Friefeld, K. Hair raiser. *Health,* Vol. 18, December 1986, p. 64 + .

Gordon, R. S. Growth arrest through tryptophan deficiency in the very young chicken. *Sixth International Congress of Nutrition,* Edinburgh, 1963, p. 471.

Guroff, G. *Growth and Maturation Factors.* Wiley, New York, 1983.

Holehan, A. M., and B. J. Merry. Aging of the female reproductive system: The menopause. Chapter 13 in P. S. Timiras, ed., *Physiological Basis of Aging and Geriatrics,* Macmillan, New York, 1988, pp. 203–231.

McCay, C. M. Chemical aspects of ageing and the effect of diet upon ageing. In A. I. Lansing, ed., *Cowdry's Problems of Ageing,* 3rd ed., Williams and Wilkins, Baltimore, 1952, pp. 139–202.

McCay, C. M., M. F. Crowell, and L. A. Maynard. The effect of retarded growth upon length of lifespan and upon ultimate body size. *Journal of Nutrition,* Vol. 10, pp. 63–79, 1935.

McCay, C. M., L. A. Maynard, G. Sperling et al. Retarded growth, lifespan, ultimate body size and age changes in the albino rat after feeding diets restricted in calories. *Journal of Nutrition,* Vol. 18, pp. 1–13, 1939.

McRoberts, M. R. Growth retardation of day old chickens and physiological effects at maturity. *Journal of Nutrition,* Vol. 87, pp. 31–40, 1965.

Nadakavukaren, M. J., K. L. Fitch, and A. Richardson. Rat corneal epithelial cells as markers of physiological age: Dietary restriction retards age-related increase in cell areas. *Gerontologist,* Vol. 26, special issue, p. 157A, October 1986.

———. Dietary restriction retards age-related decrease in cell population of rat corneal endothelium. *Proceedings of the Society for Experimental Biology and Medicine,* Vol. 184 (1), pp. 98–101, 1987.

Nelson, J., R. Gosden, and L. Felicio. Effect of dietary restriction on estrous cyclicity and follicular reserves in aging C57BL/6J mice. *Biology of Reproduction,* Vol. 32, pp. 515–522, 1985.

Ooka, H., P. E. Segall, and P. S. Timiras. Histology and survival in age-delayed low-tryptophan-fed rats. *Mechanisms of Ageing and Development,* Vol. 43, pp. 79–98, 1988.

Ross, M. H. Nutrition and longevity in experimental animals. In M. D. Winick, ed., *Nutrition and Aging,* Wiley, New York, 1976, pp. 43–57.

Segall, P. E. Aging as a programmed cascade of specific cell death. *AGE,* Vol. 7, p. 149, 1984.

Segall, P. E., and H. Sternberg. Aging: A CNS-endocrine perspective. In A. V. Everitt and J. R. Walton, eds., *Regulation of Neuroendocrine Aging. Interdisciplinary Topics in Gerontology,* Vol. 24, Karger, Basel, pp. 9–20, 1988.

Segall, P., and P. S. Timiras. Age-related changes in thermoregulatory capacity of tryptophan-deficient rats. *Federation Proceedings,* Vol. 34, pp. 83–85, 1975.

———. Patho-physiologic findings after chronic tryptophan deficiency in rats: A model for delayed growth and aging. *Mechanisms of Ageing and Development,* Vol. 5, pp. 109–124, 1976.

Segall, P. E., P. S. Timiras, and J. R. Walton. Low tryptophan diets delay reproductive aging. *Mechanisms of Ageing and Development,* Vol. 23, pp. 245–252, 1983.

Segall, P., and H. D. Waitz. Long term tryptophan deficiency and aging retardation in the rat. *Fourth Annual Meeting of the American Aging Association AGE,* Vol. 1, no. 1, 1974.

Sharma, R. Theories of aging. Chapter 4 in P. S. Timiras, ed., *Physiological Basis of Aging and Geriatrics,* Macmillan, New York, 1988, pp. 43–58.

Sherwood, N. M., and P. S. Timiras. Comparison of direct-current and radio-frequency-current lesions in the rostral hypothalamus with respect to sexual maturation in the female rat. *Endocrinology,* Vol. 94, pp. 1275–1285, 1974.

Sladek, J. R., and D. M. Gash. Nerve cell grafting in Parkinson's disease. *Journal of Neurosurgery,* Vol. 68, pp. 337–351, 1988.

Sternberg, H. Aging of the immune system. Chapter 8 in P. S. Timiras, ed., *Physiological Basis of Aging and Geriatrics,* Macmillan, New York, 1988, pp. 103–122.

Sternberg, H., P. E. Segall, V. Bellport et al. Glutamic acid decarboxylase activity in discrete hypothalamic nuclei during the development of rats. *Developmental Brain Research,* Vol. 34, pp. 316–317, 1987.

Timiras, M. L. Aging of the skin and connective tissue. Chapter 23 in P. S. Timiras, ed., *Physiological Basis of Aging and Geriatrics,* Macmillan, New York, 1988, pp. 371–379.

Timiras, P. S. Aging of the skeleton, joints and muscles. Chapter 22 in P. S. Timiras, ed., *Physiological Basis of Aging and Geriatrics,* Macmillan, New York, 1988, pp. 349–370.

Walford, R. L. *Maximum Life Span.* Norton, New York, 1983.

————.*The 120 Year Diet Plan: How to Double Your Vital Years.* Simon & Schuster, New York, 1986.

Walker, R. F., K. M. McMahon, and E. B. Pivorun. Pineal gland structure and respiration as affected by age and hypocaloric diet. *Experimental Gerontology,* Vol. 13, pp. 91–99, 1978.

Weindruch, R. H., and R. L. Walford. Dietary restriction in mice beginning at 1 year of age: Effect on lifespan and spontaneous cancer incidence. *Science,* Vol. 215, pp. 1415–1418, 1982.

Weindruch, R. H., R. L. Walford, S. Fligiel et al. The retardation of aging in mice by dietary restriction: Longevity, cancer, immunity and lifetime energy intake. *Journal of Nutrition,* Vol. 116, pp. 641–654, 1986.

3. SUSPENDED ANIMATION: BREAKING THE ICE

Andjus, R. K. Suspended animation in cooled, supercooled and frozen rats. *Journal of Physiology,* Vol. 128, pp. 547–556, 1955.

Batten, M. Life spans: Can science slow the hands of time? *Science Digest,* Vol. 92, February 1984.

Bridgeman, P. W., *The Physics of High Pressure.* Dover, New York, 1970.

Fahy, G. M. Biological effects of vitrification and devitrification. In D. E. Pegg and A. M. Karow, Jr., *The Biophysics of Organ Cryopreservation,* Plenum Press, New York, 1988, pp. 265–297.

Fahy, G. M., D. I. Levy, and S. E. Ali. Some emerging principles underlying the physical properties, biological actions, and utility of vitrification solutions. *Cryobiology,* Vol. 24, pp. 196–213, 1987.

Haff, R. C., G. Klebanoff, B. G. Brown et al. Asanguinous hypothermic perfusion as a means of total organism preservation. *Journal of Surgical Research,* Vol. 19, pp. 13–19, 1975.

Haneda, K., R. Thomas, M. P. Sands et al. Whole body protection during three hours of total circulatory arrest: An experimental study. *Cryobiology,* Vol. 23, pp. 483–494, 1986.

Hero. A clinically doggone beagle, medical miracle Miles is a former chilly dog back from the beyond. *People,* Vol. 27, no. 16, April 20, 1987, p. 85.

Hochachka, P. W., and M. Guppy. *Metabolic Arrest and the Control of Biological Time.* Harvard University Press, Cambridge, Massachusetts, 1987.

Klebanoff, G., R. G. Armstrong, R. E. Cline et al. Resuscitation of a patient in stage IV hepatic coma using total body washout. *Journal of Surgical Research,* Vol. 13, 159–165, 1972.

Musacchia, X. J. Comparative physiological and biochemical aspects of hypothermia as a model for hibernation. *Cryobiology,* Vol. 21, pp. 583–592, 1984.

Rall, W. F., and G. M. Fahy. Ice-free cryopreservation of mouse embryos at −196 degrees by vitrification. *Nature,* Vol. 313, pp. 573–575, 1985.

Resch, G., and X. J. Musacchia. A role for glucose in hypothermic hamsters. *American Journal of Physiology,* Vol. 231, pp. 1729–1734, 1976.

Rogers, P. D., and H. Hillman. Increased recovery of rat's respiration following profound hypothermia. *Journal of Applied Physiology,* Vol. 29, no. 1, pp. 58–63, July 1970.

Schmid, W. D. Survival of frogs in low temperature. *Science,* Vol. 215, pp. 697–698, 1982.

Segall, P. Preservation and storage of biologic materials. U.S. Patent 3,677,024, July 18, 1972.

Segall, P. E., H. Sternberg, and H. Waitz. Blood substitute. U.S. Patent Pending.

Segall, P. E., H. D. Waitz, H. Sternberg et al. Ice-cold bloodless dogs revived using protocol developed in hamsters. *Federation Proceedings,* Vol. 46, no. 4, p. 1338, 1987.

Smith, A. U. *Biological Effects of Freezing and Supercooling.* Williams and Wilkins, Baltimore, 1961.

———. Viability of supercooled and frozen mammals. *Annals of the New York Academy of Sciences,* Vol. 80, pp. 291–300, 1959.

———. Studies on golden hamsters during cooling to and rewarming from body temperatures below 0° C. I–III. *Proceedings of the Royal Society of London,* Vol. 145, Series B, July 24, 1956, pp. 391–442.

Sternberg, H., P. E. Segall, H. Waitz et al. Interventive gerontology, cloning and cryonics: Relevance to life extension. Annual Spring Symposium on Biochemistry, George Washington University, 1988, manuscript submitted.

Storey, K. B. Freeze tolerance in terrestrial frogs. *Cryoletters,* Vol. 6, pp. 115–134, 1985.

Susman, E., F. D. Ruehl, and J. Oppenheimer. Experts in dog-freezing experiments predict humans can be frozen and revived! *National Enquirer,* April 21, 1987, p. 2.

Waitz, H. D. *The Effects of Low Temperature on Yeast at High Pressure.* Ph.D. dissertation, University of California at Berkeley, 1982.

Weisburd, S. Beyond the cutting edge of cold. *Science News,* Vol. 132, August 29, 1987, pp. 138–141.

4. CLONING: BORN AGAIN

Allen, C. L. Answering call for organs raises critical questions. *Insight,* July 11, 1988, pp. 16–18.

Balinsky, B. I. *An Introduction to Embryology,* 4th ed. Saunders, Philadelphia, 1975.

Berger, J. Pope warns health workers against straying. *New York Times,* September 15, 1987, p. A18.

Briggs, R., and T. J. King. Changes in the nuclei of differentiating endoderm cells as revealed by nuclear transplantation. *Journal of Morphology,* Vol. 100, pp. 269–312, 1957.

————. Factors affecting the transplantability of frog embryonic cells. *Journal of Experimental Zoology,* Vol. 122, pp. 485–503, 1953.

————. Transplantation of living nuclei from blastula cells into enucleated frogs' eggs. *Proceedings of the National Academy of Science, USA,* Vol. 38, pp. 455–463, 1952.

Cloning offers factory precision to the farm. *New York Times,* February 2, 1988, p. 1.

Edwards, R. G., and P. Steptoe. *A Matter of Life: The Story of a Medical Breakthrough.* Morrow, New York, 1980.

Fehilly, C. B., S. M. Willadsen, and E. M. Tucker. Interspecific chimaerism between sheep and goat. *Nature,* Vol. 307, pp. 634–636, February 16, 1984.

Freedman, N. M. *Joshua, Son of None.* Dell, New York, 1978.

Gordon, K., E. Lee, J. A. Vitale et al. Production of human tissue plasminogen activator in transgenic mouse milk. *Biotechnology 5,* pp. 1183–1187, 1987.

Grady, D. The ticking of a time bomb in the genes. *Discover,* June 1987, p. 26+.

Gurdon, J. B. *The Control of Gene Expression in Animal Development.* Clarendon Press, Oxford, 1974.

————. The developmental capacity of nuclei taken from intestinal epithelium cells of feeding tadpoles. *Journal of Embryology and Experimental Morphology,* Vol. 10, pp. 622–640, 1962.

————. Nuclear transplantation in Amphibia and the importance of stable nuclear changes in cellular differentiation. *Quarterly Review of Biology,* Vol. 38, pp. 54–78, 1963.

————. Nuclear transplantation in eggs and oocytes. *Journal of Cell Science,* Supplement 4, 287–318, 1986.

————. Transplanted nuclei and cell differentiation. *Scientific American,* Vol. 219, no. 6, pp. 24–35, 1968.

Gurdon, J. B., R. A. Laskey, and O. R. Reeves. The developmental capacity of nuclei transplanted from keratinized skin cells of adult frogs. *Journal of Embryology and Experimental Morphology*, Vol. 34, pp. 93–112, 1975.

Hodgkinson, N. Doctors set to transplant brain tissue. *Sunday Times* (London), January 18, 1987, p. 4.

Holzgreve, W., F. K. Beller, B. Buchholz et al. Kidney transplantation from anencephalic donors. *New England Journal of Medicine*, Vol. 316, no. 17, pp. 1069–1070, April 23, 1987.

Hoppe, P. C., and K. Illmensee. Microsurgically produced homozygous-diploid uniparental mice. *Proceedings of the National Academy of Sciences, USA*, Vol. 74, pp. 5657–5661, December 1977.

Huxley, A. *Brave New World.* Doubleday, Garden City, New York, 1932.

Illmensee, K., and P. C. Hoppe. Nuclear transplantation in *Mus musculus:* Developmental potential of nuclei from preimplantation embryos. *Cell*, Vol. 23, pp. 9–18, 1981.

Kahn, C. Double takes. *Omni*, Vol. 11. no. 1, p. 58 +. October 1988.

Kolata, G. Federal agency bars implanting fetal tissue. *New York Times*, April 16, 1988, p. 1 +.

Lenard, L., The frozen zoo. *Science Digest*, Vol. 89, pp. 76–79 +, June 1981.

Leonard, R. A., N. J. Holfner, and M. A. DiBerardino. Induction of DNA synthesis in amphibian erythroid nuclei in *Rana* eggs following conditioning in meiotic oocytes. *Developmental Biology*, Vol. 92, pp. 343–355, 1982.

Lewin, T. Medical use of fetal tissue spurs new abortion debate. *New York Times*, p. 1 +, August 16, 1987.

McGrath, J. B., and D. Solter. Inability of mouse blastomere nuclei transferred to enucleated zygotes to support development *in vitro.* *Science*, Vol. 226, pp. 1317–1319, 1984.

McKinnel, R. G. *Cloning of Frogs, Mice and Other Animals.* University of Minnesota Press, Minneapolis, 1985.

Muggleton-Harris, A. L. Cellular events concerning the developmental potentiality of the transplanted nucleus with reference to the aging lens cell. *Experimental Gerontology*, Vol. 6, pp. 279–285, 1971.

Pittius, C. W., L. Hennighaus, E. Lee et al. A milk protein gene promoter directs the expression of human tissue plasminogen activator cDNA to the mammary gland in transgenic mice. *Proceedings of the National Academy of Sciences, USA*, Vol. 85, August 1988, pp. 5874–5878.

Prather, R. S., F. L. Barnes, M. M. Sims et al. Nuclear transplantation in

Bibliography 235

the bovine embryo: Assessment of donor nuclei and recipient oocyte. *Biology of Reproduction,* Vol. 37, pp. 859–866, 1987.

Rhein, R., Jr. Biotech's bid to build a better mouse. *Business Week,* November 9, 1987, p. 102.

Rorvik, D. *In His Image: The Cloning of a Man.* Lippincott, Philadelphia, 1978.

Rosenstein, J. M. Neocortical transplants in the mammalian brain lack a blood-brain barrier to macromolecules. *Science,* Vol. 235, pp. 772–774, February 13, 1987.

Spemann, H. *Embryonic Development and Induction.* Yale University Press, New Haven, Connecticut, 1938.

Sullivan, W. Fetal tissue implants in brain seen. *New York Times,* July 1, 1987, p. A20.

Willadsen, S. M. Nuclear transplantation in sheep embryos. *Nature,* Vol. 320, pp. 63–65, 1986.

5. LIFE AFTER DEATH: RESUSCITATION AND REGENERATION

Aleksandrova, M., L. V. Polezhaev, and L. V. Cherkasova. Allotransplantation of disassociated embryonic brain cells into brains of rats subjected to hypoxia. *Doklady Biological Sciences,* Vol. 275, pp. 224–226, 1984.

Borgens, R. B. Mice regrow the tips of their foretoes. *Science,* Vol. 217, pp. 747–750, August 20, 1982.

Carlson, B. M. Types of morphogenetic phenomena in vertebrate regenerating systems. *American Zoologist,* Vol. 18, 869–882, 1978.

Cerchiari, E. L., T. M. Hoel, P. Safar et al. Effect of anoxic reperfusion, superoxide dismutase and deferoxamine therapy on cerebral blood flow and metabolism and somato-sensory evoked potentials after asphyxial cardiac arrest in dogs. *Critical Care Medicine,* Vol. 14, p. 390, 1986.

Cotman, C. W., and M. Nieto-Sampedro. Cell biology of synaptic plasticity. *Science,* Vol. 225, pp. 1287–1294, September 21, 1984.

De La Torre, J. C., P. K. Hill, M. Gonzalez-Corvajal et al. Evaluation of transected spinal cord regeneration in the rat. *Experimental Neurology,* Vol. 84, pp. 188–206, 1984.

Editor. Calcium blockers given after CPR may save brains denied blood up to an hour. *Medical World News,* p. 11–13, January 18, 1982.

Fine, A. Transplantation in the nervous system. *Scientific American,* Vol. 255, August 1986, pp. 52–58B.

Gallup, G., Jr. and W. Proctor. *Adventures in Immortality.* McGraw-Hill, New York, 1982.

Goldsmith, H. S., E. Steward, W. F. Chen et al. Application of intact omentum to normal and traumatized spinal cord. In C. C. Kao, R. P. Bunge, and P. J. Reier, eds., *Spinal Cord Reconstruction,* Raven Press, New York, 1982, pp. 235–244.

Johnson, W. H., R. A. Laubengayer, C. E. Delanny et al. Echinoderms, chordates and phylogenetic relationships. Chapter 32 in *Biology,* 3rd ed., Holt, Rinehart & Winston, New York, 1966, pp. 585–594.

————. Flatworms, round worms and rotifers. Chapter 29 in *Biology,* 3rd ed., Holt, Rinehart & Winston, New York, 1966, pp. 528–543, 1968.

Kahn, C. The chemistry of self-healing. *Omni,* Vol. 10, no. 6, March 1988.

Kawamura, T., and Y. Fukui, Electrophysiologic identification of the viability of a preserved heart in a hyperbaric chamber. *Transactions of the American Society for Artificial Internal Organs,* Vol. 32, pp. 288–290, 1986.

Keeton, W. T. Development. Chapter 16 in *Biological Science,* Norton, New York, 1967, pp. 603–647.

Martin, G. B., R. M. Nowak, D. L. Carden et al. Cardiopulmonary bypass vs. CPR as treatment for prolonged canine cardiopulmonary arrest. *Annals of Emergency Medicine,* Vol. 16, pp. 628–632, 1987.

Mizelle, M. Limb regeneration: Induction in the newborn opossum. *Science,* Vol. 161, pp. 283–286, July 19, 1968.

Moody, R. A., Jr. *Life After Life: The Investigation of a Phenomenon— Survival of Bodily Death.* Bantam, New York, 1976.

Nylander, G. Tissue ischemia and hyperbaric oxygen treatment: An experimental study. *Acta Chir. Scand. Suppl.,* Vol. 533, pp. 1–109, 1988.

Pribram, K. The neurophysiology of remembering. *Scientific American,* Vol. 220, p. 73, January 1969.

Right to die initiative fails. *New York Times,* May 18, 1988, p. 23.

Ruiz, E., D. D. Brunette, E. P. Robison et al. Cerebral resuscitation after cardiac arrest using hetastarch hemodilution, hyperbaric oxygenation and magnesium ion. *Resuscitation,* Vol. 14, pp. 213–223, 1986.

Safar, P. Cerebral resuscitation after cardiac arrest: A review. *Circulation,* Vol. 74 (Suppl. IV), pp. IV 138–IV 153, 1986.

————. The pathophysiology of dying and reanimation. Chapter 1 in G. Schwartz, P. Safar et al., *Principals and Practice of Emergency Medicine,* 2nd ed., Saunders, Philadelphia, 1986.

Safar, P. , and N. G. Bircher. *Cardiopulmonary Cerebral Resuscitation,* 3rd ed., Saunders, Philadelphia, 1988.

Sealy, R., G. G. Harrison, D. Morrell et al. A feasibility study of a new approach to clinical radiosensitization: Hypothermia and hyperbaric oxygen in combination with pharmacological vasodilation. *British Journal of Radiology,* Vol. 59, pp. 1093–1098, November 1986.

Singer, M. The regeneration of body parts. *Scientific American,* Vol. 199, October 1958, pp. 79–88.

Stocum, D. L. The urodele limb regeneration blastema. *Differentiation,* Vol. 27, pp. 13–28, 1984.

6. CHANGE OF HEART: TRANSPLANTABLE AND ARTIFICIAL ORGANS

Albisser, A. M., B. S. Leibel, B. Zinman et al. Studies with an artificial endocrine pancreas. *Archives of Internal Medicine,* Vol. 137, pp. 639–649, 1977.

Altman, L. K. Heart recipient "feeling good," requests a beer. *New York Times,* November 28, 1984, p. B7.

Barnard, C., and C. B. Pepper. *One Life.* Macmillan, New York, 1970.

Borel, J. F. *Ciclosporin,* Karger, Basel, New York, 1986.

Botz, C. K., B. S. Leibel, W. Zingg et al. Comparison of the peripheral and portal routes of insulin infusion by a computer-controlled insulin infusion system (artificial endocrine pancreas). *Diabetes,* Vol. 25, pp. 691–700, 1976.

Brody, J. E. Twin boys are separated in 22 hours of surgery. *New York Times,* September 7, 1987, p. A1.

Bryner, H., I. Blohme, and I. Karlberg. *Third Congress of the European Society for Organ Transplantation, Proceedings,* Vol. 19, pp. 3531–4396, 1987.

Demikhov, V. P. *Experimental Transplantation of Vital Organs.* Authorized translation from the Russian, by Basil Haigh, Consultant's Bureau, New York, 1962.

Dobelle, W. H., M. G. Mladejovsky, J. R. Evans et al. Braille reading by a blind volunteer by visual cortex stimulation. *Nature,* Vol. 259, pp. 111–115, 1976.

Dobelle, W. H., J. Tenkel, D. C. Henderson et al. Mapping the projection of the visible field onto visual cortex in man by direct electrical stimulation. *Transactions of the American Society for Artificial Internal Organs,* Vol. 24, pp. 15–18, 1978.

Drexler, K. E. *Engines of Creation.* Anchor Press/Doubleday, Garden City, New York, 1986.

Dumbleton, J. H. *Tribology of Natural and Artificial Joints.* Elsevier, New York, 1981.

Eddington, D. K., W. H. Dobelle, D. E. Brackmann et al. Place and periodicity pitch by stimulation of multiple scale tympani, electrodes in deaf volunteers. *Transactions of the American Society for Artificial Internal Organs,* Vol. 24, pp. 1–5, 1978.

Fuller, R. A., and J. J. Rosen, Materials for medicine. *Scientific American,* vol. 255, no. 4, pp. 118–125, October 1986.

Girvin, J. P. Cerebral (cortical) biostimulation. *PACE,* Vol. 9, pp. 764–771, September 1986.

———. Current status of artificial vision by electrocortical stimulation. *Canadian Journal of Neurological Science,* Vol. 15, pp. 58–62, 1988.

House, W. F. Artificial hearing and implanted auditory prosthesis for treatment of total binaural deafness. *Transactions of the American Society for Artificial Internal Organs,* Vol. 30, pp. 11–14, 1984.

Jarvik, R. V. The total artificial heart. *Scientific American,* Vol. 244, pp. 74–80, 1981.

Levine, R., M. Gorayeb, P. Safar et al. Cardiopulmonary bypass after cardiac arrest and prolonged closed-chest CPR in dogs. *Annals of Emergency Medicine,* Vol. 16, pp. 620–627, June 1987.

Mladejovsky, M. G., D. K. Eddington, W. H. Dobelle et al. Artificial hearing for the deaf by cochlear stimulation: Pitch modulation and some parametric thresholds. *Transactions of the American Society for Artificial Internal Organs,* Vol. 21, pp. 1–7, 1975.

Mladejovsky, M. G., D. K. Eddington, J. R. Evans et al. A computer-based brain stimulation system to investigate sensory prostheses for the blind and deaf. *IEEE Transactions of Biomedical Engineering,* Vol. 23, p. 289, April 1976.

Nissenson, A. R., D. E. Gentile, R. E. Soderblum et al. Long-term outcome of continuous ambulatory peritoneal dialysis. The Southern California/Southern Nevada experience. *Transactions of the American Society for Artificial Internal Organs,* Vol. 32, pp. 560–563, 1986.

Pierce, W. S. The artificial heart—1986. Partial fulfillment of a promise. *Transactions of the American Society for Artificial Internal Organs,* Vol. 32, pp. 5–10, 1986.

Ronel, S. H., M. J. D'Andrea, H. Hashiguchi et al. Macroporous hydrogel membranes for hybrid artificial pancreas. I. Synthesis and chamber fabrication. *Journal of Biomedical Materials Research*, Vol. 17, pp. 855–864, September 1983.

Sachs, D. H. Specific immunosuppression. *Transplantation Proceedings*, Vol. 19, pp. 123–127, 1987.

Safar, P. Emergency cardiopulmonary bypass after cardiac arrest. *Proceedings of the American Academy of Cardiovascular Perfusion*, Vol. 7, pp. 124–125, January 1986.

Shaw, M. W. *After Barney Clark: Reflections on the Utah Artificial Heart Program*. University of Texas Press, Austin, 1984.

Story, K. B. Editorial: Organ preservation: Can animal models show the way? *Cryoletters*, Vol. 8, 116–117, May/June 1987.

Sun, A. M., Z. Cai, Z. Shi et al. Microencapsulated hepatocytes as a bioartificial liver. *Transactions of the American Society for Artificial Internal Organs*, Vol. 32, no. 1, pp. 39–41, 1986.

Walker, P. S. *Human Joints and Their Artificial Replacements*. Charles C. Thomas, Springfield, Illinois, 1977.

White, R. J., M. S. Albin, G. E. Locke et al. Brain transplantation: Prolonged survival of brain after carotid-jugular interposition. *Science*, Vol. 150, pp. 779–881, November 5, 1965.

White, R. J., M. S. Albin, and D. Yashon. Neuropathological investigation of the transplanted canine brain. *Transplantation Proceedings*, Vol. 1, pp. 259–261, 1969.

White, R. J., J. Austin, P. Austin et al. Preparation and performance of a non-central nervous system animal. *Surgery*, Vol. 68, pp. 48–53, 1970.

White, R. J., L. R. Wolin et al. Primate cephalic transplantation: neurogenic separation, vascular association. *Transplantation Proceedings*, Vol. 3, pp. 602–604, 1971.

7. CRYONICS: WHEN ONCE IS NOT ENOUGH

Berger, J. Pope warns health workers against straying. *New York Times*, September 15, 1987, p. A18.

Bigart, H. S. *New York Sunday Times*, January 29, 1967, p. 58.

Callahan, D. *Setting Limits: Medical Goals in an Aging Society*. Simon & Schuster, New York, 1987.

Ettinger, R. C. W. *Prospects of Immortality*. Doubleday, New York, 1964.

Fletcher, J. F. *The Ethics of Genetic Control*. Prometheus, Buffalo, New York, 1988.

Fredrickson, D. The National Institute on Aging. An orphan finds a home. Speech presented to the National Advisory Council on Aging, National Institute on Aging. The First Five Years. A symposium held May 29–30, 1980, Bethesda, Maryland, cosponsored by the National Institute on Aging and the Josiah Macy, Jr., Foundation.

Friedman, B. J. Frozen Guys. *Playboy,* August 1978, pp. 102 + .

Harrington, A. *The Immortalist: An Approach to the Engineering of Man's Divinity.* Random House, New York, 1969.

———. *Life in the Crystal Palace.* Knopf, New York, 1959.

Karow, A. M., Jr., H. I. Holst, and M. A. Ecker. Organ cryopreservation. Renal and cardiac experience. Chapter 6 in A. M. Karow, Jr., G. J. M. Abouna, and A. L. Humphries, Jr., eds., *Organ Preservation for Transplantation,* Little Brown, Boston, 1974, pp. 274–297.

Karow, A. M., Jr., W. R. Webb, and J. E. Stapp. Preservation of hearts by freezing. *Archives of Surgery,* Vol. 91, pp. 572–574, 1965.

Leaf, J., M. Federowicz, and H. Hixon. Asanguinous perfusion of dogs at 5° C for 4 hours with long term survival. Abstract #49, presented at the 22nd Annual Meeting of the Cryobiological Society, June 18–21, 1985, Madison, Wisconsin.

Lehmann-Haupt, C. Anybody want to live forever? Books of the *Times. New York Times,* June 20, 1969, p. 39.

Luyet, B. J. A review of research on the preservation of hearts in the frozen state. *Cryobiology,* Vol. 8, pp. 190–207, 1971.

Luyet, B. J. and P. M. Gehenio. *Life and Death at Low Temperatures.* Biodynamica, Normandy, Missouri, 1940.

Nelson, R. F. *We Froze the First Man,* as told to Sandra Stanley. Dell, New York, 1968.

Pohl, F. Intimations of immortality. *Playboy,* June 1964.

Rapid advances point to the mapping of all human genes. *New York Times,* July 15, 1986, p. C1 + .

Sahagan, L., and M. Arak. Cryonics center searched for clues in beheading of woman, 83. *Los Angeles Times,* January 8, 1988, p. 21.

Smith, A. U. *Biological Effects of Freezing and Supercooling.* Baltimore, Williams and Wilkins, 1961.

Sternberg, H., P. E. Segall, H. Waitz et al. Interventive gerontology, cloning and cryonics: Relevance to life extension. Annual Spring Symposium on Biochemistry, George Washington University, 1988, manuscript submitted.

Waitz, H. D., H. Sternberg, S. C. Gan et al. Improving revival of asanguinous hypothermic hamsters. Abstract #48, presented at the 22nd Annual Meeting of the Cryobiological Society, June 18–21, 1985, Madison, Wisconsin.

Waitz, H. D., H. Yee, S. Gann et al. Reviving hamsters after asanguinous hypothermic perfusion. *Cryobiology,* Vol. 21, p. 699, 1984.

Walford, R. The likelihood we shall control the aging process and the implications upon society and the individual. Presented at Life Extension and Ethical Considerations—The Perspective of the Biologist, J. Chesky, and Z. Zakari, co-chair, the 40th Annual Scientific Meeting of the Gerontology Society of America, held November 18–21, 1987, Washington, D.C.

Wilford, J. N. Body of student at N.Y.U. is frozen. *New York Times,* August 2, 1968, p. 34.

Wilson, R. A. *Cosmic Trigger: Final Secret of the Illuminati.* And/Or Press, Berkeley, California, 1977.

8. PANDORA'S ICEBOX

Bookchin, M. *Post-Scarcity Anarchism.* Ramparts Press, Berkeley, California, 1971.

Bork, R. H., Jr. He who laughs last. *Forbes,* Vol. 134, August 13, 1984, pp. 70+.

Bradbury, R. *Fahrenheit 451.* Ballantine, New York, 1953.

———. *Golden Apples of the Sun.* Doubleday, Garden City, 1953.

———. *The Illustrated Man.* Doubleday, Garden City, 1951.

———. *The Martian Chronicles.* Doubleday, Garden City, 1950.

———. *October Country.* Ballantine, New York, 1955.

Ettinger, R. C. W. *Man into Superman.* St. Martin's, New York, 1972.

Gale, R. P., and T. Hauser. *Final Warning: The Legacy of Chernobyl.* Warner Books, New York, 1988.

Malthus, T. *On Population.* G. Himmelfarb, ed. Modern Library, New York, 1960.

Mayo, J. L. *Superconductivity: The Threshold of a New Technology.* Tab Books, Blue Ridge Summit, Pennsylvania, 1988.

O'Neill, G. K. *The High Frontier: Human Colonies in Space.* Morrow, New York, 1977.

Rafelski, J., and S. E. Jones. Cold nuclear fusion. *Scientific American,* Vol. 257, July 1987, pp. 84–89.

Rifkin, J., and T. Howard. *Entropy: A New World View.* Viking, New York, 1980.

Wattenberg, B. J. *The Birth Dearth.* Pharos, New York, 1987.

9. THE CHANCE OF A (SECOND) LIFETIME

AGE, The American Aging Association, c/o Denham Harman, M.D., 42nd and Dewey Avenue, Omaha, NE 68105.

American Cryonics, The Journal of the American Cryonics Society, 1098 Euclid Avenue, Berkeley, CA 94708.

Brody, J. *Jane Brody's Nutrition Book.* Norton, New York, 1981.

Can Death Be Conquered? Cryonics Coordinators of America, Inc., 1983 Marcus Ave., Suite 260, Lake Success, NY 11042. 1-(800)-524-4456

Canadian Cryonics News, Cryonics Society of Canada, Station A., Hamilton, Ontario L8N 4C3, Canada.

Ettinger, R. C. W. *Prospects of Immortality.* Doubleday, New York, 1964.

The Immortalist, The Journal of the Immortalist Society, 24041 Stratford, Oak Park, MI 48237.

Incurably Ill for Animal Research (IIFAR), POB 1873, Bridgeview, IL 60455.

Kent, S. *The Life Extension Revolution.* Morrow, New York, 1980.

Pritikin, N., and P. M. McGrady, *The Pritikin Program for Diet and Exercise.* Grosset & Dunlap, New York, 1979.

Timiras, P. S. *Physiological Basis of Aging and Geriatrics.* Macmillan, New York, 1988.

Walford, R. L. *Maximum Life Span.* Norton, New York, 1983.

———. *The 120 Year Diet Plan: How to Double Your Vital Years.* Simon & Schuster, New York, 1986.

INDEX

ABC-TV, 49–51
Abrams, Carl, 170
acid rain, 196
Acquired Immune Deficiency
    Syndrome (AIDS), 12, 30, 69,
    103, 131, 177, 218–19
Adams, Douglas, xiii
Age of Fable, The (Bulfinch), 179
aging, xvi, 15, 36
    acceptance of, 185–86, 198,
        225–26
    causes of, 31–32
    conquest of, 58, 108, 135, 161,
        163, 185
    controlling of, 5, 18
    development related to, 28–
        32
    impact of diet restriction on,
        8, 19, 21–28, 30–33
    inevitability of, 3, 20
    legacy of, 14
    mechanisms of, 177–78
    reproductive, 24–25
    reversal of, 6
    understanding of, 18
aging theory, 23
alchemy, 4
Alcor Life Extension, 179–80
Allen, Woody, 40, 66, 167
Alliance for Aging Research, 177
All That Jazz (Fosse), 215
Alta Genetics, 89–91
Alzheimer's disease, 69, 104, 113,
    131, 135, 177

brain-cell transplantation for,
    9, 36, 106
cryonics suspension vs.
    nursing home care for, 202–3
American Cryonics Society
    (ACS), 51, 57, 68, 174–75, 218
    Board of Governors of, 55
American Paralysis Association,
    135
American Parkinson Disease
    Association, 104
American Red Cross, 40–41
Andjus, R. K., 43–44
anencephalic babies,
    transplanting organs from,
    9, 101–2, 105–7, 109, 183,
    187–89
Animal Research Station, 91
animals:
    in cloning from embryos, 7,
        10, 75, 82–93, 96–97, 99, 151,
        224
    diet-restriction experiments
        on, 8, 19, 21–28, 30–33
    endangered species of, 99
    freezing and reviving of, 8–9,
        11–12
    reconnecting spinal cords in,
        135–37, 151, 153, 183
    regeneration in, 132–33, 135–
        37
    resuscitation of, 117, 120, 124–
        25
    transgenic, 97

243